D1624998

LYNNE SEGAL was born in Sydney, Australia, and came to London in 1970 with her 14-month-old son, having received a doctorate from Sydney University for a critique of the theories and practices of experimental psychology. Since arriving in London she has taught psychology at Middlesex Polytechnic and has been very involved with the women's movement and left-wing politics. During the seventies she played an active role in setting up or supporting a variety of resource centres, campaigns and cultural and educational activities in Islington. She participated in the launching of the national Socialist Society and is a member of the Labour Party and the collective *Feminist Review*. As well as writing for many feminist and left magazines, she has also written, with Sheila Rowbotham and Hilary Wainwright, *Beyond the Fragments* (1980) and edited *What is to be done about the Family?* (1983). She lives in London.

In this controversial book Lynne Segal challenges many current feminist orthodoxies on war and peace, female sexuality, pornography, psychoanalysis and sociobiology. She argues that, in order to understand and alter the real power relations between men and women, we must look at the diverse patterns of domination and exploitation in the home, at work, and in our cultural and political lives, and work out strategies to forge a new future for women *and* men. This challenging book is an important contribution to feminist practice.

IS THE FUTURE FEMALE?

Troubled Thoughts on Contemporary Feminism

LYNNE SEGAL

PETER BEDRICK BOOKS
NEW YORK

First American edition published in 1988 by
PETER BEDRICK BOOKS
125 East 23rd Street
New York NY 10010

Library of Congress Cataloging-in-Publication Data

Segal, Lynne.
    Is the future female?: troubled thoughts on contemporary feminism
    Lynne Segal.—1st American ed.
      p. cm.
    Includes index.
    ISBN 0-87226-186-7. ISBN 0-87226-206-5 (pbk.)
    1. Feminism. 2. Socialism. 3. Sex role. I. Title.
    HQ1154.S346 1988
    305.4'2—dc 19
                                                        87-35578
                                                       CIP

Published by agreement with Virago Press Ltd.

Manufactured in the United States of America

5 4 3 2 1

Contents

Preface and Acknowledgements

Because I find the labour of writing more painful than pleasurable I have needed vast support and encouragement to write this book. I am particularly grateful to my editor Ursula Owen and my friend Marsha Rowe who each read and commented upon almost everything I wrote; I have tried to incorporate their extensive suggestions into the text. This book would not have been written without their help, and Marsha's own recollections of her involvement in the women's movement have been invaluable to me. Ruthie Petrie, Michèle Barrett, Veronica Beechey, Bob Connell, Drusilla Modjeska, Mark Nash, Anne Phillips, Denise Riley, Sheila Rowbotham and Hilary Wainwright have all made very useful suggestions on all or parts of the book. My housemates James Swinson, Chris Whitbread and Steve Skaith have been unstinting in their loving support, constant nurturing and intellectual encouragement; my son Zim has always been affirming and affectionate. Chris Whitbread typed several drafts of this book, tackling grammatical flaws, spelling mistakes, thematic illogicalities and misquotations with his characteristic and unflagging care and intelligence. I hope some time to find a way to repay the help of those who have assisted me most, and I hope, whatever disagreements they have with it, they will consider the product worthy of their efforts.

I am grateful to all the women on the *Feminist Review* collective for the stimulating though at times difficult discussions we have had over contemporary feminism. I would like to think we will soon be part of a confident resurgence of socialist feminism.

Lynne Segal,
Islington, 1986

For Iza Joan Segal,
and my housemates at Balfour Lodge,
with love

Introduction

I wanted to write this book because I was disturbed by what has been emerging as the public face of feminism in the eighties. The most accessible feminist writing today is one in which we are likely to read of the separate and special knowledge, emotion, sexuality, thought and morality of women, indeed of a type of separate 'female world', which exists in fundamental opposition to 'male culture', 'male authority', 'malestream thought', in opposition to the world of men. The central theme of this book, in contrast, is the inadequacy of such polarised thinking about women and men.

In trying to understand the return to an emphasis on natural or psychological gender *difference* in popular feminist thinking, I have read through the literature and considered the preoccupations which have most engaged feminists over the last decade (concentrating on British and North America literature as the most accessible and influential in Britain). This has been a decade of increasing fragmentation within the women's movement, with the emergence of divisions between women and the growth of Black feminist perspectives. But of major prominence, at least within white feminist writing, has been a concern with sexuality, motherhood, men's violence and the threat of nuclear war. In each of these areas feminist analysis has moved towards a new emphasis on the inevitability of men's violence and competitive power-seeking. The problem of 'male' psychology and behaviour is contrasted with a more nurturant, maternal, co-operative and peaceful 'female' psychology and behaviour. Indeed, an apocalyptic feminism has appeared which portrays a Manichean struggle between female virtue and male vice, with ensuing catastrophe and doom unless 'female' morality and values prevail. The evidence that both 'masculinity' and 'femininity' are socially constructed, and variably expressed across class, ethnic, regional and national groupings, drops out of such feminist thinking. So too does the reality that women and men relate with varying degrees of acceptance, ambivalence, tension, conflict and antagonism to social definitions of 'feminine' and 'masculine'.

What is most troubling to some older feminists such as myself is the turnaround in feminist writing from an initial denial of fundamental difference between women and men in the early seventies to a celebration of difference by the close of that decade. This is all the more troubling because a parallel cycle seems to have occurred in the first organised feminist movement at the turn of the century, when struggles for women's equality with men were gradually superseded by campaigns to revalue and improve women's position in the home. Why have our efforts to build a movement to eliminate women's position as the subordinate sex produced today, as they produced before, such contrasting feminist preoccupations and perspectives? Who, anyway, dares represent the goal and direction of feminism in the eighties? Most often, only the dogmatic or foolhardy would embark upon such a risky business. Yet who could doubt that it was the most radical force to emerge from and outlive the Western protest movements of the sixties? The women's liberation movement burst into the political arena of the 1970s with the energy and confidence to impress, and – could such things be? – at times even silence the male political voice. Times change. In the West, there is now no cohesive women's liberation movement. But feminism remains a strong, if diverse, political force.

It remains a strong force, in my view, not so much because feminists were the most ardent and committed of rebels – though many of us were that – but because the changes in women's lives, which throw up contradiction and confusion at every turn, were the most profound and continuing. It is partly the depth and diversity of change in women's lives which produce the range of feminisms we now find. The 'deconstructing' feminist academic studying the multiple meanings of 'femininity', the Cosmo journalist promoting greater choice in the lives of career women, the women in community struggles fighting the withdrawal of choice in their lives through the closure of nurseries, working-class women fighting the impact of 'privatisation' and its deteriorating job conditions, or Black women fighting heightened racism generally and increasingly racist regulations in welfare provision, all reflect the advances and retreats in the lives of different groups of women in recent years. And yet a startling feature of some of the most popular feminist writing today is its denial of any significant change in women's power in the world and control over our own lives – the belief that there has been no fundamental change in women's circumstances over recent decades, centuries or millenia. Men, it has been suggested, can always turn any apparent change to their own advantage.

Women's powerlessness, victimisation and lack of resources constitute, in this view, women's timeless history. In contrast, it seems to me, we cannot begin to think clearly about women's predicament today, and how to change it, unless we set out with very different assumptions. Women's lives, like men's, are constantly changing. Indeed, women's lives have changed much faster than men's throughout this century. Feminists today, in confronting men's power in relation to women, face a very different set of problems from those that feminists a century before encountered.

Scepticism over the importance of any objective change in women's lives goes hand in hand with the suggestion that practical struggles against women's inequality are of less significance than the need to recognise and value women's distinct ideas and experience, suppressed or ignored by the dominance of men's ideas and experience. The cultural devaluation of all that is seen as 'female', of women's most characteristic interests and activities is undeniable, and feminists have nearly always wished to assert and admire the power and strength of women and the importance of the work which women do. Contemporary feminists have also emphasised that 'the political' is more than collective actions and campaigns in the public world. The personal and subjective struggle of all oppressed people is one against being defined as inferior, marginal and deviant, in the language, discourse, myths and fantasies of the dominant culture. Women, like Black people, ethnic minorities, the disabled and sexual minorities, have always had to grapple with a subjective and collective consciousness which denies to women the most valued characteristics of 'mankind', a 'mankind' which is male, able-bodied, white and heterosexual.

In the historical and social definitions and representations of 'male' and 'female' we incorporate within us a culture which places men at its centre. Exploring and challenging how we are constructed in ideology as 'men' and 'women' has therefore always been an important project for feminism. And it is here, at the ideological level, that it can seem more persuasive to claim that little has shifted in the representation of women as the subordinate sex. The importance of women's struggle to experience and express a positive sense of ourselves is obvious in a culture which belittles women precisely as it defines us as 'woman'. But there has always been a danger that in re-valuing our notions of the female and appealing to the experiences of women, we are reinforcing the ideas of sexual polarity which feminism originally aimed to challenge. A potential essentialism, or the assertion of fixed, unified and opposed 'male' and 'female' natures, was always present in such a project. The dangers of such essentialist thinking have grown stronger within feminism as the women's movement itself has grown organisationally weaker and its perspectives more fragmented.

Ideas which express and construct men's power in relation to women are tenaciously rooted in and around us, yet they themselves are internally inconsistent, and do not determine our lives in any straightforward and static way. Men's greater power in relation to women is not simply a product of the ideas we hold and the language we use – powerful as these are when reality is conceived and named through language – but of all the social practices which give men authority over women. Ideas and language interact with other tensions and struggles between women and men in every institution of our society, both private and public. Indeed, the initial starting point for much of the feminist analysis of women's oppression in the early seventies was the significance of the separation in language and reality between the supposedly 'private' world and the 'public' world, the separation of family life from economic and political life – with women placed as central in the former and men placed as central in the latter.

And yet, individually, we are not, either as women or as men, fixed and frozen within these 'private' and 'public' institutions. Women's individual and collective actions introduce conflict, challenge, and – when they can be collectively sustained – the potential for change. It is in looking at the tensions and pressures thrown up each day in our personal lives and collective struggles as women, whether in the home, the workplace or elsewhere, that we may begin to see beyond the polarisations of 'feminine' and 'masculine', and beyond the separation of the private from the public, to a world of sexual equality.

And this brings us to the connections between feminism and socialism. The divisions between the workplace and the home, production and reproduction, serve not only to support male dominance but also to support central features of existing capitalist economic systems. The work women do in the home, though necessary for society generally, has never been valued or rewarded as an essential part of the economy. Male dominance has been a feature of all known societies, but in our own society the structures and ideologies of male dominance and the requirements of production for profit have been braided together. A vision of a world free from sexual hierarchy would require a very different economic system from any we have yet seen. It would be a world where work, pleasure, creativity and caring were no longer separated off and posed against each other, and no longer sex-linked; therefore a world no longer seriously damaging to the autonomy, authority, creativity, health and happiness of women.

This book is written to promote a socialist feminist analysis at a time when many feminists have expressed increasing doubts over any necessary connection between the two. I began writing the book in early 1984, when it seemed to me that a mood of pessimism and despair had taken a firm hold of feminist thought and action. The British anthology of women's liberation writings from 1981-1983 had just been published, in which men's violence towards women was the prevailing theme and a stronger separatist politics with its uncompromising rejection of political alliances with men was the favoured feminist strategy.[1] This pessimism over the inevitability of men's violence and greed, private and public, was being used to present a global political analysis – ranging from the threat of nuclear destruction to poverty and exploitation in the Third World. It is an analysis which suggests that women as a group are inherently opposed to, or outside, the forms of self-interest and national chauvinism which support and encourage competition between modern states, with their exploitation of the Third World externally, and their hierarchies of class, race and other social divisions internally.

It is true that some women, together with some men, have always fought for the political vision of a world free from all forms of domination and exploitation. And today there are probably more women than men fighting for international peace. Affirming the importance of the most characteristic activities and functions of women in caring for others can serve as a criticism of the militarisation of our societies, which can no longer offer us even the guarantee of a future for our children. But these same 'female' characteristics have also been mobilised in the service of war and to support other conservative economic and political goals. Most women have chosen to uphold the privileges of their particular nation, social class, region and race – often in the name of the interests of their children. And, if we accept traditional ideas about women's inclinations and potential (however much we may choose to revalue them) we fail to challenge women's exclusion from those areas of technology and science which could be developed in the interests of women. It seems important for feminists to have a historical grasp on when the social context and conditions of women have led them to organise for egalitarian and progressive goals, and when they have served to perpetuate conservative and destructive ends. We cannot ignore the women of the New Right in the USA and Britain today who, in the name of women's interests, not only oppose all moves towards the greater autonomy of women but support their countries' military obsessions.

If we are working for the liberation for all women, we can never merely celebrate the suppressed 'female' values associated with caring, unless we also embark on dismantling the social practices which maintain male dominance and social inequality generally. This means not working for a future which is 'female', but working for a future which rejects most of the social distinctions we now draw between women and men. As Cynthia Cockburn has argued:

> All the true diversity that people are capable of
> experiencing and expressing, of needing in their sexual,
> domestic and working lives and of contributing to society,
> is repressed by gender ... Gender difference is not true
> difference at all ... The good qualities deemed masculine –
> courage, strength and skill, for instance – and the good
> qualities seen as feminine – tenderness, the ability to feel

and express feelings – should be the qualities available to
all and recognised and acclaimed wherever they occur,
regardless of the sex of the person ... Any society we set
out to organise anew would surely be a celebration of
multiplicity and individual difference.[2]

In building that society feminists are going to have to engage
with the mainstream of political power – in trade unions, local
councils, and in Parliament. It is a slow and difficult process,
taking us back to the old socialist feminist emphasis on the need
to organise autonomously as women to maintain our strength,
confidence and direction, while also working in embattled
alliances to confront the power of men on the Left and in
progressive social movements. The dangers of co-option through
men's superficial or token support, and demoralisation through
their deep-rooted opposition, will continue to batter feminists'
attempts to place women's interests at the centre of political
debate and action. But I see no cosy escape from this work;
women can no longer endorse notions of 'female' virtue and
value too long associated with the lives of women and kept
separate from the lives of men.

Attempting to explore what I see as problems with
contemporary feminist theories and practices has meant that I
have needed to provide my own account of the history of the
British women's liberation movement, assessing its strengths and
weaknesses. It is bound to be a partial one, based on my own
involvement since 1971 and reflecting my position as a white,
heterosexual socialist feminist with secure employment in
London. It is also certain to displease many feminists, women
who have inspired and helped others to gain a new sense of
confidence in themselves as women. But it seems to me a time
for questioning and reassessment. We face a situation where,
culturally, women's events are popular; commercially, 'feminism' – or some versions of it – are a market success; and yet the
women's movement itself continues to fragment and weaken.

Feminists were at one time attacked from all sides; we
survived and flourished then. Today, when we are frequently
given token support (not that such support appears to change
anything very much for the majority of women) it is not a time
for complacent certainties but for open discussion and argument,

if feminism is to continue to develop in creative and challenging ways. Facing up to our different perspectives and practices for building women's liberation may make it easier to see when and how we can support each other, despite our differences.

1. Compensations of the Powerless:

The Themes of Popular Feminism

To cast out and incorporate in a person of the opposite sex all we miss in ourselves and desire in the universe and detest in humanity is a deep and universal instinct on the part of both men and women. But though it affords relief, it does not lead to understanding. Rochester is as great a travesty of the truth about men as Cordelia is of the truth about women.

Virginia Woolf[1]

Feminists have their own version of the Tower of Babel story. They feel that men have undermined women by confounding their language, the language of their bodies, their unconscious, their desire or their experience. In order to act together an authentic language of women must be forged. If there is no common language there can be no true collective action.

Deborah Cameron[2]

I have often sought power in devious ways but I have never been content to be powerless, unnoticed or simply passive. Nor has any other woman I have known. But women's sense of their own power is usually hard to sustain. Most women know only too well the feelings of being trapped, confined and devalued. Subordination to some man's authority regularly threatens to smother the strength and autonomy most of us experience at least at some point in our lives. However, the material disadvantages and cultural devaluation of women compared to men exist alongside an affirmation of 'female' values, virtues and traits. Women can and do find comfort and strength in the confirming consolations of their relative powerlessness, in the existing ideas and ideals of 'men' and 'women'.

Some of these consolations, like the genuine pleasures of motherhood and of running a home, do give women power.

1

Mother dragons may frighten or entrance the kids and may even threaten Father, at least within the confines of home, however much their real domestic lives may be based on financial dependence and social subservience. Other confirming compensations, like the glamour and pleasures of fashion, (now increasingly sought by young men) or the fantasies of romantic fiction, can enable women, if only vicariously, to experience themselves as the fiercely desired objects of those with greater power and status. Out at work, the secretary in her office may be proudly aware that a department could not function without her and that her boss depends on her knowledge of all aspects of his business. She lacks only his authority, money and prestige.

'Feminists', however, are seen as women who scorn such compensatory trappings. This perception certainly did initially apply to the second wave of organised feminism. We did want real power, in every sphere. By power we meant not the means to control and dominate others – at least that is not what most of us thought we wanted – but rather the freedom and space to express our own desires, creativity and potential: to flourish and to find 'our place in the sun'. We sought to build the collective power of all women. We wanted power to participate in the making of a new world which would be free from all forms of domination. These goals were summed up, if rather inelegantly, in the manifesto prepared for the first British Women's Liberation Conference in Oxford in 1970:

> We want eventually to be, and to help other women to be, in charge of our own lives ... We come together as groups and as individuals to further our part in the struggle for social change and the transformation of society.[3]

Today, the public face of feminism has changed. At any feminist gathering you are far more likely to hear assertions about the special nature of women and their values, with references to the separate and special 'world of women'. It may seem ironic that radical ideas and strategies should rely on conventional assumptions of 'masculinity' and 'femininity', but it is this *traditional* gender ideology which has become the *new* 'common sense' of feminism.

After two decades of feminist research, it is now easier to see that men globally have greater wealth, power and privilege than women. However, it is harder for feminists to agree on the theories or the strategies to explain this or to challenge it. We do know that everywhere, despite the liberal aspirations of the 'decade of women' (the 'invisible decade', as it has been called), women remain considerably poorer and less educated than men, and are largely absent from positions of power in *all* political, economic, religious, cultural and judicial institutions.[4] Ironically, the very popularity and acceptability of many aspects of feminist thought here in Britain across political perspectives, including the conservative, makes the continuing power of men all the harder to understand. Some men, as well as women, applaud much that feminists are saying. Some men shed tears over their own beastliness. But men's power seems all the more invincible as recognition and resistance *appear* to leave it unchanged and immutable. Is feminism itself falling back upon the traditional consolations of the powerless? Certain developments suggest to me that it is.

The Virtues of Women

The feminist writing which is now most popular in this country, which is always listed among the bestsellers in progressive literary magazines, is a new form of radical feminism. Mostly from North America, where it is known as 'cultural feminism', it celebrates women's superior virtue and spirituality and decries 'male' violence and technology. Such celebration of the 'female' and denunciation of the 'male', however, arouses fear and suspicion in feminists who, like me, recall that we joined the women's movement to challenge the myths of women's special nature.

Some of us also recall, from the history feminists have revealed, how thoroughly the attempt to revalue women's special virtues and motherhood in the 1920s and 1930s overtook and eventually crushed more confident and rebellious feminisms. Back in 1913, a very young Rebecca West was warning feminists of the 'sin of self-sacrifice', which could turn a movement 'from a march towards freedom to a romp towards voluptuous servitude.'[5] Yet today, like any Victorian gentleman, Robin Morgan, Adrienne Rich, Susan Griffin, Judith Arcana, Mary

Daly, Dale Spender and their many followers, take for granted and celebrate women's greater humanism, pacifism, nurturance and spiritual development. Robin Morgan tells us that only women can guarantee the future of life on earth. Ronald Reagan and the New Right in the US and anti-feminist conservatives here in Britain tell us much the same thing.[6] Women can save the world from the nightmares of nuclear weaponry, which represents the untamed force of 'male drives and male sexuality', through the power of the feminine mentality and the force of maternal concerns. For the right, this would not of course be achieved by those they have characterised as 'the screaming destructive witches of Greenham', but rather by a return to the traditional values of Victorian family life, where women may continue, in the words of Tory philosopher Roger Scruton, 'to quieten' the 'unbridled ambition of the phallus'.[7]

Feminist thought has always confronted intractable dilemmas in its own appraisal of women. Not only must it fight to end the subjection of women, and to eradicate the existing gender ideologies which endorse and maintain it, but it must fight to protect and respect women in their existing vulnerability and weakness. This means rejecting the cultural disparagement and insidiously false veneration of all that is 'female'. Asserting women's strength and value sits awkwardly beside an awareness that many of women's most distinctive experiences and perceptions are products of subordination.

There is, of course, nothing surprising about the observation that dignity and strength may emerge through subordination and weakness – along with inequality and diminished lives and possibilities. One of the first public declarations of British feminism, Mary Wollstonecraft's manifesto *A Vindication of The Rights of Woman*, published in 1792, portrayed women as emotionally and intellectually stunted by their lives as women and by the prevailing conceptions of true womanhood.[8] But many suffragettes just over a century later elaborated similar conceptions of 'female nature' to insist upon the benefits of enfranchising the 'mothers' of the nation. Tactically, at least, it is clear that women can push for reforms, perhaps even most successfully, without any fundamental challenge to existing gender arrangements (that is, to the social relations between women and men) and the beliefs which maintain them. But the excitement of the feminism I once knew was precisely its promise that we *could* transform our own ideas of ourselves as women, hopefully keeping what was good in what we had learned from subordination, to create quite new relations between women and men, and between women and the world. We did not want to be like men; we wanted to be something new, and better.

Such talk of transformation and change is not found in the new idealised image of women in much contemporary feminism. Here is Susan Griffin:

> We [women] can read bodies with our hands, read the earth, find water, trace gravity's path. We know what grows and how to balance one thing against another ... and even if over our bodies they [men] have transformed this earth, we say, the truth is, to this day, women still dream.[9]

It is true, of course, if we generalise, that women are in many situations warmer, more sensitive and more caring of others than men; women usually seem less aggressive and competitive than men. And men have always told us that we are. Renowned misogynists like Kingsley Amis find security and comfort in their patronising belief that 'women are really much nicer than men. No wonder we like them.'[10] The image and reality of women's 'niceness', we can all agree, is connected with women's primary involvement with mothering and caring for others. But it is women's mothering and nurturing activities, and the social beliefs which support them, which are crucial to the maintenance of women's general subordination and economic dependence. While the virtues of maternal loving and caring are obvious, they have never been materially valued but instead applauded only with the hypocrisy of cheap sentiment. Might it not be, as some feminists once forcefully argued, that the reason men do not rear children in our society is not to do with any essential incapacity but because it provides little social prestige and little power?

Moreover, the virtues of maternal love can also be problematic. In our intensely individualistic, competitive, capitalist society, love and concern for others become inappropriate outside our very own small family groupings. Class privilege and racist exclusion are most frequently justified, by both women and men, in terms of the interests of one's own children. Narrowly focused on what often seems the threatened and precarious wellbeing of each individual child, maternal behaviour can be over-anxious and controlling, clinging and possessive. Children do become the self-enhancing surrogates for their parents' abandoned dreams. Within the context of male dominance, children may be the only reparation for a woman's more general frustrations and sense of powerlessness. Women's maternal selflessness can easily become a type of unconscious maternal selfishness, and an inability to allow children to develop caring relations with others.

The weight of responsibility for one's own children can mean a contraction of social vision, an envy and resentment of the welfare of others. So, for instance, while it may be true that women are more concerned about peace and a better world for their children (and, certainly, some women are organising for peace at Greenham and in nuclear disarmament groups) this does not necessarily mean that women are any less nationalistic, racist or committed to class privilege than men. Women, in this sense, participate in the social world they share with men, however subordinate they are to men in their own group. An awareness of these contradictions was central to the feminist writing of the early seventies, when, for example, Juliet Mitchell assessed the effects of women's oppression within the family like this:

> It produces a tendency to small-mindedness, petty jealousy, irrational emotionality and random violence, dependency, competitive selfishness and possessiveness, passivity, a lack of vision and conservatism.[11]

The suggestion that any such weaknesses are bound up with the objective conditions of women's mothering is disappearing from the contemporary celebration of female virtues and values.

Women and 'Nature'

It is not so much the social realities of women's mothering which are stressed in today's popular feminism as the links between women's lives, women's bodies, and the natural order of things. The eco-feminism of the eighties, which overlaps with 'cultural' feminism and has been called a 'new wave' in feminism, suggests that women must and will liberate the earth because they live more in harmony with 'nature'. Susan Griffin, introducing the British feminist ecology anthology *Reclaim the Earth*, argued that 'those of us who are born female are often less severely alienated from nature than are most men.'[12] It is woman's capacity for motherhood which is presented as connecting her with what Adrienne Rich calls the 'cosmic essence of womanhood', keeping women in touch with the essentially creative, nurturing and benign blueprint of nature.

It is a strange projection on to nature, of course, that nature is female; that it can be seen as gentle, sensual and nurturing rather than as brutal, ravaging and indifferent to individual life and survival. We have here an inversion of the sociobiology which is so popular on the right, where nature is 'male'. And bloody.

Such differing images of nature should not really surprise us, when, as anthropologists like Marilyn Strathern and others have pointed out, 'no single meaning can in fact be given to nature or culture in Western thought; there is no consistent dichotomy, only a matrix of contrasts.'[13] In some of the symbols which we use to contrast nature and culture it is 'the male' which is seen as closer to nature: forceful, violent, animal-like and instinctive; 'the female' is the product of culture, tamed, domestic, civilised. In other symbolisations the dichotomy is reversed: 'the male' becomes the creator of culture, 'the female' becomes instinct and biology. Neither 'woman' nor 'man', then, is consistently connected with 'nature'.

The battles fought over the relation between nature and culture, between human biology and human society, are forever recurring. Each cultural period reworks the theme, and redefines the problem. Feminists have fought fiercely to demolish the significance given to the biological in determining the social inequalities between women and men, and the contrasts we draw between 'femininity' and 'masculinity'. But today some feminists, with equal passion, appear to have gone over to the opposite camp. Before puzzling over the place and significance of the biological in human behaviour, we can at least be clear that appeals to 'nature' as a guide to human action provide few secure reference points. Conceptions of the 'natural' have changed radically throughout human history. In *Keywords*, Raymond Williams argues that 'any full history of the uses of *nature* would be a history of a large part of human thought.'[14] Elsewhere he illustrates that 'it was a widespread medieval idea that common ownership was more natural than private property.'[15] Yet, today, such an idea is so seemingly unnatural to the Tory mind as to threaten civilization as they know it.

Susan Griffin and Adrienne Rich, who both emphasise the significance of female biology, do recognise, though inconsistently, that the idea of 'nature' is culturally constructed, which for them means 'man-made'. However, they believe women must learn to trust their own biological 'instincts'. For Rich, this implies that women must 'think through the body'; for Griffin, that women must express 'what is still wild in us'.[16] Bodily states, with all their physiological complexities, are indeed a part of every move we make and every sensation we receive. Nevertheless, the biological/social divide is misleading since we can only experience, describe and understand these bodily states within specific social contexts, employing the cultural meaning available to us. For example, as a severely asthmatic child, I was regularly injected with adrenalin, and although I was usually fearful of all pain and especially fearful of injections, that particular injection aroused no fear. It certainly did not 'hurt'. The subsequent respiratory ease and adrenalin-induced emotional volatility took many forms. Sometimes I reacted with deep relaxation and sensual arousal, sometimes with an instant desire for activity and effort.

The same biological conditions, even in the most simple forms of arousal, can be experienced differently depending on the context. Women's experience of bodily states peculiar to women, like menstruation, pregnancy, breastfeeding or becoming ill with an ovarian cyst, are affected by cultural factors, as well as being individually varied. Ann Oakley, for example, has written of her own experience of young motherhood as a fight against constant depression:

> The years of giving birth and breastfeeding, which should have been years in which I felt fully alive, spelled instead a kind of death. I understand why, now. I did not have the social supports that prevent depression in married women. I had not been prepared properly for the realities of motherhood.[17]

Ann Oakley goes on to explain how the birth of her third child, some years later, was to prove a very different experience.

Thus, if we listen to our female bodies, social contexts and definitions will invariably affect what we hear and how we interpret its changing states. Social definitions will affect how we feel about ourselves, even though we may consciously wish to resist them.

It is also true that as feminists we have been responsible for providing new social definitions of women's physical states. For example, pre-menstrual tension is now acknowledged as a proper syndrome by the medical profession. It has been re-interpreted by some feminists as a potentially positive experience which can be used for rest, recuperation and contemplation. Women have demanded that it be taken into account in our working lives.

The feminist search for women's harmonious union with her bodily needs and functions may, however, fail to show how the social myths of a culture which reflects men's power in relation to women affect our experiences of our bodies. The female 'instincts' of Susan Griffin and Adrienne Rich, for example, just happen to express precisely what has been most central to traditional conceptions of womanhood within male-dominated culture over the last two hundred years. Should we not be a little more sceptical of an over-emphasis on the significance of 'female biology' where the woman's body is seen entirely in terms of sex and reproduction. Yet that is how Adrienne Rich depicts it for us:

> I have come to believe ... that female biology – the diffuse,
> intense sensuality radiating out from the clitoris, breasts, uterus,
> vagina; the lunar cycles of menstruation; the gestation and
> fruition of life which can take place in the female body – has far
> more radical implications than we have yet come to appreciate.[18]

The soft-focus feminism in many of today's women's magazines shows even less critical awareness of the social definitions already surrounding women's experience of their bodies. Questions about where these definitions come from and whether it is in women's interests to endorse them are not asked. For example, as Jo Spence has illustrated, there is a much greater emphasis on women's individual self-gratification in women's magazines now, replacing the former stress on women's loyalty and service to men and children.[19] But it also encourages an essentially narcissistic attitude to the self, detached from any emphasis on women's engagement in constructing and changing any aspect of the world they inhabit – least of all, their working lives. In these magazines, self-professed feminists urge women to attend to their bodies: to keep slim, exercised and fit, to feel liberated, cheerful and autonomous. There is not necessarily anything wrong with this message, particularly if we don't take it too seriously, but we should at least be aware that it is a message remarkably similar to the one Western women have so often heard about their bodies: that we should be thin and beautiful.

A similar criticism has been made of Susie Orbach's popular therapeutic advice in her book, *Fat is a Feminist Issue*.[20] Despite her sympathetic attention to the social definitions of and demands on women, and despite the therapeutic help many women have received from her, she nevertheless accepts that being 'fat' is the real problem that so many women face. Re-learning how to listen to our bodies, which can tell us 'how to lose weight', is the solution. Our bodies talk, it would seem, at least partially to support the conventional ideals of femininity as defined with male dominance, teaching women to 'let go of the fat as a defence'.[21]

There is a further problem: the biological basis of human behaviour is not only experienced and understood through social meanings but is itself determined and transformed by human society and human action. The growth and decay of human capacities are moulded within the possibilities and constraints of particular societies. They are not two separate or separable entities. The capacities and attributes which are seen as distinctly human, the ability to use language, to write, to develop a sense of personal identity, only develop in the context of social relations.

The human body and its needs never reduce to some inevitable or simply natural process. In the Third World, for example, men outlive women; in the West these differential death rates are reversed. Human *society* has always mediated, controlled and adapted bodily needs. Food, erotic stimuli, etc, have symbolic meanings. Biological constraints, though undoubtedly real, may indeed be easier to alter than social and cultural constraints. So far, in human history, it has proved easy to invent bottles to replace breastfeeding, but not to create the social conditions whereby men would take on the responsibility to bottlefeed their infants. All social conventions come to appear natural when in reality there are no inflexible and unchanging patterns, rhythms or relationships in which human development occurs. What is most essentially human is precisely that our lives, women's and men's, are *not* just determined by biological necessity but crucially also by human action and vision.

Human needs are never simply those of the body: they equally involve emotions and intellect. The need to relate, to understand, to create, to work and to contribute – all these are needs constructed only through social interaction. It is not any more 'natural' for human beings to care for children than it is for them to plan cities or build machines (however much it is right to value and reward the former activity). Technology can either benefit or hinder human welfare depending on who controls it and whose interests it serves. Women's exclusion from education and the growing seclusion of middle class women in the eighteenth and nineteenth centuries clearly did not produce a surfeit of female engineers. But Mary Potts' invention of a new type of domestic iron in the 1860s and Mrs Cockran's invention of the first dishwasher in 1899, both in North America and therefore on record, not to mention Marie Curie's discoveries about radioactivity which formed the basis of most subsequent nuclear research, would suggest that women are not intrinsically incapable of inventing machines or discovering the most abstract of scientific principles. Dora Russell's belief that only men could have invented machines is the sort of claim feminists heard with a wry smile ten years ago; it is a view that she, as a heroic, pioneering feminist held unchanged for some 70 years. It is disturbing, however, for Dale Spender to endorse such a view uncritically today.[22]

Before we race back to reaffirming ideas of the link between 'women' and 'nature', 'man' and 'machine', we should surely feel most troubled by their pivotal place in the gender ideology of male dominance. There they serve to rationalise women's exclusion from the pursuit of knowledge and from the exercise of power. And they combine sentimentality with contempt for the effects of this exclusion. Men have been seen as distanced from 'nature' because their power in the world has allowed them greater control over their own destinies and over the destinies of others, while the more restricted possibilities open to women have been justified and regulated through the ideology of 'biological necessity'.

Women's Liberation and the Problem of Men

The idealisation of the female as both more virtuous and more natural in contemporary cultural feminist writing has, as its inevitable complement, the denunciation of the male as bad, as an enemy of nature. It is male psychology which not only oppresses women but which threatens human survival. Robin Morgan tells us that man's competitiveness and greed must be held responsible for 'the evils of sexism, racism, hunger, war and ecological disaster.'[23] 'Male' culture and 'male' behaviour, Judith Arcana writes, are 'corrupt and oppressive'.[24] Male hatred and male abuse are said to characterise *all* relationships between men and women, and men and nature. It is the imagery of violent sexist pornography which has been used to symbolise men's relations to women and to nature, and to explain how men came to have power over women.

Andrea Dworkin informs us that men wield power over women through terror:

> The reality is that men commit acts of forced sex against women systematically. That is precisely what the women's movement has been based upon – the women's movement has been based upon that recognition.[25]

Dworkin's remaking of feminist history here is misleading. Adrienne Rich, concluding an American anthology of women against pornography, claims that 'this book is in some ways a microcosm of the American feminist movement as it stands at the beginning of the 1980s'.[26] If this is true, then that movement has changed. In both the US and in Britain (and, despite the many differences between the two movements, American feminism has always had a powerful influence in Britain) feminism in the early seventies was not *primarily* a reaction to men's violence against women.

It is true that in Britain the women's liberation movement in the early seventies began to organise against men's violence against women, as feminists had over a hundred years before. In particular, feminists fought for and supported a network of refuges for battered women. Direct action through demonstrations, sticker campaigns and graffiti was taken against *all* sexist representations of women: pin-ups, pornography and the

ubiquitous stereotyped female form promoting every commodity known to 'man'. But this was alongside countless other
strategies and actions studying and attacking the social practices
and beliefs which kept women economically dependent and
socially subordinate to men. *The Body Politic*, the first anthology
of writings from the women's liberation movement in Britain
1969-1972, indicates the scope: a concern with reproductive
rights, childcare and child allowance, women's health, training
for jobs and women's working conditions. In addition the role of
the media, the law, education and state policies generally in
regulating the lives of women were under scrutiny and
constantly criticised.[27]

Feminists in the early seventies were busy uncovering the
images, ideas and day-to-day practices through which women
were subordinated. Women, we argued, occupied a cultural
landscape which both belittled and silenced them, in a world
where they were undervalued, underpaid and undermined by the
arrogance, complacency or contempt of men. But, 'masculine'
and 'feminine' identities were seen as neither fixed nor
monolithic. Feminism, it was hoped, would give birth to new
women, and to new men. Indeed an attachment to gender
stereotypes, or to any idea of a 'natural' difference underlying
them, was criticised for causing women's oppression. As Sheila
Rowbotham wrote optimistically back in 1973, 'I think we are at
the beginning of new social and personal possibilities, both for
men and for women.'[28] Many feminists then were irritated by
any talk of sexual difference, and so less likely to emphasise any
positive differences in women. This failure to acknowledge
sufficiently the strengths of women's existing capacities and
behaviour (however much they may have been forged through
subordination) left a space which the later radical/cultural
feminists would fill.

Men, unsurprisingly, were always seen as a problem by
feminists. But in the seventies, typically masculine pursuits and
behaviour were more likely to be seen as contradictory. We
wanted the skills, confidence, sense of personal responsibility and
autonomy which men seemed to have – at least in relation to
women of their own class and group. We disliked and resented
the arrogance, insensitivity, self-assertion, and lack of responsibility for the welfare and feelings of others which many men

shared to varying degrees. We always expressed outrage at men's sexist assumptions: the stereotyped images of women which defined us primarily through our attraction for or usefulness to men. It is startling today to see again the unselfconscious and confident contempt for women in films considered progressive in the 1960s, like the misogynist treatment of Julie Christie in *Darling*; or to hear again the paternalistic tones of Harold Wilson describing women before we had even re-emerged on the political agenda as 'a problem'!

In recent years it has been suggested that feminists in the early seventies were too 'phallocentric': too accepting and uncritical of typically 'masculine' behaviour and values, too rejecting and critical of typically 'feminine' pursuits, style and behaviour. There is truth in some of this. The predominantly young women who had often benefited from a middle-class education and become feminists in the early seventies certainly wanted something very different from the lives of their mothers (though we equally wanted something very different from the lives of our fathers). But I know I was not alone in finding a new pride and pleasure in my own motherhood in those days. However often we hear it denied, and however much some feminists now disagree, children and childcare were of great importance to many of us then. 'The liberation of women', as Valerie Charlton wrote in 1973, 'is inseparable from, among other things, the development of different ways of caring for and relating to children.'[29] Feminists were over-reacting to what we saw as the shackles of conventional femininity, but we uncovered enough misery and bitterness in that world to warrant much of the reaction. The women's liberation movement insisted that the stereotypes of femininity denied and distorted women's experience and aspirations, and feminists then were more inclined to see men, and 'masculinity', too, as having their own contradictions. Men expressed their adoration and need and concern for women, alongside their bullying, their put-downs and their contempt. The popular notion of 'male chauvinism' suggested something which could be shifted.

It was also more readily admitted that men were a motley crew at a time when many feminists had emerged from, and still saw themselves as part of, the then still flourishing 'counter culture' and left, radical and revolutionary movements. Men did relate variously to typical masculine ideals: sometimes with ambivalence, self-doubt, anxiety (expressed in private), and, occasionally, as in the simultaneously emerging gay movement, with outright rejection and mockery (often expressed in public). Sheila Rowbotham sums up some of the fearless if somewhat patronising confidence of those times:

> We must not be discouraged by them [men]. We must go on our own way but remember we are going to have to take them with us. They learn slowly. They are like creatures who have just crawled out of their shells after millennia. They are sore and tender and afraid.[30]

Nor was the feminist rejection of men's power and status without contradictions. There was, most obviously in heterosexual women, extreme ambivalence towards the different degrees of personal power of men on the left. We admitted our resentment of powerful men, we rejected their habitual dominance, but could we admit the attraction they held? Patterns of attraction to powerful men (and also, increasingly, to powerful women) conflicted with our desire for completely egalitarian relations in all situations. This ambivalence, which could be predicted from any admission of the infantile and unconscious entanglements of desire and attraction with the appeal of the powerful, was a factor, I believe, in the later rigorous and self-righteous repudiation of men by many feminists.

Many radical men in the early seventies changed rapidly from outraged ridicule and rejection of the very idea of women's liberation towards, at the very least, more patronising encouragement. As Juliet Mitchell wrote in 1971:

> In an effort to repudiate the days of obscene ridiculing of Women's Liberation, radical men who endorse the movement have taken up various postures in relation to it, ranging from the tilting, half-begging posture 'let us in' to the falling over backwards 'go ahead show us the way, you're the new revolutionary hope … we'll support you'.[31]

Men in the 'counter culture' appeared from the start to accept the sexual politics of both the women's liberation movement and the gay liberation movement. They refused to feel threatened by it. Many were even to chastise their women friends for any reluctance over their feminist commitments; for some men, it meant that women could now perhaps be expected to make even fewer demands of the men in their lives! But if at times men's support was partially one of surface and style, genuine assistance was offered for the campaigning work of the women's movement. Some men did listen to women, and try to change. In the organised left, though women's oppression was theorised only as a by-product of class oppression, 'women's rights' did begin to appear on every political agenda – though almost always at the end.

The majority of feminists then believed that men could, and must, change. Women's personal struggle with the men in their lives was seen as the main aim of sexual politics in the early seventies. Feminists at that time who, as I did, lived with men, battled to force men to share childcare and housework – often successfully. The men I lived and worked with in the grassroots local politics of north London, for example, did come to value the time they spent in childcare: whether it was with their own children, or with the children of friends or lovers. (The history of the success, as well as the inevitable failures of more communally shared domestic commitments has yet to be written – hopefully the children involved may soon supply it themselves!)[32]

It is true that feminists also argued with altogether more ambiguous and uncertain success that the men they were close to should abandon all their sexist thought and behaviour; that is, their former ways of thinking about and relating to women primarily as sex objects and providers of emotional and physical nurturance. But the current popularity of Andrea Dworkin's thoughts on 'the systematic sadism of men' could not be further removed from much of the early sexual politics of women's liberation. Dworkin's writing, sometimes as lurid as pornography itself, distorts and denies that politics. She writes:

> One can know everything and still be unable to accept the fact that sex and murder are fused in male consciousness, so that one without the immanent possibility of the other is unthinkable and impossible. One can know everything and still, at bottom, refuse to accept that the annihilation of women is the source of meaning and identity for men.[33]

One can know nothing and still, with certainty, know that this terrorising rhetoric is false and alarmingly unhelpful.

The issue of men's violence, and of its timeless, universal inevitability, moved to the centre of feminist thought and action in the eighties. The belief that men will never change, that male dominance is inevitable and incurable, has become a dominant view, at least within radical feminism. Angela Hamblin, for example, described this development in 1982:

> ... in Britain the belief that change is possible, and therefore worth pursuing, is a minority view within radical feminist circles ... the arguments which insist on total separation from men and the abandonment of male children as the only solution to women's oppression, have tended to eclipse the earlier radical feminist ideas which focused on forcing political change ... Feminists who are trying to bring about change in their relationships with individual men, or attempting to influence the development of their male children, are seen as squandering female energy, and have even, on occasions, been denounced as 'collaborators with the enemy'.[34]

I am aware that the radical and cultural feminist themes I have criticised have become popular in feminism today because they have given many women a new sense of confidence and creativity in their lives as women, and mobilised anger against the abusive, dismissive and oppressive behaviour of many men towards women. As we shall see in the course of this book, these themes have inspired a radical rejection of the most uncaring, irrational and destructive aspects of the world we know. But I am troubled because they have also been developed and turned into a new political project by some influential and commercially successful feminists in ways which dismiss as unimportant most of the activities of women's liberation in the seventies: activities which, I believe, were and are crucial to the future of feminism. This new and problematic project for feminism has been developed most comprehensively in the US by Mary Daly and in Britain by Dale Spender.

Mary Daly's Psychic Voyaging

The passionate intensity of Andrea Dworkin's denunciation of men is not only supported but surpassed by Mary Daly's consignment of men, and all things male, to universal execration: now and forever. No thunders from the Vatican (from the Catholic faith, which Mary Daly once professed and to whose discourse and rhetoric she remains devoted) have ever so passionately portrayed a cosmic evil, or one so entirely menacing, as the 'polluting', 'poisoning' and 'contaminating' evil of men's rule, of 'phallocracy'. It, and it alone, 'is the root of rapism, racism, gynocide, genocide and ultimately biocide.'[35] Relentlessly, Mary Daly insists upon the elemental purity of women (their 'spiritual/moral power') and the permanent pestilence of men (the 'sovereigns of the sadostate'). In *Gyn/Ecology* she documents in full and chilling detail every type of cruelty which men have ever inflicted upon women from the beginning of time. From footbinding in China, widow-burning in India, 'witch' burnings in Europe, to the contemporary abuse of women in the West through harmful gynaecology and psychotherapy, rape and wife beating, she declares that women's history is a 'history of holocausts ... (of) the multitudes of women sacrificed as burnt offerings.'[36]

Such a magnitude of male crimes against women would alone make this book memorable. They comprise the most horrifying catalogue of brutality towards women. But the impact of *Gyn/-Ecology*, published in 1978, was greater than this. It has been described by many feminists as the single most important and influential book to emerge from North American feminism since the early seventies.[37] It is important not only because it is widely read by feminists – impressed by its deliberately outrageous passion and provocation and by its startling poetics of wordplay, alliteration, metaphor and punning – but because it represents a new and very particular project for feminism. It promotes as its solution to male-domination an individual and psychic voyage, on which only women may embark, out of 'the cockocratic sadostate'. In this book, and its sequel *Pure Lust*, Daly takes us on a psychic journey into her idea of 'women's space'. Real women who are in touch with their own elementary being must embark on this journey, for 'women', as she likes to quote Virginia Woolf, 'have no country of their own'. Forsaking the logic, language and reasoning of men, women must travel to their own 'country'. A strange country, for it exists, like Heaven, without physical dimensions, a 'hagocentric psychic space' constructed out of Daly's feminist philosophy.

> The point is not to save society or to focus on escape ... but to release the Spring of be-ing. To the inhabitants of Babel, this Spring of living speech will be unintelligible ... So much the better for the Crone's Chorus. Left undisturbed we are free to find our own concordance, to hear our own harmony of the spheres.[38]

In her role as guide, Daly's primary concern is to expose the pollution of patriarchal culture and language. Above all, elemental women must learn to 'recycle' words to enable 'cleansing/depolluting of the Self by the Self'.[39] The way to end male domination and to create women's power is through language:

> Breaking the bonds/bars of phallocracy requires breaking through the radiant power of words, so that by releasing words, we can release our Selves. Lusty women long for radiant words, to free their flow, their currents, which like our own be-ing have been blocked and severed from ancestral Memory. The Race of Lusty Women, then, has deep connections with the Race of Radiant Words.[40]

For Mary Daly, reality is reduced to language: language alone creates reality. Women must subvert or 'castrate' the male meanings of words to unearth their buried female meanings: reclaiming the New/Old meanings of 'witch', 'crone', 'hag' and 'spinster', can serve again to empower women. These ancient meanings of words are, like women's own country, not traceable to any particular time or place. In reclaiming the New/Old meanings to express their inner essence, however, women rediscover something already familiar to them in the Bad/Old meanings of male-dominated culture. Women rediscover their affinity with nature: 'For we are rooted, as are animals and trees, wind and seas, in the Earth's substance. Our origins are in her elements.'[41] Men, in boundless and illimitable contrast, are 'the life-blockers ... radically separated from the natural harmony of the universe.' Men's separation from nature is so total that 'It is a trap to imagine women should "save" men from the dynamics of demonic possession.'[42]

I would love to take pleasure in this familiar nineteenth-century pagan romanticism, with all its rites this time reserved for women. I would love to chuckle along with my friends , both women and men, at Daly's so 'absolutely Anti-androcrat, A-mazingly Anti-male' fiery poetics. Many feminists have delighted in Daly's passionate promise of female fulfilment. How powerful the image of salvation she offers women! She dangles before us 'the intense joy of woman-identified bonding and creating', with her warm, cosy and apparently all-embracing notion of *'Female Be-Friending'*.[43] She unfurls the rich and colourful 'cosmic tapestries' of sisterhood, woven from the 'deep hearing by sisters'.[44] But there is a snag. Mary Daly's writing is also A-mazingly anti-woman, as well as anti-political. When we come to the end of our long journey through patriarchy's deceptions (in my view a journey largely constructed from within the discourse of those deceptions) we find, as Meaghan Morris so vividly argues, 'yet another image of the evil of Other women'.[45] Daly is crystal clear that her journey to the 'Otherworld' of the Race of Women is for the chosen few.

Not only all men, but most women, are excluded from any possible creative being or salvation. The 'Painted Birds' (the stereotypically feminine), the 'token feminists' (those seeking or offering reforms for women), the 'fembots' (female robots or professional women) and a host of other 'parasites' are too 'blinded' and 'damaged' by patriarchy to free themselves, and express their inner female biophilic being and spirituality. These women, like the Race of Men, can pollute and poison the Lusty Woman and impede her journey. Such women are not even the authors of their own evil and contaminating ways: they appear 'to be normal', but their distance from the 'telic centering principle within' establishes them as 'man-made, made-up, misbegotten'.[46] They are the women who are 'lobotomized', who are 'victimized into a state of living death',[47] who are 'trained to kill off feminists in patriarchal professions',[48] 'taken as tokens before they have a chance to be selves'.[49] They too are damned, *not* of the Race of Woman.

Daly's image of Happiness is primarily 'a life of contemplation',[50] but some forms of creative activism are acceptable: 'such as shelters for battered women, rape crisis centers, anti-pornography demonstrations, women's concerts, anti-nuclear protests, the women's health movement, female-identified rituals.'[51] Others are not. Beyond the pale of acceptable women's activity is any which seeks reform or change within existing institutions, in the world of paid work, or the state, or in any alliance with men. The 'token feminist' is thus one of the most dangerous of creatures. Her support for reforms (like equal rights, affirmative action, abortion rights, women's studies courses) can be used by the patriarchy to sap women's energy, because 'the appearance of social mobility, or progress, squelches the instinct to revolt and create radical change ... taming the radical impulse with false hope.'[52]

None can follow Daly but the pure of heart. She tells us how to recognise them: 'Gestures, witty comments, facial expressions, glances, a certain light in the eye, caresses, style of clothing, ways of walking, choices of occupation, of environment – these are a few of the signals of women's participation in Be-Friending, or of her nonparticipation in the Spinning/Weaving process.'[53] She does not say women must be affluent, highly educated, white, Western, free of needy dependents and all exhausting commitments. She does not say the weary night-cleaner cannot enter into her Gnostic Nag-Nation of Dreamers, as she dreams only of sleep. She does not give it a single solitary thought! Daly's voyage is also offensive to Black feminists who have been saying for some time now that they are up against more than male abuse, more than male power. For as Audre Lorde powerfully rebukes Mary Daly: 'beyond sisterhood is still racism.'[54] Women's oppression is not everywhere the same. The differences are as important as the similarities. Audre Lorde succinctly summarises her own criticism in *An Open Letter to Mary Daly*:

> The oppression of women knows no ethnic nor racial boundaries, true, but that does not mean it is identical within those boundaries. Nor do the reservoirs of our ancient power know these boundaries, either. To deal with one without even alluding to the other is to distort our commonality as well as our difference.[55]

Daly's voyage of the mind, possible only for the few, could hardly be further removed from the grassroots, anti-elitist activism flourishing in the early days of the women's liberation movement in the US and Britain. Not Big, Strong, Lusty women, but the lives of the most exploited and most oppressed women were the focus of much of this activity. Campaigns with women living on social security pittances, or with those working anti-social hours, with the homeless or in support of women in prisons or mental hospitals, were common engagements of feminists then.

But feminist critics of Daly's chauvinist and anti-materialist elitism are easily dismissed by her supporters. Dale Spender, for example, tells us that to criticise Mary Daly's work for disregarding the realm of the material (as indeed is its own proud boast) 'is to evaluate her work against patriarchal standards'.[56] However Frightfully and Fearlessly Frank/Forthright/Funny we may try to be about Mary Daly's exclusion of all men and most women from any serious claim to humanity, we would be ignored by the faithful.

Mary Daly herself ignores all her critics. She refuses to discuss or debate with them: she does not talk with 'stupid women', as she told an audience in Sydney, Australia, in August 1981.[57] So she and her followers have ignored, for example, the lucid and witty critique of her type of linguistic determinism by Meaghan Morris.[58] Introducing new words, or subverting isolated signs, as the linguists would say, does not on its own transform the way meaning is produced within language, let alone transform reality.

Meaghan Morris's argument against Daly's feminist linguistics is extremely powerful. Meanings, 'patriarchal' or otherwise, are not carried by individual words. They are produced by the particular types of linguistic contexts or 'discourses' in which they occur: the way words are customarily connected up within different types of speech. For instance, we could refer to the discourse of Catholicism, with its polarities of Good and Evil, Purity and Sin; the discourse of nineteenth-century roman-ticism, which sees the individual, placed at the centre of the social world, as the agent of his or her own fate: the discourse of naturalism, which connects (though inconsistently) women with nature and men with culture. All these discourses of the male-dominated individualistic culture of capitalism are adopted, uncritically, in Mary Daly's feminist metaphysics. And they explain her exclusion of so many women – the 'corrupted', the 'damaged' and the 'parasites' – from the Race of Woman. For they are discourses which exclude and deny any notion of how inequality is a product of social structures and social relations, not reducible to individual evil, incompetence or alienation from nature. (Just as language itself is integrated with social life generally, and not the sole determiner of our individual perceptions and experience.)[59] They are each discourses incompatible with any feminist project aiming to include all women. The predicaments and concerns of most women could not possibly be seen as separate and separable from the material world they inhabit. It is a world which they share, to a considerable extent, with men of their own class, race, religion or sexual orientation. It is a predicament which is determined by factors other than their sex.

Dale Spender and the Separate World of Women

Mary Daly's work has encouraged new ways of thinking and writing in North American feminism, as Susan Griffin[60] and many other popular feminist writers have acknowledged. And, like most things born in the USA, it has had repercussions well beyond its own birthplace.

In Britain, however, it is the prolific Australian feminist Dale Spender who has most successfully popularised the idea of feminism as a cultural movement for freeing women from the imposition of 'male values'. Like Mary Daly, she argues that women's experience and values have been suppressed by men. The project of feminism should be to allow women to rediscover our own knowledge, 'to reclaim our minds':

> A feminist is a woman who does not accept man's socially sanctioned view of himself ... feminism refers to the alternate meanings put forward by feminists.[61]

It is men's control over language which in Dale Spender's view denies women's experience and values. Men's control over 'meanings' creates men's power: language itself causes women's oppression.

My problem with Spender's analysis is that, like Mary Daly's, it suggests purely idealist rather than any practical solutions to the universal reality of male domination. There is no talk of struggle, success or even progress in Spender's works. She coyly asks, 'Is winning the issue?' It is not, she responds, since our idea of 'winners and losers' is patriarchal; patriarchy created the idea (forget about the reality) of dominance and oppression.[62] Class struggle never appears in Spender's writing, and racial oppression is reduced to the unjust 'white value system'.[63] In her opinion 'Marxism and capitalism [are] two sides of the same economistic coin that glorifies male achievement and reduces human and life-enhancing values to the periphery, in the interests of technological conquest.'[64]

Dale Spender's philosophical idealism, which collapses the notion of 'objective reality' into the subjective ways we see and describe it, underpins all her writing, and continually threatens to reduce the reality of women's oppression to little more than a set of ideas. A type of toothless liberalism results. It is clear in her conclusion to *Women of Ideas (And What Men Have Done To Them)*:

> I do not seek a victory over men. I do not wish to deny in full their values and their creations but I do want to deny, again and again, that their values and their creations are the only ones that society can outline. I want co-existence.[65]

Later on in the same page she adds, 'I want men to be "irrelevant" to our enterprise of constructing our own knowledge …'[66] Her goals, it seems to me, pose little or no threat to the minds, pockets or powers of men. But is winning the issue?

Spender tirelessly asserts and documents the over-riding importance of women's ideas. In *For the Record* she gives her reason for writing her history of our own recent women's movement: 'It is for now and for the future a declaration that women have wonderful ideas.'[67] It is important to Spender to insist that women's wonderful ideas never change: 'Great strength and great joy can be derived from the knowledge that a little over 50 years ago, many women felt much the same about male power as many women do today.'[68] Why? Great weakness and great sorrow would seem a more appropriate reaction if indeed all we as women could claim, while men have continued to dominate us, is that we have noticed the fact.

Spender takes comfort from the belief that women's ideas have remained unchanged for centuries, perhaps for ever. From Mary Astell in the seventeenth century to Mary Wollstonecraft in the eighteenth century to Sheila Rowbotham and Adrienne Rich in the twentieth century, women have been saying the same thing; anticipating what Dale Spender is herself saying: asserting the timeless, over-riding and unchanging significance of gender. Women's lives and experiences remain essentially the same, dictated by some inner essence of womanhood. Time and circumstance pass us by, the many social divisions which appear to determine very different prospects and priorities for different women are unimportant. Spender thus denies any significant change in women's lives. For women, she feels, 'progress' is an absurd concept: 'if it has any meaning it applies only to men.'[69] The only progress women have seen is in men's ever more sophisticated account of female inferiority. Women live, in Dale Spender's philosophy, in men's heads. No wonder she wants to escape.

In complete contrast to these views, I agree with those feminists who argue that even our ideas of 'woman' and woman's consciousness, as well as the lives of women, have changed constantly. Australian historian Jill Matthews, for example, criticises any ahistorical category of women's experience:

> I would argue instead that women and men and the nature of misogyny and oppression are all qualitatively different in different times and places. The sense of similarity, of easily drawn parallels, is illusory. Women themselves change: it is precisely the differences in circumstances that [are] crucial to the meaning and sense of being a woman. We must therefore understand the particularity of our own circumstances in order to understand ourselves.[70]

Women's lives have been transformed under Western capitalism in the last few centuries. The degree of independence and autonomy many women now experience was almost unthinkable to the eighteenth and nineteenth century feminist. It is quite false to suggest, as Spender does, that 'There is little to distinguish us from our foremother Mary Wollstonecraft, who made much the same argument that I am making here ...'[71] Mary Wollstonecraft's pleas for the education of girls alongside boys have been met. The problems of women and education today are not the same as those which she faced. Wollstonecraft's contempt for the degradations of 'femininity' could hardly provide a starker contrast with Spender's faith in the 'meanings' and 'values' of women.

Even at the turn of the century the choices feminists had in Britain were quite different from those today. Cicely Hamilton's *Marriage As A Trade* (1909) outlines what she saw as the alternatives for women of her class. For her, as for all single middle class women of her time, the price of a career was celibacy and childlessness.[72] Cicely Hamilton's struggles were for access into the professions of men.

Spender's unchanging categories of experience distort or deny the vast differences in women's lives and experiences even within the same periods and places. Until the First World War, for example, there remained a huge gulf between the domestic life of the bourgeois woman under capitalism and the lives of her servants. This was before childcare or housework had acquired the sanctified status they were later to have, and before the focus of feminist concern shifted to the needs of mothers and their children. Today it is not so much the domestic circumstances of women, but rather the very different job prospects open to them, determined primarily by their ethnic and class positions, which provide the major contrast in women's lives.[73] This is why Spender, and other cultural feminists, ignore women in the workforce. For it is there that dramatic contrasts are so sharply revealed in the degree of self-assertion, authority and creativity different groups of women may exercise, and in the level of respect and reward they may receive.

Spender's dismissal of material circumstances as irrelevant to the realm of 'ideas' removes us from any analysis of the many, and changing, institutional sites where women have fought for *and won* significant changes in their lives. More worryingly, Spender denies the significance and value of many of these struggles with her formula: 'NO MATTER WHAT WOMEN DO [Spender's emphasis] it can be arranged to suit patriarchy.'[74]

In her own chosen terrain, that of women and language, Dale Spender has rightly been praised for publicising the extent to which our conventional use of language excludes, trivialises and demeans women. The publication of *Man Made Language* in 1980 alerted many people to the sexism of language. 'Man', not 'Woman', provides the norm for humanity. (The odd male journalist with feminist sympathies has even been known to boast of his computer program designed to eliminate the 'male-as-norm' fault from his word processor.)[75] Our use of language does reflect the centrality, power and authoritativeness of men, and of all things seen as 'male', in human social relations. 'Yes, sir' cannot be feminised without a lowering of the tone of respect, which is why women officers newly admitted to the elite Sandhurst military training college must be addressed as 'sir' and not 'madam'. 'Woman' and all things regarded as characteristically feminine are usually negatively valued (or romanticised) in language. Language, as Dale Spender suggests, is systematically sexist. It does play an active role in the symbolic positioning of women as inferior to men and therefore in constructing and perpetuating that reality.

But other feminists have revealed gaps and weaknesses in Spender's work on language. Spender wants to argue that even the abstract, semantic rules of language are imposed by men. The first male semantic rule of language, she asserts, is that 'man' must represent the norm of humanity. A second semantic rule makes it a contradiction 'to formulate representations of women's autonomy or strength'.[76] But Spender's semantic rules are not rules at all. We can easily, even unsurprisingly, paraphrase Blake to affirm, '*She* reminds us all once again that ... Mercy has a human heart, Pity a human face.' We would thereby contradict Spender's first rule for assigning meanings. We can as easily and intelligibly contradict Spender's second rule: 'Girls/women are powerful/beautiful/wonderful/smart', or whatever else we like. Men have not determined the semantic rules for assigning meaning in the way Spender suggests.

Maria Black and Rosalind Coward have convincingly criticised Spender's work, pointing out that she confuses the underlying rules and structures of language with what are the conventional *uses* of language.[77] Her 'rules' are not so much rules as conventions, habits and traditions of language use; they are familiar terminologies or types of discourse. Such conventions govern or guide the way we customarily connect words within specific types of contexts. The familiar devaluation of women in language is not a rule of language, but is a linguistic link to the presence and power of men in all the social institutions which produce these discourses; whether academic, legal, medical, bureaucratic or religious. They reflect men's historic and continuing positions of power within these separate institutions, and hence men's way of representing the world with themselves as the norm and women as deviant. Black and Coward conclude, therefore, that it is not meanings but 'discursive practices' which need analysing since they express and partly constitute men's power, and women's place within language as inferior. It is possible, however, to expose or 'deconstruct' the male-centred assumptions of different discourses, to explore all the hidden meanings which presuppose a male subject. It is even possible to attempt to make women visible rather than hidden, central rather than peripheral, positive rather than negative within such discourses – though the reconstructed discourse itself, like talk of 'God the Loving Mother', may become barely recognisable in the process.

The connections we make between experience, language and reality are crucial to understanding the political implications of Spender's work. She believes that there is a disjuncture between women's experience and language, and hence between women's experience and 'reality'. 'Reality' is constructed out of men's language. Meanings and 'reality' already exist, separate from the individual, but defined by men. Women's experience is alienated. In contrast, Black and Coward believe that experience cannot arise outside language and the meanings available to us for interpretation. Our experiences and our sense of individual identity are therefore themselves a product of language. Thus, although from opposite positions, both Spender and her critics Black and Coward give language a pre-eminent role in determining reality.

In a useful overview of these contrasting perspectives within feminist linguistics, Deborah Cameron has recently criticised all forms of linguistic determinism. She rejects the idea that language alone determines perception and reality, whether or not we see language as male-defined and women as alienated from it.[78]

Cameron opposes the linguistic theories of Saussure and Whorf which feminists have drawn upon, both of which see meanings as fixed and static within the system of signs which constitute a language. Instead she argues that there is always scope for creativity in language use, and that meanings do shift:

'It is clear that as conditions alter, speakers can and do modify both their frame of reference and their language ... [a] remoulding [of] our linguistic classification system is constantly being undertaken.'[79] For example, where once 'work' was a concept applied to activity outside the domestic sphere, feminists have raised the issue of 'workers' in the home. Where once 'the personal' was defined in contrast to 'the public' and 'the political', feminists have spoken of 'personal politics', and stressed the gaps and distortions behind such dichotomies. Language, therefore, does not determine reality in any fixed way. It does, though, provide the dominant frames of reference and the dominant meanings we attach to experience at any particular time. But language creation and use interact with other power relations of social life. As Cameron explains, it is not that women have problems with language but rather that they usually lack the power to participate in the construction of particular types of privileged, dominant and authoritative uses or 'registers' of language. Most women have been excluded, for a variety of historical reasons, from the institutional contexts where 'learning' and 'high culture' are produced. They are also rarely powerful within state-controlled mass media or private oligarchies of journalism and advertising.

Rather than write, as Spender does, of men's transhistorical and universal control over meanings, I feel we would do better to study how particular groups of people are able to control the specific institutions which construct dominant frameworks of meaning. We would then see that it is rarely *all* men, but only men from the dominant social groups – white, middle-class, heterosexual and able-bodied – who have power in these institutions. And it is not only women who are so often excluded from what is positively valued and made central within authoritative or dominant discourses. All subordinate groups are similarly placed; which is why, for example, working class and ethnic minority speech has often been treated as linguistically inadequate. It is also now possible for us to begin to investigate the extent to which a growing feminist access to privileged areas of knowledge, in psychology, biology, history, literary criticism and elsewhere, has begun to shift the focus and nature of description and explanation in these areas.

Spender's belief that women have their own separate

experiences but are unable to encode or express them in language leads us into all sorts of dead ends. If women had separate experiences, even separate 'knowledge', why should they be incapable of finding the words to speak about them? If men's power denies women their own linguistic resources, and it is the power to control meanings which determines power in general, then women must be forever doomed to silence and subordination. With apparent equanimity, Dale Spender writes herself, and all women, into corners such as these, from which there is no escape: 'Men won't cease to be exclusive authorities until women have authority – and women won't have authority until men cease to be the exclusive authorities. Full circle again.'[80] Men have power because men generate meanings; men generate meanings because men have power. Full stop. We are told that changes in material circumstances make little difference to men's power. Men can simply generate new meanings: 'So even if women were to be allowed the scope for equal achievement, in the end it could be valued at less than the male achievement.'[81] Men's control over meanings is decisive: there is nothing either true or false, but men's thinking makes it so!

The crux of Spender's argument is that men and women experience the world differently, not simply that they have different experiences. Her ideal goal is that they should each 'be "authorities" on their own sex.'[82] It is not impossible that there is some fundamental difference in the way women and men experience the world, but we have nothing beyond faith and the assurances of Dale Spender and like-minded feminists that this is so. It is precisely the very different circumstances in the lives, and therefore experiences, of women and men, and the very different ideals for acceptable female and male behaviour, which should prevent us from assuming such fundamental differences of capacity. For Spender, however, it is a philosophical truth that we can never move beyond subjective experience towards a greater objectivity. Feminist knowledge differs from patriarchal knowledge, she tells us, in its belief that 'there is no one truth, no one authority, no one objective method which leads to the production of pure knowledge.'[83]

Ironically, Spender almost certainly acquired this relativist and idealist philosophy from the fashionable 'patriarchal' authorities of the 1960s. When she and I and many other feminists were students in those years, this was the progressive wisdom of our time. From Ronnie Laing to Howard Becker, all the male intellectual gurus of those days advanced what Spender now labels 'feminist knowledge'. She borrows from them the idea of 'participant observation', declaring it the model for feminist research, and one which suggests the researcher must always share the experiences of those they study, must be of them, to know them. As Carol Smart has pointed out, this would exclude most feminists from any research on the powerful – whether the police, politicians, the judiciary or whomever.[84]

Such an approach, however, characterises what many others have come to see as a 'feminist methodology' in academic feminism today. It is outlined, for example, in the writing of Liz Stanley and Sue Wise. Like Spender, they argue that 'truth' is a social construct, in the same way that 'objectivity' is; and both are constructed out of experiences which are, for all practical purposes, the same as 'lies' and 'subjectivity'.[85] They insist, usefully, on the importance of attending to personal experience, suggesting that other theorists of social structure lose sight of the fact that oppression occurs at an interpersonal level. But they add, incorrectly in my view, that 'there is no going beyond the personal'; social structures do not exist outside interpersonal relations. And they abandon the possibility of any criteria for rigorous and objective theorising. Strangely, we are returned to a type of primitive positivism, forbidden to move beyond immediate sense impressions. Such a method is weakened by its refusal to question, reconceptualise, or even sift and compare data. The rejection of any useful criteria of objectivity or rational arguments turns 'feminist knowledge' into something which we merely accept if we like it and ignore if we don't. Spender tells us that 'a feminist framework is no more "true" than a patriarchal one', but it is 'a good deal better'.[86] This is in keeping with what I see as an inevitable result of Spender's general philosophy: that two evils are better than one. If men's knowledge is biased and androcentric, women's knowledge will be biased and gynocentric.

Spender's work is indeed so full of tautologies, inconsistencies, half-truths and outright contradictions that grappling with it is like tackling a hydra. Although she rejects 'male thinking', 'male truths', 'male logic' and 'male scientific measurement', she feels free to draw upon these 'male' machinations explicitly when it suits her purposes. She writes that 'even according to male ideology, less than half the human population has been designated as "aggressive" and in need of "conquests" ', and that therefore 'there is a strong feminist argument for the desirability of the introduction of co-operation and peace.'[87] Suddenly male definitions are of use to us.

Spender tells us that the emergence of women as a reference group in the 1970s enabled them to take back the power of controlling meanings which men had appropriated. If, on the one hand, this process is possible, how is it that women's meanings have hitherto remained outside language? Women have nearly always had some type of reference group: whether within voluntary associations, the ladies' sections of their churches or political parties, on the factory floor, in PTAs, in women's colleges or in borstals. Women are rarely completely isolated from other women as a reference group. And if, on the other hand, controlling meanings really does enable one to control reality, why hasn't feminism changed the world – at least for feminists? Spender tells us that 'It is obvious that religion declines once people cease to believe in God: it follows that male dominance will decline when people cease to believe in male supremacy and authority.'[88] Some will spot the obvious difference. God lacks the material resources of men with which to fight back!

Spender believes that her ideas are the same as those advanced by most feminists in the women's movement. There is much in common, she argues, between herself and Mary Daly on the one hand, and, on the other, what Sheila Rowbotham was claiming back in 1972. But what Sheila Rowbotham was saying was in fact rather different: language is neither disconnected from nor alone determining of women's social reality. 'The language which makes us invisible to "history" is not coincidence, but part of our real situation in a society and in a movement we do not control.'[89] Spender, in contrast, says that material circumstances are irrelevant to women's subordination. There is no reality outside language and ideology in Spender's perspective: 'Yet if we didn't know about hierarchies, if our value system was not founded on distinctions between superior and inferior, then we would have no way of perceiving male supremacy, and sex differences could well be meaningless.'[90] It is 'patriarchal thinking which predisposes us to arrange the world in hierarchical order';[91] the material basis of race, sex and class oppression is not the problem. This means, too, that women can never be blamed for their participation in any form of injustice, coercion, discrimination or even for their own nasty habits; it wasn't women who thought up these nasty things to begin with. This also means that male dominance will cease when women cease to believe in it: 'Would men be content to agree among themselves that they are dominant, if women gave no credence to such male belief?'[92] Mass hypnosis, it follows, would be the speediest, most effective strategy to end male dominance.

Many feminists, I realise, will feel that these criticisms of Dale Spender's ideas are unfair and unnecessary, not to mention 'patriarchal' and unsisterly. I know that there is some truth in what Spender says. All areas of knowledge and culture that we see as authoritative and edifying, or simply as the dictates of good 'common sense', have tended to ignore or misrepresent the experiences and struggles of women. (They have equally, it must be added, ignored or misrepresented the experiences and struggles of all other subordinate groups.) As Genevieve Lloyd argues, 'What is valued – whether it is odd against even numbers, "aggressive" as against "nurturing" skills and capacities, or Reason as against Emotion – has been readily identified with maleness.'[93] Our ideals of Reason, Lloyd elaborates, have been designed to exclude what has culturally been defined as feminine. But this does not take us to Spender's conclusions that reality consists of two types of experience and knowledge: two separate cultures, each with their separate languages and sets of meanings and values. And we do have to take very seriously indeed the political consequences of these conclusions, for they have a firm hold on the contemporary feminist imagination. They have become the popular, 'acceptable' face of feminism in Britain today.

There are two fundamental reasons why I believe Spender's conclusions are not just inadequate but significantly misleading. The first is that the separate female experience which Spender and others believe in is not separate at all, but constructed out of the same meanings, and from within the same space, which women have been allotted within our male-dominated traditions. There is not a single 'feminine' value or experience which Spender claims for women that is at odds with that old-time religion of patriarchy. When she tells us that 'for generation after generation women have tried to assert the feasibility of a human society in which procreation, nurturance, warmth, security and creativity are fostered',[94] we hear the voice and the values of our fathers just as strongly as that of our mothers. The belief in the unchanging nature of women, of an opposition between women and progress, lies at the very heart of the traditional mythology of 'woman'. Discussing the dominant influence of Spender's ideas in feminist theatre today, Michelene Wandor despairs:

> This phenomena is mind-blowingly perverse: a soft-edged radical feminism is aligned with exactly those 'feminine' virtues of passivity and dependence based on nurturing that the gutsy radical feminism of the early 1970s sought to transform.[95]

Women value nurturance, warmth and security, or at least we believe we ought to, precisely because of, not in spite of, the meanings, culture and social relations of a world where men are more powerful than women. Women's and men's experiences and values are shaped by the same ideologies and the same meanings handed down to us from the past, though we are placed differently in relation to them. They are also shaped by the changing social practices and circumstances of our lives in the present. It is important, though Spender rejects this as 'not an issue', to see how women came to value nurturance.[96] Indeed, it is precisely *the* issue if we are seriously interested in how feminists might collectively organise to change existing economic, sexual and social arrangements which have served men's interests at the expense of women's. It is only when we abandon all hope of any real change in the lives and the experiences of women that we may console ourselves with the reassuring, complacent belief in women's essential superiority.

The second fundamental problem is that Spender writes women out of any active engagement in most of human history as surely as the 'patriarchal' or 'malestream' history she attacks. In her view, women have truly participated in history only at those times when their actions can be seen (often rather curiously) as illustrative of 'women's values'. Women who have been jingoistic, racist, sexist or committed to privilege for their kith and kin are not seen as part of this feminist history. For Spender tells us that 'any feminist framework needs to take into account the extent to which women are prepared to go – for all sorts of reasons – to uphold male values.'[97] Thus Spender (unlike Daly, perhaps without really intending to) sets us the project of separating off the experiences of women in touch with their own true 'female values' from those of other women who are alienated from themselves and promote 'male values'. But any need to distinguish women who have 'real female values' from women blinded by 'male values' encourages a distinctly puritanical, repressive politics, sadly not unfamiliar in gatherings of feminists today. More importantly, it frustrates what I see as the necessary project which *would* begin to restore women's place in the making of history.

This would not simply focus selectively on the experiences of women, although it would take women's experiences very seriously. It would not reject the existing criteria for objectivity and intellectual rigour. It would entail vigilant attention to the claims of alternative theoretical frameworks. It would begin by reassessing or, as they say now, 'deconstructing' all existing conceptual frameworks and bodies of thought to expose the assumption of a male subject or viewpoint. We would need to look for the power relations between men and women as a basic category of analysis, cutting across and modifying other social categories. We would be equally aware that other social categories like those of race, class and nationality cut across and modify the generalisations we make about women and men as groups.

Such a feminist project is quite unlike that which seeks to uncover the separate worlds of men and women: either to substitute 'women's' knowledge for 'men's' knowledge or, as Spender has suggested, to pursue a form of 'co-existence'. If, for example, we see official 'men's' history as irrelevant to female experience, and focus only on what has most sharply differentiated the lives of women from those of men, we endorse rather than challenge the exclusion of women from most historical research. If, however, we begin to alter this bias and uncover women's actual participation in history, we discover an array of new challenges and contradictions. For, as Elizabeth Fox-Genovese has argued:

> The undervaluation of women has not only led to the slighting of
> women's participation in slave revolts, *jacqueries* [peasant revolts],
> strikes and revolutions; it has led to the slighting of their
> formidable contribution to the building of slave societies, the
> suppression of *jacqueries*, the consolidation of big business and the
> efforts at counter-revolution ... In this sense, women's history
> challenges mainstream history not to substitute the chronicle of
> the female subject for that of the male, but rather to restore
> conflict, ambiguity and tragedy to the centre of historical process:
> to explore the varied and unequal terms upon which genders,
> classes and races participate in the forging of a common destiny.[98]

Such ambiguities and conflicts in women's lives disappear
altogether in the writing of cultural feminists. We will not find
them in Andrea Dworkin's satanic image of male sexual
domination from which 'there is no way out, no redemption'.
We will not find them in Mary Daly's Manichean vision of
female good besieged by male evil, nor in Dale Spender's softer
focus on the 'different and autonomous' meanings and values of
women and men. And we do not find them in *Sweeping
Statements*, the latest anthology to be compiled of writings from
the British women's liberation movement, 1981-1983. The most
insistent themes in the collection concern the dangers
surrounding women and the damage done to them at the hands
of men: '... all women have been sexually assaulted, we're all
kept in fear by men's sexual violence, we're all threatened by
men, we're all hurt and damaged by pornography and the
objectification of women.'[99] Women's common and inescapable
victimisation is repeated in most of the articles, 'the basic first
principle of feminism [is the belief] that we are *all* sexually
oppressed by men.'[100] This same article continues 'it is male
sexual minorities (transsexuals and paedophiles) who are most in
the vanguard of oppressing women.'[101]

Such outrage is contagious, but only for the true believers.
Other women exclude at least the men they know from the
category of rapist. Many women have not been raped or sexually
assaulted; some do not feel sexually oppressed by men – they
may even desire sex with men. It is simply perverse to describe
transsexuals and paedophiles as the leaders of male domination,
when they are one of its most popular victims. It is insulting to
women who have been raped to imply all women have been

raped; it diminishes rather than clarifies rape's hideous reality and prevalence.

A feminism which emphasises only the dangers to women from men, which insists upon the essential differences between women's and men's inner being, between women's and men's natural urges and experience of the world, leaves little or no scope for transforming the relations between men and women. Neither any alliance with groups of men nor any struggle to change relations with men individually would seem to follow from such a feminist perspective. Feminism of this kind encourages a defensive, even reactionary politics because it places women outside all mainstream political struggle, with its advances and retreats against class, race and gender domination. It denies all the contradictions and tensions in existing relations between the sexes, both in and between different social groups, although these are exactly what we need to locate in order to push more successfully for change.

A politics of despair and retreat seems to pervade this new cultural feminism, reflecting the pessimism many feminists were feeling in the early eighties. It is a despair and retreat which can be softened for some by asserting the superior virtues of women. But I cannot connect my own feminism with either its methods or its message.

2. *Not Advancing but Retreating:*

What Happened to Socialist Feminism?

Feminism in its non-socialist forms is immensely more powerful and influential than we are … Indeed it seems to me that our most pressing political project should be to try and win back what is effectively lost ground for socialist feminist ideas in the women's movement.

Michèle Barrett[1]

I recognise that theories cannot always in themselves be 'easy' to understand, but surely it is necessary to re-assert the earlier emphasis put on the links between theory and practice and to remember how deeply rooted early discussions and actions were in questions of ideology.

Sue O'Sullivan[2]

We, as black/Third World women, do not need your opinion, your approval or disapproval of our Third World/black feminism, politics and actions, especially from uninformed ignorant white feminists. *We* can judge for ourselves what is best for us. You cannot.

Shaila, with support from Third World/Black
Feminist Groups and the Black Lesbian Group.[3]

It would seem strange, I think, to the visiting spaceperson, that a more conservative and pessimistic vision should have arisen in feminist thought from the late seventies, a vision which serves to widen what it sees as the large and inevitable gulf between the needs and values of women and men. For at least at the ideological level, many men's attitudes have changed. Feminist issues are no longer ridiculed and rejected out of hand as they were in the early seventies. The issues of sexual harassment, childcare, abortion and women's equality generally are on the agenda of most trade unions, many local councils, the Labour Party and the European Assembly. Feminist goals have become 'respectable'. They are genuinely supported by at least some men of goodwill, whatever the hostility they arouse from others. Pornography, violence against women and overt sexist behaviour are now taboo for some of the young generation of men who have been influenced by feminism.

The situation has become even more ironic since some socialist men have begun to argue that it is feminism which must provide the basis for any renewal of socialism. Herbert Marcuse, who was the most decisive influence on the New Left of the sixties, endorsed this view in 1978, two years before his death, announcing dramatically that 'far more attention should be paid to the women's liberation movement.'[4] He had come to believe that the socially conditioned 'feminine qualities' of 'non-violence, receptivity and tenderness' could transform society. In France, André Gorz quoted sociologist Alain Touraine to echo this theme in his vision of the way forward for socialism. The women's movement could be the 'vanguard' of the 'post-industrial society'. But – and here his argument also echoes those of cultural feminists – they can do so only insofar as they assert 'the centrality of non-economic values and autonomous activities ... [for] women's activities and qualities prefigure a post-capitalist and post-industrial society, culture and civilisation.'[5] In Britain, futurologist James Robertson welcomed 1984 on national television with his version of a SHE future: sane, humanistic, ecological – more female. Robin Morgan likes to quote physicist Fritzof Capra in her latest writing since he believes that 'the feminist movement is one of the strongest cultural currents of our time and will have a profound effect on our further evolution.'[6] His words support her claim that feminism is 'the key to human survival and transformation',[7] the next step in human evolution.

More mundanely, Tony Benn, in or out of Parliament, mentions the strength and success of the women's movement in most of his speeches. Few men on the left fail to pay the movement due respect. Ken Livingstone (once voted the most popular man in London after the Pope) is passionately pro-feminist and committed to sexual politics. He argues, quoting Andrea Dworkin, that male violence and male power are central political problems; men must begin at once to change 'the nature of the relationships they have with the women they live with'.[8] Of course, we might accuse these men of 'mere lip service to feminism'. When it comes to sharing housework and childcare, for example, many men think they have changed more than their actions corroborate. But since feminists have always stressed the force of ideas, it seems odd to dismiss completely the shifting thoughts of at least some men on what is appropriate 'male' behaviour.

The new popular feminism gave up on men, it seems, just when more men appeared more willing to embrace its ideas. Many feminists began losing hope for any real change, just when some men began to look to feminists as a source of change.

This is not insignificant. I don't mean to suggest, as we could instantly conclude, that the male embrace crushed the hopes of many feminists. Not at all. But perhaps it became harder to accept men's support for feminist goals as genuine, or authentic, when for most women the possibility of achieving these goals was as far away as ever. Neither the increasing social acceptance of demands for women's formal equality with men, nor men's chivalrous applause for the 'gentle', nurturing ways of women, have undermined the power relations between men and women. Ideological victories for feminism have not been matched by any significant material change.

Uneven and Unequal Progress

In spite of this some changes in women's lives have given them greater autonomy, and seem permanent. It is now the norm for women to work outside the home. And no matter how often and with what passion we hear it denied, most women do value both the sociability and the economic independence this brings them. (Angela Coyle documents just how desperately 'redundant women' miss their jobs. Sue Sharpe records the enormous sacrifices 'working mothers' with young children will make to return to some form of employment – though the pitiful wages and the inadequate childcare provision make their 'double identity' such a complex and difficult one.)[9] State benefits for married women no longer always assume a male breadwinner, though not all legal discrimination has been removed. Social attitudes have begun to shift, hopefully for ever, on rape, domestic violence, and the treatment of its victims (despite the obscene contempt for women which can still issue from the judiciary and other male authorities). Men are more involved in childbirth; 80 per cent of fathers watch the birth of their child in the 1980s, compared to 1 per cent just over a decade earlier, and many fathers now have a closer relation, physically and psychologically, with their children.[10]

The right of women to choose whether to embark on motherhood, in or outside marriage, is more widely accepted, despite the continuing organised opposition to abortion and the pro-family rhetoric of the right. Abortion legislation since 1967 has meant that women in Britain who become accidentally pregnant are less often either forced to bear a child they do not want or risk death through unsafe abortion. (This is why so few babies are available for adoption and consequently fertility problems loom so large in this country.) The *Daily Mirror*'s agony aunt Marge Proops assures us from the thousands of letters written by women over the years: 'Women's lives have changed enormously.'[11] She adds: 'It does annoy me when people keep saying that liberation for women has been a purely middle class preoccupation ... there has been a real revolution in attitudes and expectations.'[12] Women today, in her view, are more aware of their rights, less ready to be exploited and more aggressive.

However, the liberal optimism of many a professional woman cannot dispel the weary pessimism of many an older feminist. It is also true that most women remain relatively impoverished, domestically isolated and often sexually harassed – as overburdened with work as they always have been. Some women today may find their situation is worse than ever. This decline has not taken the form we might anticipate in a time of recession, retreat into full time housework. (Contrary to common opinion, women's ejection from the labour force did not occur even in earlier recessions.)[13] Instead, recession has further entrenched women in the lowest paid, less secure and least attractive jobs. In recent years the only creation of new jobs in Britain has been the steady increase in part time employment for women in low waged service work.[14] These jobs are so poorly paid that they do not even begin to take women out of poverty, particularly where women are contributing to the support of others. There is also an increasing number of women raising children on their own, who either have to work full time on top of their domestic commitments, or who cannot, without net financial loss, undertake any paid work. The currently existing possibilities for women's employment are therefore not a solution to women's economic dependence. They are very much a part of the problem.

The legislation which was supposed to improve women's economic situation has had a limited impact. This should hardly surprise us because it was never designed to tackle women's situation outside the workforce. (The legislation ignored the fact that over 40 per cent of women are classified as 'part time' workers – although they may work perhaps 30 hours a week – compared to a mere 5 per cent of men. And they are part time because of domestic commitments.) The legislation has also failed in its own terms. The Equal Pay Act, passed in 1970 and made enforceable in 1975, and the Sex Discrimination Act of 1975, both designed to create wage equality and equal opportunity for women, ignored the reality of a workforce already divided by sex, in which women's jobs are *by definition* the low paid ones. (More positive anti-discrimination legislation on 'equal pay for work of equal value' has yet to be implemented in Britain.) The maternity provision contained in the Employment Protection Act of 1975 does not give adequate protection for part time workers, and it has been eroded further by subsequent Tory legislation. The segregation of women into a narrow range of the worst paid jobs has actually increased since these reforms were passed; after an initial rise, women's wages have begun to lag even further behind men's. Financially then, while a very small number of 'skilled' women are now better off (a mere 7 per cent of women, for example, work in skilled manual jobs) the majority of women are worse off.[15]

A false and hypocritical 'acceptance' of women's formal equality is now used at times to exacerbate women's deprivation. Former safeguards are being withdrawn, safeguards which recognised, though they did little to alleviate, women's economic disadvantage. For instance, the proposed Divorce Reform Bill in Britain restricts women's access to financial support from her husband after divorce, and so ignores how a wife's domestic and childcare commitments within marriage disadvantage her employment prospects but benefit the husband's. In reality, divorce settlements in the past – on which men could and would frequently renege with impunity – never did protect many divorced women and their children from living in poverty. But today, more women are expected to support themselves and their children on wages which average little more than half those of men.

Struggles which have focused on women's equal rights outside the home seem forever doomed to be ineffectual unless they also take account of women's domestic and familial responsibilities; but this is very difficult when women still have negligible power in the trade union movement, national government, the Labour Party or any other political party. Individuals or small groups of women have to seek equality within structures already dominated by men, structures designed and accustomed only to defending men's interests. This was always an awesome task. Barbara Ehrenreich, for example, has written of women's realistic fears that 'liberation' has 'freed men first', that is, freed men from their traditional family commitments before, and perhaps without ever, improving the situation of women.[16] She describes the increasing impoverishment of women trying to support themselves and their dependants without men's higher wages. Men's continuing resistance to taking on domestic and caring responsibilities, the realities of recession and, in this country, a Thatcher government determined to dismantle welfare services and allow massive unemployment, have forced women on to the defensive. The recent feminist emphasis on women's difference from men, accompanying a retreat from public politics to focus on women's personal and domestic lives, chimes in with such fears.

The Rise and Fall of Socialist Feminism

It is socialist feminism which might have been expected to understand, to explain, perhaps even to predict such uneven, complicated, contradictory developments in the lives of women. Where different types of oppression are connected in such complex ways, progress can never be linear or smooth, particularly in a time of recession when yet other factors become involved. Yet the voice of socialist feminism is now remarkably silent in popular feminist debate, a change which has taken many socialist feminists by surprise. In the early seventies, radical socialist politics of some sort were integral to a feminist outlook in Britain. According to Ellen Willis, this was also true in the US, since most feminists in the early seventies considered themselves 'leftists of one kind or another'.[17] How else could we fight, as we then sought to do, all forms of social domination? In Britain, at first, feminists avoided the two labels 'radical feminist' or 'socialist feminist'. The distinction stemmed from whether we believed women's oppression was primary and underlay all other forms of domination, or whether it was interconnected with other equally basic forms of oppression in capitalist class society. As Angela Weir and Elizabeth Wilson have pointed out, nearly all feminists who had contact with the left hoped to push both the left and the working class towards a broader form of socialism which would genuinely include women's liberation;[18] feminists in general shared a vision of the future free from social hierarchies and any notion of cultural inferiority. All but those who did not accept the need for an *autonomous* women's liberation movement hoped to achieve this by uniting all women, through a shared 'sisterhood', in loosely structured, open-ended, non-hierarchical groups. We mostly rejected notions of 'leadership' and what we saw as the obsolete dogmas and authoritarian tactics of existing socialist groupings. Libertarian socialists as many of us were – emerging out of the student radicalism of the sixties – we criticised 'reformism' and all things 'bourgeois' to stress instead self-help, and popular, grassroots, localised, direct control over resources. A fear of the dreaded contamination of 'co-option' accompanied any assistance we received from the state.

Although most feminists in the early years shared these assumptions on methods and goals, by 1973 a strong socialist feminist current had formed in Britain which was to hold five national conferences over the next two years. Many feminists believed that to open up socialism to feminism, we needed to understand classical marxism, which, as a body of political thought, seemed to strive for a total analysis of capitalism, however much it had failed to theorise adequately the specific situation of women. Some socialist feminists at this time were members of parties and groups on the left, but the majority, like myself, were not. We were united in our attempt to understand the connections between women's subordination and capitalism, and to create a movement of and for *all* women, but not only for women – also for all oppressed groups and peoples and for men. Lee Comer captures the all-embracing aspirations of many socialist feminists then:

> The Women's Liberation Movement is not and never has been about the amelioration of the position of women *vis-à-vis* men in a capitalist society … Because the Women's Movement analyses and questions the very fundamentals of human experience – the division of labour between the sexes, the tenets of 'masculinity' and 'femininity', the sexual objectification of women, the exclusion of women, children and old people from the 'real' world, the Protestant work ethic, the distribution of wealth, the separation of men from emotionality and women from rationality, the competitive and individualistic morality which divides people from each other while propping up a capitalist economy, and the oppressive nature of a society divided by class, sex and race – the Movement, unlike any before it, confronts both the minutiae and the totality of human experience … women bring the actuality of their experience, pinioned at the base of the family unit and in the lowest sector of the workforce, into a *political* awareness of the totality of oppression.[19]

We thought, with the political idealism which survived the sixties, that we could tackle everything. As we saw things then, the issues, tactics, language and lifestyle of all those fighting for socialism needed to be challenged and transformed to encompass the struggle of women for their liberation. This also meant that many women moved towards a socialist politics through becoming involved in the women's movement – women who became feminists first, then socialists. For instance, Marsha Rowe, who with Rosie Boycott founded the first commercial women's liberation magazine *Spare Rib* in June 1972, recalls that her first women's group at that time was a 'political study group', where they read not only Juliet Mitchell and other feminist writers but also Marx's *Capital* and Wilhelm Reich.[20]

The feminist magazine *Red Rag* also emerged around this time, in June 1972, as an explicitly marxist feminist publication. First initiated by women in the Communist Party, its collective was soon to include a variety of other socialist feminists, who were then immersed in the various feminist campaigns and activities. It had both descriptive resonance and theoretical clarity. Describing itself as 'feminist first and foremost because feminism is the political movement which emerges as women's response to their own oppression', the collective nevertheless argued that 'women's oppression is only part of a class and racist society whose total formation we must understand if we wish to change it.'[21] The dominant themes covered in *Red Rag* were struggles over childcare, family allowance and other welfare campaigns, women organising in paid work, and the demand for women's complete control over their own fertility and sexuality.

Socialist feminism seemed to flourish in these years, yet from the start the conferences threw up a whole range of problems which were never adequately resolved. Some of these problems were to lead to the distancing of socialist feminist theory from the active feminist movement. The socialist feminists who had formed women's political study groups from around 1972 aimed, in the words many of us used then, 'to liberate marxism from the dead hand of male orthodoxy'. But this was exactly what did not happen. The first socialist feminist conference in Birmingham in 1973 swung into action by transforming the feminist critique of housework into a debate on domestic labour. It discussed whether or not work done by women in the home contributed in a specific, (potentially) accountable form to the real value of labour, and thus to 'surplus value' and private profit; and whether this could be incorporated into marxist analysis. But this form of economistic categorisation buried everything else at issue, including the isolation, drudgery, dependence and not infrequent violence women experienced in the home.

The debate arose in response to Maria Rosa Dalla Costa and Selma James's pamphlet *The Power of Women and the Subversion of the Community*[22] which had developed a classically economistic, though heretical, marxist argument that women's oppression was located in the 'surplus value' it produced for capital. Since Selma James theorised that housework produced a 'commodity', labour power, which could be exchanged on the capitalist market, wages for housework was her solution. Revealingly, the Wages for Housework campaign, as it then became, later brought the same strange economism to its analysis of sexual relations: prostitution became the paradigm of women's engagement in sex with men. And certainly the combination of a simple and intransigent economism (women want money) with the equally intransigent economism and indefatigable interventionism of Selma James has always proved a powerful attraction for a small group of determined supporters. Wages for Housework flourishes to this day, although it was a campaign and an analysis which every women's liberation conference and every open socialist feminist grouping rejected.

Other socialist feminists countered Selma James's analysis in various ways, mainly arguing that women's domestic work produces only 'use values'. That is, housework is essential and necessary for the functioning of a capitalist market, but does not produce things which can be exchanged. On this view, domestic labour is necessary for the reproduction and servicing of future and present wage labourers, as well as for socialising children into acceptance of capitalist social relations. There were many problems, however, with such a use of the marxist theory of value to provide a general explanation of women's subordination. It is worth exploring them, as they hold a clue, I believe, to many subsequent problems for socialist feminism. They were problems which would not disappear, even after ever more sophisticated versions of European marxism and French psychoanalysis swept aside this initial debate.

It was important at that time, as it still is today, to assert that housework does have an *economic* function, in the sense that it is socially necessary and essential work for the smooth functioning of any society. (Combined with childcare, it is also emotionally engulfing, time-consuming and demanding work.) But the mode of analysis was narrow and academic. Most obviously, all participants were advancing strictly marxist 'functionalist' accounts, that is, they were looking only at how women's work in the home served the interests and needs of a capitalist society, and thereby also ignoring how it served more specifically the interests and constructed needs of men. This gave considerable force to the argument of our radical feminist critics that socialist feminism avoided the question of men's power over women, the question of 'patriarchy'.

A second problem, which now seems equally obvious, was the

distancing effect of using the most abstract and difficult marxist language instead of a more accessible and concrete language of women and men in specific contemporary situations. It committed socialist feminist theory to many of the existing weaknesses of marxism. The whole debate was largely unintelligible to the majority of feminist activists at the time who, like me, were simply bewildered by the marxist terminology, and unable to grasp what significance it had. A third problem was the exclusive focus on the housewife and on her relation to capitalism. This meant that socialist feminists were selecting out some single or root cause of women's oppression (though we had often accused radical feminists of doing just that in their focus on men's desire for power) and that we too were ignoring the complexity of factors involved. As a group of socialist feminists were later to write 'it is worth remembering that socialist feminism has emerged as a distinct tendency precisely because it has refused [the] kind of simplistic analysis which concentrates exclusively on finding "root" causes of oppression, whether of class, gender or patriarchy.'[23] Finally, though, ironically, perhaps of less significance at the time, feminists failed to see that the domestic labour debate was not universally applicable. Others who have rethought women's situation since then have argued that capitalism does not necessarily require women's unpaid domestic labour in the home.[24] For example, the most exploited workers, such as migrant labourers, rarely have housewives at hand to service them or their own homes to be serviced in.

This focus on the housewife was reflected in much current socialist feminist writing. Most of the *Red Rag* editorials located women's oppression first and foremost in *the home*: in their 'imprisonment in the home as wives and mothers – still their basic role under capitalism as in all other societies.'[25] This encouraged a fundamental dualism in socialist feminist thought which distinguished women's oppression as a sex (located in the family) from the separate reality of capitalist class exploitation (located in the workplace). Most socialist feminists were soon to argue that it was capitalism which confined women to unpaid domestic labour, which used them as an industrial reserve army of labour and categorised their jobs in the labour market. It was patriarchy, however, which subordinated women to men.

'Patriarchy' has been defined in a variety of ways within different feminist frameworks and discourses: as a social system of male domination, as the power of the father in the family, as the universal principle and symbol of male domination, or as men's power to exchange women in order to form kinship groups.[26] But central to all these definitions of patriarchy was men's power over women's sexuality and fertility. The quest for the exact connection between the two systems set the agenda for socialist feminist theoretical work from the mid seventies. By the end of the decade many if not most socialist feminists were convinced that patriarchy was at least as basic a structure as capitalism: 'the one describing the area of sexual relations and the mode of social reproduction, the other describing the area of economic relations and the mode of social production.'[27] But socialist feminists who used the term continued to search for, yet fail to find, one fundamental cause of patriarchy, just as they searched for and could not find any single correct analysis of the relationship between capitalism and patriarchy.

It was precisely the persistence of women's subordination to men through all historical periods and differing economic and political structures which made many of us believe that we needed to point to some specific and continuing basis for 'patriarchy' as a separate structure, independent of all other social arrangements. It was harder to conceptualise how women's subordination might be created and consolidated anew in different historical periods, throwing up a variety of quite new ideas and practices which institutionalised women's subordination, growing out of, but perhaps superseding, earlier ones.

The theoretical problems which perplexed socialist feminists in attempting to illuminate women's situation by extending marxist concepts of production and exchange into the area of 'reproduction' and 'domestic labour', were accompanied by other strategic problems. Women in some of the marxist groups (particularly in the tiniest Trotskyist groups), though few in number, tended to dominate conference debates with their own, usually rather simplistic, strategic perspectives.

By the fourth socialist feminist conference in September 1974, destructive, sectarian analyses were appearing in the conference agenda itself, disguised as debate. For example, feminists were asked by the conference organisers to consider: 'Do we see the women's movement as some kind of vanguard movement or as a petty-bourgeois movement which may be ideologically useful but is essentially marginal to the main political struggle?'[28] And by the fifth conference of this series, held in 1975 in Mile End in London, women from these same small Trotskyist groupings had taken over the organising of the event. The conference degenerated almost immediately, as socialist feminists resisted their destructive efforts to persuade the rest of us that the only way forward was to form a central committee to push the whole of the women's movement into a mass single issue campaign — the campaign for abortion on demand. To achieve this they had planned the conference almost entirely in large plenaries with platform speakers, along the lines of traditional left organising; this left little space for the smaller workshops which the rest of us had anticipated would be run along the lines of feminist practice to encourage maximum participation.

Interestingly enough, some of these women *still* propose a very similar formula around the issue of abortion to this day, only now I hear them make their proposals from within the Labour Party. It is little more than amusing today: you can't teach an old vanguard new tricks! But what was so destructive about these manipulative manoeuvres then, from such a tiny group of women, was that they rejected out of hand almost all the principles and practices which socialist feminists in general shared with all other feminists. They rejected, for instance, the importance we attached to 'private' life and to personal politics in shifting women's perceptions of themselves as powerless, passive and inferior. They declared instead: 'We need to change the very nature of capitalism which oppresses women and not look for short cuts to our personal liberation through changing life styles or through community action.'[29] So destructive was the hijacking of this conference that socialist feminists did not meet again nationally for another three years. As the editorial collective of *Scarlet Woman* (the journal of the socialist feminist current of the women's movement started by the Tyneside Coast women's group in 1976) was later to write, 'The idea of having another national Women's Liberation and Socialism Conference was opposed because of fear of a repeat of the Mile End one ...'[30]

It is interesting to note that at this time the organised socialist feminist current in the US was also being irrevocably damaged as a result of the activities of various marxist-leninist and maoist groups. Barbara Ehrenreich describes a startlingly parallel history of US socialist feminism from 1975 to 1977 thus:

> ... sectarian groups joined and harassed or merely attacked from outside more than twenty socialist feminist women's unions around the country, dragging almost all of them down to their deaths in arcane squabbles over the 'correct line'. I have never seen an adequate – or even inadequate – account of this nasty phase of left feminist history that addresses why the sects decided to go after socialist feminist organisations at this time, and why socialist feminist organisations, including the successful and level-headed Chicago Women's Liberation Union, crumbled in the face of so much bullshit.[31]

I would suggest it was the *success* of socialist feminism at that time which attracted women in the sectarian left. It was feminism and not any form of traditional socialism which was bringing new people into active political engagements in those years. (The 50,000-strong march of 1975 against James White's anti-abortion bill proved this for the left.) And it was the open and unstructured principles of feminist organising which made us so vulnerable to determined takeover tactics. (At least, once women in these left groups had learned that they themselves must attempt to take over feminist platforms and leave their men at home, unlike the early maoist intervention at the national Women's Liberation Conference at Skegness in 1971 when the men had come along, and been ejected.) Perhaps these women were also relieved to escape from the authoritarian structures of their own small sects, in which they had so little power. But sadly, their interventions in socialist feminist organisations and campaigns reproduced the same depressingly authoritarian style of politics of the groups from which they had come. Their activities culminated in a widespread reaction of hostility or resentment towards women in any mixed left group, with one South London socialist feminist group deciding to exclude such women from their meetings.

For three years after the Mile End Conference there were some regional gatherings of socialist feminists, most regularly in the North of England. Socialist feminists were then mainly active on single issue campaigns like the National Abortion Campaign (NAC), or in trade union work, like the Working Women's Charter Campaign which, initiated in 1974, flourished briefly in those years. Others, like myself, were also active in our local women's centres or in other types of women's self-help groups; we were also beginning to join the campaigns against the welfare cuts that the Labour government was implementing. But an increasing distance was developing between those engaged in the various campaigning activities and those engaged in intellectual or theoretical work such as setting up women's studies courses and seeking to understand the formations and interconnections of 'patriarchy' and 'capitalism'.

The absorption of Althusser, Lacan, and later of Foucault, into marxist and academic feminist theory increased this distance.[32] Academic feminists who were influenced by these developments began to reject the importance of women's testimonies of their own lives and experience on which the feminist practice of 'consciousness raising' in small groups of women as a central part of the movement was based. Instead, they turned to language itself as the determining factor, as in itself not only expressing but 'constructing' consciousness. Thus they stressed that it was through language that women were made inferior to men. Here, on the surface at least, there is an obvious parallel with the arguments of Dale Spender.

For these academic feminists, the previous emphasis on individual change and struggle was superseded by a study of the non-unitary, contradictory and unstable subjectivities construct-ed through particular discourses. Put more simply, what was being suggested was not so startling: that our notion of the individual 'self' as a fixed, single being, an 'I' separated off from the rest of reality, is an illusion; that it is rather 'composed' of a bundle of different and contradictory images we have received of ourselves from the conceptual frameworks available for describing experience. But when elaborated, as it was, for example, in the difficult language of the theoretical feminist journal *m/f* (begun in 1978 to examine tendencies within 'marxist feminism') the project of discovering 'how women are produced as a category' was a daunting one.[33]

It would of course be quite wrong to expect such theoretical work to have to relate explicitly to ongoing political action.

Some of the growing talk of 'the problem of academic feminism' stemmed from an extreme anti-theoreticism associated with radical and activist strands of feminism. But much of the intellectual work undertaken by socialist feminist theorists of that time, like that of male marxists, was overwhelmingly abstract. Not only did any notion of the 'individual' in struggle become suspect in favour of the 'subject' constructed 'through discourse', but soon, too, any notion of 'society', or of 'basic social structures' was rejected as unhelpful and false, as being totalisations of diverse and contradictory power relations. Some, of course, would argue that their political engagements were helped by such an analysis of the infinite and subtle interplay of multiple power relationships without any simple set of organising structures. Others, however, had little time to spare from the intellectual work of keeping up with and making sense of the shifting theoretical fashions and fragmentations.

At any rate, the inaccessibility of socialist feminist theoretical work was a dominant theme when socialist feminists did finally come to meet together again nationally in Manchester in 1978 and London in 1979. A proposal for discussion at all the workshops during one session at the London conference put the problem in this way:

> At the moment, work on new definitions of socialist feminism is done by a small number of study groups and individuals in isolation. There are no channels for *ongoing* development of these ideas and how they would apply to political issues. Until these channels are set up we will never overcome the present division of labour between study groups and action groups.[34]

Other papers also pointed to the dangers of emphasising theory at a time when the changing nature of the women's movement 'no longer presents concrete activity alongside theoretical concerns',[35] or wondered why it had proved so hard to 'break out of established left jargon when writing theory.'[36]

The conference itself was very successful. Attended by over a thousand feminists, there were varied and useful workshops on all aspects of social policy, employment, sexuality and male violence. Socialist feminism still seemed to be the dominant tendency within the British women's movement, but we never did manage to create those channels to overcome the 'division of labour' which many of us had sought.

By this time socialist feminists were active in an even wider variety of political campaigns. Alongside the nursery campaigns, NAC groups and women's legal and welfare rights campaigns, many other issues were assuming a new importance. The racist violence of the National Front in the late seventies drew many socialist feminists into anti-racist, anti-fascist work. The withdrawal of welfare services engaged us in anti-cuts work, for instance in London to save the Elizabeth Garrett Anderson women's hospital. Some socialist feminists helped set up or service women's refuges and rape crisis centres for supporting women against men's violence. The campaigns against nuclear power and nuclear missiles were emerging with the support of socialist feminists. And committed groups of women were now engaged in anti-imperialist solidarity work. The range of these campaigns meant that it was often hard for socialist feminists to hold on to any clear sense of political identity and coherence – either analytically or in practice.

Amidst this diversity, the women in anti-imperialist solidarity work developed a fierce criticism of Western feminists' perspectives and priorities. It is perhaps hard to avoid a stance which is self-righteous when struggling against the brutality of the US-backed, military power operating in Chile, Nicaragua, Angola, Namibia and other Third World countries, or, closer to home, when supporting those women who experience the daily violence of British military occupation in Northern Ireland. The overwhelming threat and apparent intransigence of military force and imperialist power against any progressive movements in the Third World allows little space for appreciating the significance of other struggles. And many socialist feminists began to understand that white-dominated Western feminism had failed to incorporate into its own analyses the different perspectives and experiences of Third World women, as Black feminists were also telling us. The anti-imperialist women's groups were therefore able to push for the next and final socialist feminist conference to have an anti-imperialist focus.

But the problem which some socialist feminists had foreseen and publicly warned against emerged at that last conference.[37] The conference planning group in its pre-conference publicity statement was highly critical of most of the activities of feminists in Britain, seeing them as having been engaged in campaigns making mainly reformist demands on the state.[38] Thus, as had happened in 1975, but for different reasons, the engagements of most socialist feminists were overshadowed, this time by a call for solidarity with anti-imperialist struggles worldwide.

Within the wider women's movement, socialist feminists were attacked for underplaying the reality of male power and male violence. Within socialist feminism, some attacked others as ethnocentric and reformist. By and large, we lacked any theoretical or practical perspectives which could clarify or connect the diverse political engagements, or sort through the muddles and antagonisms. From the outside, this confusion was growing as the Thatcher government, elected in 1979, allowed unemployment to rise dramatically, destroyed traditional industry, cut back the service sector (on which women in particular depend) and threatened economic and civil rights generally. Thatcher's primitive monetarist policies were backed by a new rhetoric of authoritarian populism which relied upon anti-permissive morality and appeals to the traditional family ideal. Many feminists feared (as it turns out, wrongly) that the left and the labour movement would now abandon whatever shaky commitment they had to feminist politics. Socialist feminism as a distinct and coherent political tendency began to disappear amidst fear, pessimism and conflict.

There is still important political work being done by socialist feminists, both theoretical and practical. But to be a socialist feminist now is to claim a personal and political identity which is insecure and unsure. It is a position often treated with disdain by other feminists as either boring or redundant. It is not unusual to hear sentiments such as that expressed in the still flourishing feminist magazine *Spare Rib*, describing a debate at the Feminist Bookfair in 1984: ' "Socialist feminism" seemed to mould the discussion into the terms of the *men*'s left, and so be almost out of touch with the live issues of the women's movement.'[39] I was at that meeting, where Beatrix Campbell described the problems of making her way as a female journalist and Sheila Rowbotham spoke of her work at the Greater London Council (GLC) arguing for the expansion of socially useful jobs and for better services over which people felt some measure of control. The *Spare Rib* report was, in my view, an unfair but revealing one.

The Fragmentation of the Women's Liberation Movement

The problems which troubled and fragmented socialist feminists were also connected with the decline of the women's movement itself. It has been many years since we could talk meaningfully of any single entity called 'the women's movement'. National conferences of the entire women's movement were abandoned after the apparently unresolvable and fierce confrontations between feminists at the final conference in Birmingham in 1978. The movement also began to decline in many local areas as lack of support led to the closing down of women's centres, NAC groups, women's health groups and other autonomous women's groups which had formed a loose part of the once thriving alternative socialist and feminist networks in many localities up to the late seventies.[40] The collapse of these groups was part of the more general withering away of many campaigns and organisations around welfare, housing and opposition to government cutbacks as political optimism departed along with the seventies.

Those who believed that reaction to a government of the far right would be to mobilise resistance could hardly have been more wrong. However, this was a view advanced by many a passionate revolutionary. In 1980 some feminists, including myself, were travelling around the country trying to unite what we called 'the fragments', hoping to build up and co-ordinate networks of women and men active in any progressive struggles without abandoning our feminist perspectives and ways of working.[41] We too failed to foresee the extent of the disarray and despair the Thatcher government would succeed in creating. As the political climate shifted to a defensive protection of the inadequate incomes and services we already had and were about to lose, many feminists gradually began (often with considerable reluctance) to test out the only remaining political forum still speaking even the language of reform. We joined the Labour Party.

It is true (as we shall see in Chapter 6) that some groups and activities of feminists have fallen apart only to rise again, funded, at least for a while, by a left Labour council or metropolitan borough. But these new women's centres and campaigns are inevitably more isolated. They do not have any national or regional forums of the women's movement from which they might learn, to which they are accountable or to which they could contribute. Despite this, feminism is still a powerful social influence. Its ideas now appear, if in a new jargon, in many popular women's magazines. As Anne Karpf reported:

> ... at the *Spare Rib* relaunch [in October 1985], novelist Zoë Fairbairns recalled that in the far-off 1970s, people were chastising *Spare Rib* for being extreme, but now no women's magazine is untouched by the issues *Spare Rib* and the women's movement campaigned for.[42]

But feminism's influences are so dispersed that it is hard for us to have any sense of ourselves as a movement. The original four demands of the women's liberation movement, drawn up in 1971, were for equal pay, equal education and job opportunities, free contraception, abortion on demand and free 24-hour nurseries. Three subsequent demands were added: legal and financial independence; an end to discrimination against lesbians and the right of all women to define their own sexuality; and finally in 1978 (together with some modifications to the sixth demand) freedom from intimidation by the threat or use of violence or sexual coercion, regardless of marital status, and an end to the laws, assumptions and institutions that perpetuate male dominance and men's aggression towards women. Nowadays, however, there are women who see themselves as 'feminists', sometimes even staffing the new women's centres,[43] who are opposed to abortion rights, against nursery provision, and indeed reject most of the demands of the women's movement. There are others who might well support all those demands, but who equally adamantly deny that they are 'feminists'. It is much less clear today what the moods and motives of feminists are supposed to be, or what it is to be a feminist.

The early years of the women's movement had generated amazing levels of energy, excitement and pleasure. It was altogether new at that time for women collectively to find a voice to assert our own passionate determination to break through the devaluation of women we had felt and witnessed all our lives. I was not the only stranded single mother a long way from 'home' to find a new self-confidence and a great deal of personal support from my involvement with the movement. Within a few years, for instance, three of us single mothers meeting at the women's centre in Islington, one Irish, one Scottish, one Australian, were living with our children under the same roof. We all changed and grew in leaps and bounds, and not one of us could doubt the personal strength and confidence we gained from those days. It is a common experience when individuals engage in collective action of any sort. Goodbye, for a while, to cynical indifference, to isolation, and the narrow social horizons which customarily confine us. Few things are more uplifting than the strengthening of identity, coherence and purpose which collective struggle and action can at times create. But that is in the early days, the days when victory or change seem possible: it is then that we feel we are consciously participating in the making of history.

History, however, is not made painlessly, directly or according to conscious plan. Setbacks do not spring solely from the more obvious obstacles and enemies. They rise up unexpectedly, in our victories as much as in our defeats. Many other factors, which only in hindsight appear inevitable, had contributed to the fragmentation of the women's movement. It was not just a symptom of the general decline of radicalism in the chilly winds of recession. The power and confidence of Western feminism in the early seventies very quickly extended beyond its predominantly white ex-student base as newer feminist voices began to be heard. Black women, working-class women, Jewish women, lesbians, younger, older, disabled, and many other women began to speak, write and organise around their specific oppression. They spoke of domination not just by men, but by groups of women who were more powerful than they, including feminists. Although universally subordinated as women within their own class and ethnic groups, their lives were also affected by women who held power and privilege in the wider world. But since feminism had always stressed the possibility of a universal sisterhood, how were we now to analyse women as a separate group and to build a movement for the liberation of all women? This need to theorise about women as a separate group became fraught with the difficulties of going beyond the fate of women as a gender, to encompass these other forms of domination. The significance of race and class, for example, always held the threat of engulfing and destroying the strength and urgency of the struggle against men's power over women.

The disputes between feminists of different racial, ethnic, class or national groupings proved extraordinarily divisive and painful. As the primary target of British racism (still such a central feature of Britain's post-imperial culture and society) Black women were particularly embittered when white feminists failed to support anti-racist struggles adequately or to confront their own racism. When a number of Black women joined the *Spare Rib* collective the resulting conflicts of perspectives and priorities were so difficult to handle that it resulted in one issue appearing with two separate editorials, one written by the Black women and one by the white women. But other fierce divisions between women also ripped the old assumptions of sisterhood to shreds. We witnessed bitter confrontations between Israeli Jewish women and pro-Palestinian women, between political lesbians and heterosexual women, between mothers and non-mothers, we heard the anger of working-class women, Irish women, disabled women, and others.

The concluding section of the anthology *Sweeping Statements* is headed 'Challenges', and it catalogues the different varieties of ever more specific oppressions women face. This would be a good thing if it helped us to understand the particular situations of different groups of women. But the anger expressed by 'Challenges' is against other feminists. It focuses on tensions and conflicts between women, as though these were generated only from within feminist groupings and activities. It seems to me that, paradoxically, some of the most important feminist ideas actually contribute to the problem. The method feminists have used to outline or describe differences between women is the same as the one used for consciousness raising. The specificity of race, class and other divisions are reported as women immediately experience them in situations where feelings can be most easily expressed. Women's liberation has always stressed that women use their own feelings, experiences and perceptions to make their analyses. We attached importance to the personal and the interpersonal (assuming that from there we could move to the social and the political). And this was necessary. It was necessary if we were to throw off the mythology of male 'expertise'. It was necessary to create an openness which would enable all women to participate on an equal footing. It is always necessary at least in the early stages to enable any oppressed group to understand and transform its internalised psychological subordination and to assert itself. It has proved however a source both of strength and of weakness within feminism.

It was a strength when the small groups which feminists like to work in were relatively homogeneous. The emphasis on our common experience of inferiority, frustration and social ineffectualness was literally empowering. It generated closeness, warmth and solidarity – if also some competitiveness, envy and accusations of elitism against women who slid too easily into leadership positions. It became a weakness when the emergence of differences and conflicts between women not only produced enormous distress but became immobilising. Either it silenced those who felt guilty for being articulate and privileged or it encouraged the defensive re-assertion of some common oppression, like the experience of male violence, which could be thought to over-ride the significance of race, class or any other structures of power and privilege. There are women who have insisted, for example, that we must accept that genocide and racism have been a far more destructive force than the oppression of women. There are others who declare as passionately that gynocide and the abuse of women is the more ancient and ubiquitous evil. I find the deployment of such scales of injustice, the drawing up of hierarchies of brutality and oppression, unhelpfully divisive and pointless. And we certainly cannot understand the abuses and atrocities of human history only by the passionate assertion of our own experience of the world. Black feminist Pratibha Parmar has criticised this tendency in British feminism:

> One of the results of only focusing on separate oppressions has been retrogressive. Women have got into hierarchies of oppression saying, 'I'm more oppressed than you because I've got more labels and more oppressed status'. I think that has been totally wrong and negative. What worries me is that now more and more young women in the movement are operating with this politics.[44]

Within the women's movement the validation of personal experience and talk of 'common oppression' often hides straightforward ignorance of the lives of other women and of the factors beyond gender which determine women's lives. In the words of Black feminist theorist bell hooks, 'Sisterhood became yet another shield against reality, another support system.'[45] For if we rely on personal experience alone we cannot explore how that experience is itself shaped by the frameworks of thought of those immediately around us. These frameworks are not static or inflexible: there is conflict and disagreement within the groups we are born or move into over ways of living and relating to others, ways of interpreting and experiencing the world. We cannot, however, easily step outside our own specific culture. Our experience is also shaped in various ways by interests and desires of which we may be unaware. With the best of intentions, we are self-deceiving. The very act of communication across cultural groups is often difficult, even without formal language barriers. Again, bell hooks argues, contrary to some feminist ideals, that women find 'common bonds' of affinity more easily with men of their socioeconomic and cultural group than they do with women across barriers of class or race.[46]

So resentment and mistrust would seem to be eternal and inevitable features of feminism were we not also able to move beyond individual experience. But we are able to generate theories on how our experiences are formed through the ideologies or sets of discourses available to us. And we are able to generate theories about the structures of domination in which we ourselves, and others outside our own experience, are enmeshed. An emphasis on interpersonal behaviour, on racism or on class privilege within feminism is misleading if it encourages only individualistic, moralistic self-blame, and proposes only personal solutions. For we are up against something much larger if we want to confront the underlying structures of class or race, or of gender domination.

Black Feminist Perspectives

Of the new feminist voices in Britain it is without doubt those of Black women which have been the most powerful and effective, and which have created a collective self-confidence as well as the organisational structures to fight against the entrenched racism of

Western capitalism. Black feminism has flourished both culturally and politically in the 1980s. The first Black women's conference was held in 1979, and Black women have written and campaigned against racism in the health service and in education, as well as against state repression of Black people, particularly through racist immigration laws and police violence. Several bitterly prolonged deportation cases, like the one in Manchester over Anwar Ditta's children, united both Black and white feminists in passionate protest. Black feminists have also supported anti-imperialist struggles, and criticised the misuse of sterilisation and contraception techniques on Black and Third World women for the purposes of population control, as have some white feminists. Since March 1982, a racially mixed collective of feminists has worked together to produce the monthly women's newspaper *Outwrite*, which covers anti-racist, anti-imperialist campaigns and women's struggles internationally. And from 1984, Sheba Feminist Publishers has operated as a racially mixed collective, prioritising Black women's writing.

However, some Black feminists have accused white feminists of 'colonising' Black women, of demanding, in the words of the first three Black women on *Spare Rib*, that they 'fight patriarchy on white women's terms ... white women want the benefit of patriarchy through racist privilege *and* the termination of patriarchy.'[47] When a group of Black feminists took over editorial control of one issue of the socialist feminist theoretical journal *Feminist Review* in 1984, they too argued that 'a particular tradition, white, Eurocentric and Western, has sought to establish itself as the only legitimate feminism in current political practice.'[48] Valerie Amos and Pratibha Parmar added that the priorities of white feminism concerned issues which 'in the main have contributed to an improvement in the material situation of a small number of white middle class women often *at the expense* of their Black and working class "sisters", e.g. short term gains such as equal opportunities and job sharing' (my emphasis).[49] They argued, as have many other Black women, that white feminists use racist and stereotyped perceptions of Black and ethnic women, or ignore them altogether, assuming a unity across ethnic groups which does not exist. In illustration, Parita Trivedi pointed out that white women's perception of Asian women as 'passive' and 'submissive' is a racist myth.[50] Most

Black feminists would now agree that white feminists have developed perspectives on 'women's' situation in the family and the workplace, on welfare rights, on men, motherhood, abortion and sexuality which distort or even betray the situation and interests of Black women.

In criticising family ideology, for instance, white feminists have often failed to emphasise the crucial role of Black family groupings in providing protection against the surrounding racism of white-dominated societies. Black families, many white feminists failed to see, were frequently attacked rather than supported by the British state, whose racist policies served to prevent, or to delay for as long as possible, children and other dependants from joining their Black relatives in Britain. In campaigning for improved welfare benefits, white feminists have often ignored the situation of many Black and immigrant women in Britain who, while paying taxes, receive no benefit at all for the children they support in countries abroad. Moreover, feminist positive discrimination campaigns in employment are of less use to Black (and working class) women who are more likely than white middle-class women to be segregated off into the worst paid, 'unskilled' jobs, with little chance of promotion. But where white feminists have been most directly implicated in condoning racist thought and practices has been in their failure to take on board the reality of police racism in their demands for 'better policing' to protect women from attacks by men. Despite the protests of Black women, for instance, the Reclaim the Night marches organised in the late seventies sometimes marched through Black areas, thus confirming the racist stereotypes of Black men threatening white women which is held by police and media alike. They remained insensitive to the fact that for Black women 'police protection' of their communities is more of a threat than a safeguard, more likely to involve insult and abuse, if not, as in the more recent cases of Cynthia Jarrett and Cherry Groce, death or serious assault.

There is now, belatedly, some rethinking being done by white feminists. Michèle Barrett and Mary McIntosh, for example, have acknowledged that 'our work has spoken from an unacknowledged but ethnically specific position ... its apparently universal applicability has been specious.'[51] They illustrate from their own earlier work how easy it is to ignore the situation of Black and ethnic women, or else to slide into ways of expressing things which negate their existence and experience. Many white women involved in feminist campaigns have tried to take on board the criticism from Black feminists. Women split from NAC in October 1983 to form the Reproductive Rights Campaign; this was a move away from the particular priorities of white feminists, to stress (as, to be fair, some of them always had) the situation of Black and Third World women and to confront population control strategies and the use of dangerous contraceptives like Depo Provera that are mainly directed at Black women. There is now more attention given by feminists in childcare and health campaigns to accommodate a wider range of women's needs, particularly those of Black and Asian women. For example, the GLC, pressured by the feminists who worked there, backed a conference on childcare in Wandsworth in February 1985 which stressed the need to combat racism and involve Black parents in childcare initiatives as its first priority.[52] The Women's Unit of Camden Council in London, realising its initial ignorance of the politics of race, has ensured that 50 per cent of the workers it employs are Black.[53]

Paying more attention to the needs of Black women on a practical and descriptive level, constantly being vigilant about old assumptions that 'we' women are all white, has become an important aspect of feminism in the eighties. But it has not been easy to make theoretical connections between race, class and sex. Black women themselves are in disagreement. There is even disagreement on how and whether to employ such an obviously complex category as 'Black', with its false overtones of a physiological rather than a cultural understanding of 'race'.[54] Some Black women employ a primarily class analysis of race. For example, the Brixton Black Women's Group wrote in 1978:

> We concluded that our oppression arose with the emergence of class society; and in our particular case, [it arose] with the initial impact of colonialism, (our slave experience), then the subsequent neo-colonial and imperialist oppression of our people.[55]

Others would say that race oppression is autonomous, distinct from class oppression, and that it is at least as basic as (or more basic than) sex oppression in capitalist and non-capitalist societies. Gloria Joseph for example has written, 'Ample evidence indicates that relations between the races have a long and important history which cannot be exclusively reduced to an analysis limited to sex or class.'[56]

Socialist feminism might be expected to offer a fuller analysis of how the oppressions of race, class and sex intersect than a feminism which analyses gender as the primary over-riding form of domination. But race was not a preoccupation of socialist feminism at its height. And since then, the idea that people can speak only from their *own* experience of oppression, and that white women have no right to attempt to theorise the situation of Black women, remains a strong influence on both Black and white feminist thought. Adrienne Rich argued eloquently that white women can and must identify with Black female experience. But she overstates her case by insisting that: 'Women share their suffering across the barriers of age, race, nationality, culture, sexual preference, and ethnic background.'[57] White women do not 'share' the sufferings of the targets of racism, indeed many directly cause it, and they all indirectly benefit from it.

The End of an Era

However, it was not race but the issue of sexuality which produced the final and fundamental rift between feminists at the end of the 1970s and which shattered any potential unity about the nature, direction and goal of feminism. Opposing attitudes to heterosexuality and to the significance of male violence blew apart the women's movement of the seventies.

There had always been some tension between lesbian and heterosexual women from the start of the contemporary women's movement. Lesbian women rightly resented the complacency of heterosexual women over the social acceptance, relative privilege and partial safety accorded heterosexual women in the wider world. (This could, of cause, be a precarious 'safety', as any battered wife would testify.) Lesbianism was nevertheless a very important issue to many feminists because it symbolised women's right to an autonomous sexuality, outside men's control or men's desire. Some feminists, like the North American

Jill Johnstone, had always preached a separatist sexual practice.[58] But the closing years of the seventies saw the growth of 'political lesbianism' and its call for sexual separatism. Heterosexuality was explicitly *theorised* as the root cause of women's oppression and linked, inevitably, with male violence against women. This issue of the primacy of sexuality and male violence as the cause of women's oppression lay behind the closing confrontation between political lesbians and others at the 1978 conference in Birmingham. It was the end of an era. Any possibility of further constructive national conferences of the women's movement or of a united women's movement had gone.

I see the current hegemony of the new radical or cultural feminism, with its passionate rhetoric about male violence and female virtue, as an attempt, though perhaps not always a deliberate one, to recreate a sense of sisterhood in the face of so much fragmentation. The particular emphasis on the dangers of pornography, which accompanied this shift within feminism, could be used – again consciously or otherwise – to provide a single focus on which some feminists hoped all women could unite. And it has served as a very effective way of appealing to (and directing) women's anger, despite the lack of any wider feminist organisational or political cohesion. But then, over ten years ago, the breadth and vision of the women's movement came precisely from the opposite situation. It came from the fact that we could claim in 1975 that 'women's liberation has no single over-riding issue or panacea. Our vision of social change is both utopian and more comprehensive in its analysis of women's oppression.'[59] And so, indeed, it was. Today, with such deep internal divisions among feminists, the wish to point the finger of blame at one, single, concrete enemy, strong enough even to turn women against each other, seems all the more compelling. It's HIM, over there!

Meanwhile, in my view, the most useful work which has been done by socialist feminists since the closing years of the seventies has moved away from the traditional marxist arguments and categories, away from the search for a single synthesis of marxism and feminism, or for the missing link between socialism and feminism. This is not to say that feminists have nothing to learn from marxism. In particular, it seems crucial to insist, against so many varieties of idealism which are now prevalent in feminism (from Mary Daly to Dale Spender and beyond) that *all* social relations and social practices are connected with the specific material and concrete world in which they occur, and are affected by changes in that world. They are not simply a product of the evil thoughts or tender sentiments of men or of women. But now, in analysing relations of exploitation or oppression, socialist feminists should, I think, begin by asserting the very different problems of diverse groups of women and stress the contradictory changes which have taken place in women's lives. We should not be looking for the primacy of sex, class or race, nor to isolate them as separate structures when they have fused together historically. Socialist feminists in Britain need to start from the contemporary reality of a racially and sexually *divided* capitalist class society. We could then see that sexual hierarchies are embedded in *all* social practices and institutions: they do not stem from any one institution or any single set of ideas.

Socialist feminists, for example, have studied more recently how the workplace, and not just the household, has helped shape the power relations between men and women. Cynthia Cockburn has shown how male print workers have historically organised their work practices in ways designed to exclude women and to confirm their own 'manliness'.[60] Studies have revealed how subordination has been built into many of the jobs designed by employers for women, which, like the assembly line work described by Ruth Cavendish, bear no relation to domestic skills.[61] It is in this context that sexual harassment has been exposed as a way of confirming the sexual hierarchies of the workplace, and of keeping women subordinate.

Today many socialist feminists can still be found, as politically active as ever, in their trade unions or in unemployment and trade union resource centres. Many more are pushing for improved welfare resources in pressure groups like 'Under 5s' or 'Health Emergency', for social policy change in groups like Rights of Women, or for job training schemes and greater protection from sexual abuse through local government Women's Committees. In the 1980s, particularly after the election of a number of left Labour Metropolitan and local councils in 1982/3, more socialist feminists have been working within the formal structures of mainstream politics. They have been caught up in a variety of activities which mean working, or at least negotiating, with men. Although feminists have tried to create open, collective and co-operative patterns within these structures, the task is daunting and difficult: the constraints posed by men's resistance to change and the demands for bureaucratic efficiency are almost overwhelming. This means that socialist feminists have been less involved in creating the cultural spaces where alternative feminist support networks and identities can flourish. With its elected chairpersons, committee structures, and fixed agendas, feminist work in trade union or local government politics could hardly be further removed from the alternative lifestyle and countercultural community politics of the early seventies.

Much of the energy and enthusiasm, as well as the exhaustion, pain and problems of women's liberation in its early days came from the way feminists worked together then. The excitement was in meeting together in our own space at women's centres, staying up late at night to prepare for the next demonstration or meeting, socialising afterwards at women's discos, forming women's bands and music workshops, developing new and important friendships, and establishing joint living and childcare arrangements with other women. But such practices were more possible for, and more appealing to, some women rather than others; they also tended to keep us marginal to the mainstream politics still dominated by men.

Cultural feminism today, at least in principle (although distinctions are often blurred in practice), holds out the promise of this former culture of feminism. At that time, finding a collective voice as women also meant, for a while, finding an identity as well as a politics. The explicit goal of cultural feminism is the expression of 'female' power, the creation of 'female' values, lifestyle and communities, cleansed of the language and values of men. Its emphasis on women's culture, on entertainment, writing, aesthetic works and social life, is both personally enriching and can provide a secure moral basis and a sense of belonging. Women working on Judy Chicago's Dinner Party, for example, were given a sense of total immersion in archetypal 'women's' work. Such an affirmation of womanhood is also strengthened by a clearly identifiable enemy, a clear and polar opposite.

But the cultural politics of the two periods is different. That of the early seventies was extraordinarily, if naively, optimistic that as women we could change our lives and those of others once we saw through 'male lies'. Many feminists were eagerly attempting to change every aspect of their lives; how we lived with and related to other adults and children, how we worked and developed new skills, how we saw ourselves. Even cutting one's long hair off could give feminists a sense of freedom then.[62] Much of the cultural feminism of today, in contrast, is less concerned with change: it calls upon the timeless truths of women's lives, sufficient in themselves, but threatened by the perpetual and invasive danger of men. It suggests that women do not need to change their lives, other than to separate themselves from the lives of men, and that there is little hope of men themselves changing.

The uneven, sometimes widening gap between what feminism had seemed to promise and women's still vulnerable, and for some increasingly impoverished position in the world, fits most neatly with a biologistic and fatalistic interpretation of the inevitability of men's power. The sense of danger aroused by the emphasis on male violence parallels, and has underlying it, the fears of this more conservative time when we hear only that change is impossible. 'It is precisely in times such as these,' Gayle Rubin has written, 'that people are likely to become dangerously crazy about sexuality.'[63] The conflicts over sexuality which occurred in feminism at the end of the seventies, which I shall describe in the next chapter, are very much a product of such times.

3.   Beauty and the Beast I:

Sex and Violence

> We found ourselves continually returning to the centrality
> of male sexuality as an issue, its form and function in the
> social control of women.
>
> > Lal Coveney et al, Patriarchy Study Group[1]

> If 'all men' are seriously to be taken as a political category,
> about the only thing they actually have in common is their
> penises. The biological fact of maleness thus gets attached
> to the social fact of power, not by historical analysis but by
> definition. Conversely, the biological fact of femaleness
> becomes the central way of defining the experience of
> women.
>
> > R.W. Connell[2]

> Only now, from a different time and place in the feminist
> debate over sexuality, does that apparently unanimous
> agreement among young educated women that sexual
> pleasure, however achieved, was an unproblematic desire
> seem curious.
>
> > Cora Kaplan[3]

The greater emphasis on the separate experiences of women and
men during the late seventies derived above all from a re-analysis
of sexuality. The identification of sexuality as 'the primary social
sphere of male power'[4] was to have far-reaching, and disastrous,
effects on the feminist analysis of heterosexuality, lesbianism and
the possibilities for combating power relations between men
and women. It was disastrous in my view, because it encouraged
'all women' to identify themselves as the victims of 'all men'. It
therefore rejected any serious attempt to examine the
complexities and confusion of our experiences as women and
men. It underestimated the significance of the many factors
which cut across women's experience simply as women. Above
all, it submerged the earlier feminist assertion that the collective

power of women could help transform all practices of domination, including the sexual.

The pull of the sexual is magnetic. All the more so when the meaning of 'sex' is puzzling, ambiguous and obscure. Is sex primarily some need for communication, for a relationship, a state of passion or arousal, an expression of buried desire, or the ultimate physical pleasure to be sought after and dreamed of? The need for affection, support, communication, understanding, as well as nagging feelings of emptiness, futility, hostility and neglect, all attach themselves most readily to thoughts of sex in our society. Indeed so many human desires are collapsed into sex that it becomes almost inevitable that our thoughts should continually return to it.

Sex has been placed at the centre of our lives. It appears to define who we are as individuals. Havelock Ellis summed it up at the start of the twentieth century, 'There is considerable truth in the dictum: "A man is what his sex is." '[5] Michel Foucault has argued that from the beginning of the eighteenth century 'sex' became 'the truth' of our lives.[6] But it is a truth which he saw as historically constructed by society. I believe he is right to suggest that 'sex' has only an illusory unity, being the product of all the discourses used to describe the body. It is this complexity of 'the sexual', combined with the endless discussion of sex which makes it such a powerful force in our lives. Whether provoking fear and danger, aching despair, unfathomable longing, the search for new pleasures or the need for the comfort of the familiar, the discussion of sex has a remarkable capacity to threaten our tranquillity.

We see sex as the most 'natural' and private part of our lives. But the power of the cultural images which define it and the variety of legal, medical and welfare practices which regulate it, mean that our sexual lives are always intricately shaped by the society we live in. Sex, as it is socially defined and controlled, is also, without doubt, tied in with all the social practices and institutions confirming men in their power over women.

It is not surprising, then, that the issue of sexuality has so violently divided the feminist movement. Divisions also appeared in the first wave of organised feminism at the turn of this century. And it has seemed to feminists, both past and present, that women do share a common awareness of men's power and control over women's sexuality – that sex is indeed the site of women's difference from men. Is sex not, in the intimate last instance, the solid base from which men's social control over women is built?

In most societies, although in very different ways, a host of sanctions and constraints – legal, social and ideological – surrounds every aspect of women's sexuality. From bottom-pinching to coercive sex, men's greater power in the world is manifested in, and often mediated through, sexual encounters. It is manifested, and, in the relentless inescapable ideology and iconography of the erotic, endlessly celebrated. The searching stare, the crushing lips, the strong embrace, the final, forceful, hard and thrusting penis – ever erect, ever active – are women's and men's inevitable language and imagery of 'male' sexuality. In stark contrast, the provocatively posed but constructed passivity of the female body, used in our society to promote the sale of every possible commodity from BMWs to drainpipes, is offered up, to be endlessly contemplated and endlessly consumed. For the truth of our lives in the West is also the truth of a capitalist market, and how it has been able to harness sexuality for its own ends, creating and stimulating new 'needs' and desires. The impact of feminism and other forces of change over the last ten years has thrown up new representations of the female body, like the sexually knowing virgin *and* whore, victim *and* aggressor, found in the pop star Madonna's image.[7] But it is still the *female* body which remains the primary sex object for commercial exploitation. There could not, it would seem, fail to be a connection between the traditional imagery of male and female sexuality, and the reality of men's control and dominance in the world.

But what has fashioned the image, and what really is the connection? Is it, as is still conventionally assumed, some overpowering all-conquering male instinct to be sexually aggressive and assertive? Or is it (if we reject the biological as never alone determining human action) some need for power somehow restricted to men? Could men consciously and wilfully control women through the threat of sexual violence, while concealing their desire for power over women through their perennial propaganda for the joys of heterosexual sex? Many feminists today seem to think so: 'women's sexual "desire" for the penis has been inflicted on us by a male dominated culture', the Lesbians Against Pornography Group write.[8] And, more lyrically and persuasively, Adrienne Rich argues the same thing when she suggests, 'for women, heterosexuality may not be "preference" at all but something that has been composed, managed, organised, propagandised, and maintained by force.'[9] Men, it is true, are physically stronger than women, but how does something so vulnerable and fragile as men's *genital* equipment (for it is well known that a tiny tweak of the testes or a knee to a man's groin never fails to produce shrieks of pain) transform itself into something which appears as a potential weapon, an instrument to dominate and control, the very basis of men's power? How do men control women through sex? The answer, I would argue, is far from obvious.

The Route to 'Sexual Liberation'

At least on the surface, women's experience of sexuality changed dramatically in this century. And yet, seen from the aspect of feminist discontent, the more it changes, the more it stays the same. A central theme of the suffragette campaign in the early stages of this century was the urgent need to change sexual relations between men and women. Christabel Pankhurst's passionate call for sexual purity in men, alongside votes for women, was a call to reform men in line with the Victorian ideal of the sexual purity and spirituality of the bourgeois woman. It was echoed by most, though not all, feminists of her day. A small group of feminist sexual radicals in the early twentieth century, like the fiery young Rebecca West and the editors of *The Freewoman*, did seek greater sexual freedom for everybody, and rejected the traditional stereotypes surrounding men and women.[10] But the overwhelming majority of suffragettes stressed the asexuality and moral superiority of women. As feminist historian Catherine Hall has argued, this reflected the general portrayal of the bourgeois woman developed in the nineteenth century: 'woman's project was to be moral, and to save men from immorality.'[11]

But the cry for sexual purity in those days was not surprising when it seemed to offer the best protection for married women against continuous and debilitating pregnancies and infection from venereal disease. It was also a protection against that grim counterpart to the Victorian 'moral home' and 'perfect wife', the even harsher fate awaiting the unfortunate unmarried and pregnant woman – frequently forced into prostitution through social disgrace and economic destitution. Unwanted pregnancy, syphilis and congenital disease in children were the apparent and constant confirmation that the sexuality of men involved the brutalisation of women. Sex, as Victorian morality proclaimed, was a Sin.

Today, in contrast, the physical dangers of pregnancy and disease do not loom so large as 'the inevitable consequences of sin' in women's experience of sex with men. There are those who still want retribution for a woman's sexual life outside marriage, and retribution for any unorthodox sexuality. Their opposition to sex education for the young and their attempts to halt greater public awareness of the varieties of sexual practice, have served to promote ignorance and fear of sex. In the 1980s a more conservative climate gives space to those who would confine sexuality within the traditional male-dominated and authoritarian family. The delayed medical response in seeking a cure for, or suggesting how to prevent AIDS, a disease still primarily affecting men through homosexual encounters in this country, is part of this punitive and regressive attitude to unorthodox sexual practices. And the increasing cervical cancer rates in women have served the cause of the sexual conservatives. There are persisting inadequacies in modern contraception (still seen as primarily women's responsibility, whatever the dangers to our health and sexual spontaneity) which mean that heterosexuality is not free from physical problems, especially for younger and sexually inexperienced women. But, despite the more visible and vocal moral right of the eighties, the dominant trend throughout the twentieth century has been to make a separation between sexual pleasure and conception, and between sex and disease. In parallel, despite inevitable reactions, there has been an insistent reversal of Victorian attitudes towards women's sexuality, and towards sexuality in general. Sex, in the contemporary Western metropolis, is no longer a Sin.

The Western sexual reform movements of the twentieth century, together with the steady growth of a literature and practice of marriage counselling, took as their starting point an emphasis on the joys of, and indeed necessity for, sexual satisfaction for both men and women within marriage; sex free from fears of conception. Women's satisfaction was, to be sure, described as uniquely responsive to men's competent, skilled and if necessary virtuoso performance. In no sense was it seen as self-initiating or self-directed; nonetheless, it was seen as essential for true marital harmony or 'marital bliss' as Marie Stopes, Van de Velde and others wrote in the 1920s.[12] This attitude had the repressive consequence of a growing scorn for the unmarried woman and the need for a 'cure' for the supposedly 'frigid' woman. But the public encouragement of women's sexual pleasure within marriage always held the threat that it might break free from its marital enclosure into pre-marital or extra-marital sexual encounters. The floodgates of women's eroticism were being dangerously weakened.

There was a fear of women's sexuality and of a decline in the position of men amongst some of those who argued for sexual reform. It is reflected, for example, in the writing of D.H. Lawrence, with his anxiety that women of a sexually independent nature, like Lady Chatterley, were in danger of losing their 'femininity' – their tenderness and receptivity. It was not until the 1960s that women's sexuality otuside marriage became publicly acceptable. The new wave of egalitarianism and permissiveness accompanying the more economically secure sixties ushered in a variety of new sexual reforms, and transformed the lives of women. The abortion reform bill of the late sixties, alongside the marketing of the oral contraceptive pill for women over sixteen, made women's sexual engagements with men an altogether less risky pursuit. This remains so today, despite important regional differences in availability of abortion facilities and fears about the effects of 'the pill'.

It was the combination of 'sexual liberation' and the student protest movements of the sixties which provided the seeds from which the women's liberation movement was to flower at the close of the decade – both affirming and rejecting much that had given rise to it. The predominantly young women who became feminists in the late sixties and early seventies mostly emerged into feminism from the anti-imperialist, anti-authoritarian and co-operative 'counter culture' which had flourished particularly between 1967 and 1972.[13] Sexual liberation was fundamental to its politics. Capitalism, in counter cultural ideology, needed sexually repressed people for the realisation of its life-negating, endlessly acquisitive, and destructive goals. It required self-restraint and compulsive work: both at odds, it was thought, with any liberated or spontaneous sexual expression.

Recalling the Sixties

In an affirmation of the sexual radicalism of the sixties, feminists in the early seventies took their own search for sexual pleasure very seriously. If we could not quite match the solemnity and zeal of Masters and Johnson as they meticulously recorded and advised upon women's route to orgasm, we were at least impressed by their deference to the clitoris, and their damning dismissal of much of men's customary sexual practice. If women had not been enjoying their sexual experience with men, not having their share of orgasms, it became easier to reject what we had usually been led by men to see as our own problem – and one we were unable to discuss with men. Feminists soon began to suggest that it was necessary for women to explore and express their real sexual feelings, needs and desires, and, if engaging with men, to begin to re-educate men as well. Sexual satisfaction, feminists argued in these early days, could give women greater confidence in themselves and more power in the world – an idea lifted directly from the raunchy Reichian sixties, when the first English edition of *The Function of the Orgasm* became a bestseller.

There has been some considerable feminist rewriting of women's engagement with the sexual radicalism of the sixties. It has become a new orthodoxy, strangely enough of radicals and conservatives alike, that women eagerly participated only briefly in what Beatrix Campbell has referred to as 'men's clamour for sex': that we were quickly disillusioned and disappointed.[14] But that was not my own experience, nor that of other women recording those times for us. The reality was, as usual, more ambiguous. We have not only Germaine Greer's ballsy bragging of her own predatory passions and carnal conquests in *The Female Eunuch*, which is critical of other women who cannot share her own desire to 'embrace' the penis, but other reflections on those times.[15] The New York writer and feminist, Ellen Willis, reflecting on her own writing on Bob Dylan in 1968, recalls how she identified with men's promiscuous sexual exploits and shared their anti-possessiveness: 'I understood men's needs to go on the road because I was, spiritually speaking, on the road myself. That, at least, was my fantasy; the realities of my life were somewhat more ambiguous.'[16] Her compatriot, Deirdre English, has also discussed the ambiguities of those days: 'The sexism was there, but women were actually having more sexual experience of different kinds and enjoying it.'[17]

It was my own experience in the sixties, and that of most of my women friends, that we greatly enjoyed being able to live openly in sexual relations with men, and also enjoyed the more or less frequent forays we chose to make outside our central relationships at any one time. I was then involved with the Sydney libertarian 'push', a small but influential radical bohemian social and political movement which flourished in Sydney, Australia, in the late fifties and early sixties. We were passionately anti-authoritarian anarchists committed to a philosophy of 'free love' and 'permanent protest'. A group of women from the 'push' recorded their experiences of those days for the Australian Broadcasting Commission in 1982.[18] Recalling the very early days in the fifties, Judy Smith pointed out 'Our battles then really were breaking down sexual barriers: other battles came later.' But, she added, 'I enjoyed it, because the alternative in most societies was so dreadful; it was the push or suburbia.' Rosanne Bonney, reflecting on her life in the push in the early sixties, also concludes, 'I don't think I share what is the fashionable contemporary feminist view of what men did to me … indeed I think I benefited greatly from it.' The general feeling all the women interviewed expressed was that they had enjoyed taking responsibility for themselves and the sexual and intellectual freedom this had meant.

It was rather less enjoyable, I would now add, once a woman decided to have a child or children, when the philosophy of individual responsibility and the pursuit of personal pleasure were to prove disastrously unsupportive and rejecting for many women. But certainly I look back with no flicker of regret, except occasionally at its passing, to those years in the 1960s when I rarely slept alone and devoted much of my leisure time to bedding my favourite man of the moment. However strange it now seems to recall, it was not usually the men who initiated these erotic encounters. Sexual coercion is not what was happening amongst that little band of sexual radicals (even though Australian women have been described as 'the doormats of the Western world'). Like Mary Ingham[19] recalling those times in Britain, I suspect our sexual conquests – for that is how we saw them – were most satisfying for the social status they conferred on us rather than the physical pleasure they provided (seducing one's professor was usually the most boring experience of all, I remember, and not to be repeated). But some women did start to feel more sexually relaxed and confident in those years. Indeed, as I have been assured by many feminists of my own age, it was quite frequently our desire for new sexual experiences coming up against the unexamined double standards of men, and especially men's inability to cope with their own sexual jealousy, that led women into women's liberation.[20]

I think we can assume from women's recollections of the sixties that at least some were enjoying sex with men. Many more were probably more ambivalently enjoying sex with men, though unable to discuss its attendant frustrations. Some, no doubt, found little or no satisfaction in their sexual encounters with men. These differences were to feed later conflicts between women as ambivalence over heterosexuality deepened, and guilt-tripping of women who enjoyed sex with men strengthened. Nevertheless, however real or illusory the joys of sex with men, all feminists in the early 1970s were rejecting, and rejecting with anger, other practices which had been celebrated in the name of 'sexual liberation'.

In the late sixties a harder and more aggressive male radicalism had replaced the (superficially at least) softer focus of earlier years. Large numbers of feminists were soon to put an end to the male-centred, cock-crowing soft porn which had festooned much of the underground press in the sixties and early seventies, with its tits, bums, gang bangs and macho bravado. We exposed this as an expression of men's contemptuous and aggressive objectification of women. At the office of the radical socialist magazine *Black Dwarf*, Sheila Rowbotham, back in 1968, had been provoked to pin up the following poem: 'Let us put pin-ups in Black Dwarf/Let us wank into Revolution … Let us stick cunts/On our projecting egos/Calling this comradeship/And the end of exploitation ...'[21] And other underground magazines, like *Oz*, were seen as serving more to underline than to undermine society's general oppression of women, with certain added new twists. Young women (the younger the better) were depicted as little other than the sexual servicers of men; yet, like men, they were expected to equate fucking with their own liberation. Women with children could be eulogised as earth mothers but were expected to make no financial demands on men, and even less to expect men to take turns with the mop. Women in general were seen as providing emotional warmth and support but could expect no commitment or security from men. This could be a mugs' game for women, as Janis Joplin's self-flagellating, sobbing, throbbing, throaty wails warned us.

When Robin Morgan thundered forth her farewells to the sexist ignorance and arrogance of male radicals in 1970 and with other women took over the New York underground paper *RAT*, the wind that cooled the cocky confidence of many an old rebel fanned the flame of collective passion for many a new feminist. By the end of 1971, women working in the underground press in London had begun to meet together, which led within six months to the production of *Spare Rib*. Women's sexuality was to be reclaimed for women. Or so it seemed.

Women's Liberation and the Search for Sexual Pleasure

The first problem with sexuality, as feminists saw things back then, was that it was 'male-defined'. Our conception of the sexual act itself was, literally, the moment of penile penetration of the vagina. But, as Anne Koedt and a host of other pamphleteers soon proclaimed, this may, but very often may not, be the source of sexual arousal in women. Pointing out that the clitoris and not the vagina was 'the centre of sexual pleasure' for women, Koedt argued:

> We must begin to demand that if certain sexual positions now defined as 'standard' are not mutually conducive to orgasm, they no longer be defined as standard. New techniques must be used

or devised which transform this particular aspect of our current sexual exploration.[22]

Women, it was felt, had been kept in the dark about their own sexuality, and in the dark they could not assert their own sexual needs. It was also clear that the language of sex, of fucking, always assigned activity and control to men, and passivity and surrender to women. It therefore served to symbolise the power relation between men and women in the world. It was the purest form of sexist imagery: dominant male, submissive female. The task for women in the women's liberation movement, Pat Whiting wrote in 1972, was 'to "decondition" men, to rid ourselves of the double standard and to establish a more realistic image of female sexuality than that offered by the male society.'[23]

Reappraisal of the sources of women's sexual pleasure and rejection of the double standard which disparaged or denied sexual assertiveness in women while celebrating it in men, was at the heart of the feminist critique of standard heterosexual practice in the early seventies. Wedded to this critique was the belief from the sixties that there was a connection between suppressed sexuality and social powerlessness. The Women's Liberation Workshop paper *Shrew*, in December 1972, carried the bold banner headline THE SUPPRESSED POWER OF FEMALE SEXUALITY. It began:

> Women have a capacity for sexuality far in excess of that of men. But thousands of years of patriarchal conditioning has robbed us of our sexual potential and deceived us about the true nature of our sexuality.

And it concluded:

> A woman who is directly in touch with her own forceful sexual capacities can no longer tolerate being told that she is inherently passive, essentially masochistic, and that she will only find true fulfilment in submission to men. To such a woman these ideas would be absurd ... Having finally come to realise the reality of her own power, she would never again relinquish it.[24]

Or, as Beatrix Campbell argued the following year:

> Women's sexual passivity and objectification undermines their functioning as autonomous individuals ... Acknowledgement of

lust, acceptance of so-called promiscuity must be recognised as potentially inevitable stages in women's escape from sexual conformity.

More optimistically still, she concluded:

> The intervention of women in determining how sexuality is expressed need not simply end in evolving 'new response patterns', for this can just as easily end in exchanging one mechanical blueprint for another. The potency of women's intervention in the sexual arena lies in the possibilities of shedding the whole mythology of masculinity and femininity.[25]

The *Shrew* issue on sexuality had carried as its special Christmas treat 'PRICK: The Magazine for the Randy Woman' featuring gigantic male nudes, RAM dildos and RAPIER razor blades, thus mocking pervasive male sexual fantasies, but with a type of confident ridicule which would soon disappear altogether from feminist writing – to be replaced by pure rage. Such mockery of men's sexual obsessions also appeared in early issues of *Spare Rib*.

The second aspect of feminist analysis of sexuality in the early seventies stressed the significance of women's historic lack of control over their own fertility. This made sex with men a potential danger and problem for women, and was seen as the central mechanism through which men gained power and control over women. More basic than the extent to which men had defined existing ideas of sexuality were the ideas and arrangements surrounding reproduction and childcare. These placed women's fertility, and ultimately, therefore, women's lives, in men's hands.

Women could not, with any level of social acceptance and support, choose to give birth to a child except within marriage and the family, which legally, economically and socially, established men's power and authority over women. Equally, women who were sexually active with men could not choose *not* to give birth to a child with any confidence or security. Historically women had been denied access to adequate contraception; and were still, if accidentally pregnant, denied the right (usually by male authorities) to humane or unproblematically available abortion facilities. This analysis made free contraception and abortion on demand key issues for women's liberation in its early days, the bottom line for women controlling their own destiny. Rosalind Delmar wrote in 1972, 'Today, the right to free contraception and abortion on demand is inscribed on the banners of every women's movement.'[26] And in these early days of hope, all the feminist campaigns over sexuality, fertility and childcare seemed to hold the promise of a brand new future for women. As Monica Sjoo summed it up,

> For women to be able to control their fertility questions the functions of the father-centred family and women's past within it as a source of unpaid labour – and so ultimately it questions the entire structure of the society we live in.[27]

While women's rights to free contraception and abortion became perhaps *the* symbols of women's liberation in its early days – and the demand which many men on the left and in trade unions came to support – it was always connected with wider campaigns concerning women's health, sexuality and issues of childbirth and childcare. By the mid seventies women's centres were being opened in almost every major city of Britain. Often the most active groups in the centres were women's health groups, which, along with promoting self-examination and self-help for women, were to expose the chilling inadequacies of the obstetric and gynaecological care women were receiving. These groups were in the forefront of opposition to the way in which women were denied active control over the process of childbirth and were frequently subjected to degrading and humiliating experiences in the hands of authoritarian, mostly male, doctors. Health care in general was seen as a crucial political issue. These women's health groups prefigured much of the current preoccupation with more holistic approaches to health and the proliferation of acupuncture, naturopathy and keep fit classes, all stressing the connections between physical, psychological, social and political factors. With their emphasis on self-help and alternative medicine, many of these initiatives necessarily involved working outside as well as inside the institutions of the National Health Service.

Women's health groups also encouraged and developed better sex education for young women in schools, stressing the need for more positive and independent images of women's sexuality. Feminists were busy seeking greater knowledge of and control over their own bodies, while at the same time fighting for better social provision and social benefits for childcare. They were also, of course, demanding men's greater involvement in childcare and domestic work. 'A Woman's Right to Choose', which became the slogan of the National Abortion Campaign (NAC) set up in 1975, was a shorthand for a lot more than legal abortion.

By the mid 1970s socialist feminist theory in Britain and the US was fairly consistently arguing that it was the social arrangements for having and rearing children which created the material basis for men's power over women. In capitalist society reproduction is organised through the 'private' sphere of the family, and, seen as the primary responsibility of women, this serves to separate women from any central or dominant role in the public sphere of production, and control of the market. It is this separation, and its related ideologies, which were identified as the basis for women's economic, social and political dependence on men. Men had thus gained control over women's sexuality and domestic labour; the key to their power over women. The power relations between men and women are enshrined in the rights given to men within marriage, and (a point most socialist feminists were always at pains to emphasise) are manifested in and daily experienced through the strength of received ideas about men and women: their separate spheres, distinct capacities, contrasting desires and emotions. Within this theoretical framework, our ideas about men's and women's sexuality were seen as one very distinct aspect of the more general ideologies of sexual difference. Socialist feminists therefore stressed the need to analyse and attack existing ideologies, and were later increasingly to emphasise the role of the unconscious in sustaining them, and in determining behaviour.

It is one thing, however, to search for a theoretical framework in which to locate men's control over women's sexuality in the material world and its dominant ideologies: it is another to provide a more detailed and specific theoretical understanding and explanation of human sexual relations. It is quite another task again for each of us in practice to grapple with the doubts, dilemmas and difficulties we face individually concerning sex.

Our problems were not immediately theoretical ones, but rather, for most heterosexual feminists, were to do with the hopes, fears and resentments many of us experienced in sexual relations with men. And it is here of course that radical feminist approaches to sexuality had, and have, an immediate and accessible appeal. In radical feminist theory all relations between women and men are, and always have been, determined by men's collective effort to assert and maintain power over women. This is the nature of patriarchy – the first and most fundamental power relation in all societies. In the early radical feminist writing of Kate Millett and Shulamith Firestone, men's sexuality was, above all else, directed towards the conquest of women. It involved exploitation and domination. Firestone wrote, 'Yes, love means an entirely different thing to men than to women: it means ownership and control ...'[28] Kate Millett saw patriarchal power as essentially phallic power, expressed most clearly in men's sexual exploitation of women. She portrayed what she termed the 'sexual cannibalism' in the writings of Henry Miller, D.H. Lawrence and Norman Mailer, as a true 'literary reflection' of the reality of patriarchy.[29] These authors exposed the real nature of men's designs on women as sadistic, abusive, controlling, and subordinating.

Radical feminist thought here is persuasive because the violent and sadistic sexual fantasies flowing from the pens of these eminent men are familiar to us all. And even if, as other feminists have since pointed out, works like *Lady Chatterley's Lover* are not in any clear sense abusive of women, other texts from the literary canon handed down to us most certainly are.[30] Radical feminist 'exposure' of male sexuality is not so different from 'common sense' assumptions about sexuality: that it is aggressive and male. When Roger Scruton writes of 'the unbridled ambition of the phallus'[31] or Enoch Powell informs us – quoting from the Book of Genesis – that 'the imagination of man's heart is evil from his youth',[32] they express similar thoughts. It is a common sense which creates, as much as it reflects, the reality it describes.

What was to shock and enrage feminists, eventually to the point of hopeless despair, was the initial public denial and persisting public tolerance of men's sexual violence towards women, especially from men in authority. The blindness towards this reality was expressed, ironically, in the early writing of Germaine Greer. It encapsulates perfectly the nonchalance of liberals and particularly of sexual radicals towards questions of men's violence:

It is true that men use the threat of physical force, usually histrionically, to silence nagging wives: but it is almost always a sham. It is actually a game of nerves, and can be turned aside fairly easily.[33]

Such statements could perhaps themselves be cast aside as naive, a failure of perception induced by a commitment to promote more positive attitudes towards sexuality, were they not also coupled with some knowledge of the reality of men's sexual violence towards women and collusion with the myth that women were ultimately to blame. So Greer informed us: 'Women are always precipitating scenes of violence in pubs and dance halls';[34] 'Many of the vile and cruel things which men do to women are done at women's instigation';[35] 'If women would only offer a genuine alternative to the treadmill of violence the world might breathe a little longer with less pain.'[36] In these comments which, hopefully, must sound a little strange even to the most confirmed sexist today, Greer was merely reflecting what was still the current opinion of most people in the early seventies. The popular psychiatric wisdom of Anthony Storr, for example, had quite recently informed the world that 'The nagging, aggressive woman is often unconsciously demanding that which she most fears' – men's sexual domination and aggression.[37] But in undertaking to shatter this particular 'common sense' mythology, feminists were to find it increasingly difficult to hold on to any progressive sexual politics at all.

Confronting Men's Sexual Violence against Women

It was the issue of men's domestic violence against women and children which feminists were forced to confront early in the 1970s. The first Women's Aid refuge was opened, without actually being planned, when a number of battered women sought help and safety after the Chiswick Women's Centre opened up in 1971. Over the next few years dozens of other local groups of feminists helped to set up and support similar refuges for women trying to escape from violent men. They were always democratically and collectively run to ensure maximum autonomy for and participation from all women. In 1975 the

National Women's Aid Federation was formed from 35 of these groups. Its aims were to provide temporary refuge for all battered women and their children, as well as to publicise the rapidly growing evidence of the appalling extent of domestic violence: 25 per cent of all violent crime is wife assault. Women's Aid also campaigned for changes in the law, in public housing provision and in social policy to protect and provide for battered women. Feminists in Women's Aid saw the problem of violence in the home and women's difficulty escaping from it as the result of the general social subordination of women, and the particular economic and legal dependence of married women on their husbands (especially married women with young children). Women's domestic dependence upon men, it was stressed, was organised through and insisted upon by the state via inadequate child benefit and the absence of nursery provision; the low wages paid for women's jobs were also part of this dependence.

But however much women were trapped and weakened by their greater economic and social powerlessness, and however much some men were brutalised by existing social conditions, the abominable cruelty and persistent sexual abuse many women suffered in the one place they most needed safety and security triggered a stronger and sharper hostility from feminists towards men. A rhetoric of battle emerged in some feminist writing, particularly from feminists working with battered women. Women were taking up arms against the collective terrorism of men. The old sex war (part joke, part serious) between individuals was being organised on a new, collective and deadly serious basis. From 1974, alongside the work with battered women which was pioneered in Britain and which spread to the US, Canada and elsewhere, feminists in Britain began similar work in relation to rape, this time drawing upon work already begun in the US. By 1975 the first Rape Crisis Centre had opened in London, to provide support and counselling for women victims of rape. It also campaigned to change legal, police and medical practices which, firmly in the hands of male authorities, accepted the mythology that many women in some sense provoked, colluded in, or deserved sexual violence from men. Some women, the myth went, were 'innocent', but many were 'guilty'; guilty, feminists concluded, of appearing to men as independent, actively sexual people.

Feminists urgently needed to understand the prevalence of rape in our society, and to see how a mythology of men's sexual needs could serve so readily to blame the victim and not the perpetrator of sexual outrages against women. As with domestic violence, feminists began by seeing rape as an extension of women's general social subordination. Discussing 'the rape controversy' in 1975, Anna Coote and Tess Gill wrote:

> Like the battering of women in the home, rape is primarily a social problem, rooted in centuries of male predominance and in the links our society has fostered between property, sex and violence ... The problem cannot be tackled effectively unless changes are made in the social conditions that encourage violence and keep women in an inferior position.[39]

However, the enormity of so many evil crimes against women, and the hypocritical, contradictory reactions or dismissive contempt of the media, courts, police, doctors and others towards them, once again fuelled feminist rage towards men.

The tigers of wrath may be wiser than the horses of instruction. When it comes to showing men what women think of male indifference to the suffering of women, rage is appropriate; but nevertheless, for understanding men's and women's sexuality – 'perverse' or otherwise – rage alone has proved inadequate.

By 1975, some feminists in the women's liberation movement, particularly those connected with Women's Aid and Rape Crisis Centres, had increasingly more to say on one aspect of men's sexual behaviour: its coercive and violent manifestations. But other feminists, especially those who had sexual relations with men, felt increasingly less able to talk about their own sexual practices and experiences. Since the need to explore personal life and experience was at the heart of the 1970s feminist movement, and sexuality certainly still preoccupied most feminists – whether lesbian, celibate, or still predominantly heterosexual – this silence was clearly a sign of trouble. The British feminist anthology *No Turning Back* covering the years 1975 to 1980 contained not a single article on heterosexuality.[40] A subsequent project by Sue Cartledge and Joanna Ryan in 1982 to gather together all that had been written more recently by feminists specifically on sexuality had to be abandoned when they discovered how little there was. They chose instead to solicit new articles for their book *Sex and Love*.[41]

Anna Coote and Beatrix Campbell reflected upon this silence in *Sweet Freedom*, their history of women's liberation. They attributed it to a frustrating and futile struggle fought out between 'heterosexual chauvinism' and 'lesbian separatism', which they believed had produced stalemate and disappointment for the majority of feminists who could identify with neither position.[42] But their account of heterosexual chauvinism relied solely upon Germaine Greer's *The Female Eunuch*, which, though very influential, is surely a pre-feminist text or at the very least an unusual feminist text in that it was known to have little, if any, connection to the contemporary women's movement. (Despite popular opinion *The Female Eunuch* is unrepresentative of women's liberation in its early days; the movement predominantly rejected Greer's individualistic anarchism and dismissal of collective action.) The strengthening of a lesbian separatist analysis of sexuality, on the other hand, was most influential only after 1978, and was, it seems to me, as much a product of the silence over heterosexuality as its cause.

Sexology and Feminist Theorising of Sexuality

I think the silence on heterosexuality in the late seventies has a more general explanation, not one simply based on the women's liberation movement. It is linked to the inadequacies of the theories of sexuality available for feminists to draw upon, and consequent weaknesses in feminist sexual politics. Feminist thought on sexuality in the 1970s was, as I have suggested, influenced by the ideas and research which the 'science of sexology' had been popularising over the last hundred years. We can understand many current debates better if we return to the history of these ideas.

It was the classic case studies of Krafft-Ebing, recording in horror the pitiful plight of the sexual 'perverts' paraded before the law courts of Vienna in the 1880s, which had pioneered this new area of research and theory. In Britain, also in the 1880s, Havelock Ellis began his massive global survey and categorisation of all the known varieties of sexual performance. He presented his resulting display of human 'sexual deviations' as the product of some core essence of each individual. People were born with different types of sexual desires and proclivities. For Krafft-Ebing and for Havelock Ellis the single most salient feature of sexuality was its over-riding significance for the individual and for society generally. (Few subsequent sexologists have demurred from this view.) The new emphasis on 'private life' which accompanied the development of capitalism, suggested that it was indeed sexuality which provided the key to most of the problems which can disrupt society. People's personal lives in the domestic sphere were seen as necessarily split off from the public and rational world of production and the market, and a potential threat to that world. In line with contemporary Darwinian theory, which stressed the evolutionary base of human behaviour, sexual behaviour was seen as driven by an inner 'natural instinct', and one of almost overpowering and uncontrollable strength. (At least, that is, as it manifested itself in the human male.)

The founders of sexology thus provided instinctivist and essentialist explanations of sexual behaviour, seeing it – however complex and varied its manifestations – as flowing directly from some inner biological essence. This is an idea which should be familiar to us, corresponding as it does to all our common sense assumptions about sexuality to this day. As Jeffrey Weeks argues, setting out to record and classify what they saw as 'the truth of the sexual', sexology has played its part in promoting the idea of sex as the centre of identity.[43] Sexologists in the twentieth century were to modify some of the emphases of their forefathers, and, in particular, to distance themselves from the pervasive pessimism of Krafft-Ebing (and of Freud), with their grim vision of the potentially dangerous and anti-social nature of the sexual impulse. They stressed instead its beneficial effects for humanity, in serving to cement (so they believed) the ties of matrimony. But they rejected neither the biologism nor the essentialism of Krafft-Ebing and Ellis.

Alfred Kinsey in the 1940s and 1950s, and Masters and Johnson in the 1960s, undertook their own 'authoritative' investigations of human sexual behaviour at a time when behaviouristic stimulus-response psychology had replaced the earlier instinctivist psychology as the dominant theoretical framework of psychology. This meant they set out to describe and quantify the specific types of physical stimulation which were effective in producing what they could label – and for them, more importantly, measure – as the definitive sexual response: the physical contractions of orgasm. Taking their lead from contemporary behaviouristic social learning theory, both Kinsey and Masters and Johnson stressed the role of learning in determining which types of stimulation were sexually arousing. But their description of the sexual process was, if anything, even more physical and biologistic than their predecessors.

'Relax, stroke gently, if you want to come.' The booming sexual therapy courses offered by Masters and Johnson from the mid-sixties served as the model for countless other programmes, with the apparently successful formula of 'sensate focusing', to prepare partners in search of better sex for the learning of new sexual techniques. Indeed, better sex, within the monogamous heterosexual couple relationship, was to become everybody's birthright in the crusading publications of Masters and Johnson.[44] (It was also presented as a cure for all social ills, seen in Britain and in the US as stemming from the ever upwardly spiralling rate of divorce.) Most centrally of all, Masters and Johnson stressed that *women* must now be given their fair share of physical sexual release – if no other release – within the heterosexual union. Orgasmic equality! This was the goal devoutly sought by the new school of sex therapists, fully aware as never before, through Kinsey's depressing surveys and the many which had followed them, of how profoundly unequal and unjust orgasmic distribution between the sexes appeared to be. The old beast within, the dangerous sex impulse itself, could, in their view, be tamed and trained, could even serve to nurture better and fairer social relations between the sexes. Such was the optimistic, if mechanistic and misleading, message of contemporary sexology.

Feminists, though quick to pick up on what Masters and Johnson pictured as the magnificently expansive and recurring orgasmic contractability of the human female, were not fooled by Masters and Johnson's propaganda for fucking, that is, for heterosexual normality. Masters and Johnson had insisted that 'penile thrusting' in the vagina should be adequate stimulation for female orgasm, due to the resulting movement of the clitoral hood over the clitoris. To this assertion, feminist sex researcher Shere Hite had retorted that we might just as well say that the pulling of a man's testicles should be adequate stimulation for male orgasm. Shere Hite's own survey *The Hite Report* suggested that only 30 per cent of women could have orgasms regularly through intercourse, direct stimulation of the clitoris being necessary for the majority of women to reach orgasm.[45] This meant, as most feminists perceived with pleasure, that as far as orgasmic stimulation was concerned, men were physically irrelevant: women could as easily go it alone, with each other, or however else they wished. (That physical stimulation might have absolutely nothing to do with the dynamics of desire, which are largely unconscious, was something which most feminists at that time seemed not to have noticed. Or, if we had, we could not find a 'public' way of saying so in the feminist discourse of the day.)

Many feminists were fooled, however, by the crude and simplistic behaviourist psychology of Masters and Johnson, corresponding as it did to much that passed for explanation in psychology in general in both Britain and the US. Not only was sexual behaviour reduced to physical techniques and bodily sensations, separated off from their cultural and social meanings or their context within social relations, but human consciousness was reduced to sets of attitudes which could be conditioned at will. Whilst Shere Hite's findings were different from those of Masters and Johnson, she shared their behaviourist approach. With 'great joy', so she told us, she concluded from her four years of research into human sexuality that:

> There is no great mystery about why a woman has an orgasm. It happens with the right stimulation, quickly, pleasurably, and reliably ... The whole key is adequate stimulation.[46]

This was to prove a misleading type of optimistic voluntarism for feminists. It paved the way for the pessimistic reversal of much of the earlier feminist thought on sexuality which occurred in the late seventies: the shift from an emphasis on women's sexual pleasure to an emphasis on the dangers which might accompany it.

A crop of self-identified feminist advice books and articles were published and eagerly consumed by feminists in the early seventies, most originating from the US. In Betty Dodson's *Liberating Masturbation*, Lonnie Barbach's *For Yourself: The Fulfilment of Female Sexuality*, and Barbara Seaman's *Free and Female*, it was, as the titles suggested, repeatedly emphasised that women could (and for their mental health and fighting spirit most certainly should) learn to acquire the skills which would enable them to fulfil their own, unique 'sexual needs'.[47] The message was always the same: women can, through exploration of their own bodily and genital sensations, find out about their 'true needs'; having done so, they will know how to get what they want from sex; women do not need to wait for somebody else to fulfil their sexual needs, they can do it quite adequately for themselves.[48] Once aware of your own *unique* bodily sensations (if you're having trouble finding an identity, you could probably find it here) and once you have learned to throw off any remaining old-fashioned perceptions of self (simply by deciding to), these books all suggest that satisfaction can be guaranteed – with or without a sexual partner. Here, the idea of women's sexuality as some type of 'inner essence' or 'body electric', a source of individuality and identity, completely submerges any notions of sexuality as a type of communication, understanding or relationship.

Romantic aspirations, in any case, were dismissed in these early years of feminism as dangerous delusions, promoted only to trap women into marriage or other types of emotional dependency on men, a dependency which could never be satisfactory for any real feminist because of the inevitable inbuilt inequality of overestimating or idealising one's sexual partner. Women only formed romantic attachments with men because they had no secure sense of themselves. As Verena Stefan wrote in the feminist bestseller *Shedding* in 1975:

> I was still in love with Dave, lying there in the hospital with a urinary tract infection. He regretted the fact that we wouldn't be able to go to bed with each other for a while. I did too. *I needed him because I didn't have my self.* [my emphasis][49]

There is little wonder and even less desire in such feminist reflection on sex. Indeed there is little emotion of any intensity at all in this bland optimism about women reclaiming their bodies, and hence themselves. Yet such writing, it must be admitted, did have a liberating effect on many feminists, at least for a while. It was encouraging to believe, as Hite reassured us, that 'controlling your own stimulation symbolises owning your own body, and is a very important step towards freedom.'[50] Eleanor Stephens was partially right when she concluded in *Spare Rib* in 1975 that:

> Amongst all the issues raised by the women's movement, the feminist approach to female sexuality is one which has, for many women, completely transformed our feelings about ourselves ... The implications of taking responsibility for our sexuality reach into all areas of our lives, giving women a new sense of autonomy and power.[51]

Spare Rib by this time had replaced its confident ridicule of men's sexual obsessions with personal descriptive pieces, which were then phased out to be replaced by pieces on the mechanics of sex and how to have orgasms. So by the mid seventies heterosexual sex was taken out of the context of personal relationships and put in terms of individual needs which were being met, or not met. Alongside this was the growing importance of articles on women's refuges and rape crisis centres, stressing men's violence.[52]

Yet in the early years of women's liberation many feminists did, at least some of the time, feel a sense of collective power and autonomy which made us a lot less desperate. Less desperate, anyway, to find some man to provide a sense of meaning and satisfaction in our lives. We could feel such autonomy so long as sisterhood was blooming, when it felt secure, exciting, and stimulating to fill up each and every moment with living the feminist struggle.

Again, it is the rhetoric of Robin Morgan, whose collected poems *Monster* were published here in 1973, which celebrates some of the easily eroticised excitement of those times:

> I want a women's revolution like a lover
> I lust for it, I want so much this freedom
> this end to struggle and fears and lies
> we all exhale, that, I could die just
> with the passionate utterance of that desire.[53]

Less theatrically, and perhaps more characteristically, Sheila Shulman's *Pome to Jackie* written in 1974 sums up a more restrained but similar ecstasy:

> When I say (meaning you) 'my sister',
> some childhood loneliness is healed.[54]

It was, I think, the shared embrace of feminism itself and not the emergence of any individual, unique and liberated bodily sensations which felt something like the promise of a new kind of loving. It was not some new authentic female sexuality of our own we had discovered, but the desire to bring into being the love of womankind for herself.

When, by the mid seventies, it became essential to integrate this optimistic feminist vision of women's powerful inner sexuality with the depressing awareness of men's sexual violence towards women and the misogyny and sexism embedded within the imagery and language of heterosexuality, it was almost inevitable that these opposed preoccupations with the sexual would collapse into the idea of opposed sexual natures.

The early enthusiasm for women reclaiming their 'authentic sexuality', expressing a sexuality which was 'essentially female', soon took a prescriptive tone in feminist writing. It is well illustrated in Anja Meulenbelt's *For Ourselves* published in Britain in 1981. Women's needs, as Meulenbelt illustrated them, are all positive and progressive: women want equality in sexual relations and to feel independent and in control.[55] Women's sexual sensations, she wrote, repeating what had by then become feminist orthodoxy, are mostly unconnected to genital penetration, and establish the basis for that happy 'love affair' we can all have with ourselves. Meulenbelt assured us that 'there isn't just *one* kind of liberated or emancipated sexuality', but strait is the gate and narrow is the way that leads us to it.[56] For example, observing that some women do 'make an orgasm' through movement in the vagina (and don't expect anyone to do it for you!), she adds, 'But it isn't as common as we have been taught. And even if you *can* do it like that, the question remains do you *want* to? (author's emphasis)[57] The question is loaded, hammered home for us in the interviews with individual women which the book included: 'You didn't really expect that you could come from fucking?' I should hope not! But the interviewee hastens to reassure her questioner: 'Oh no, but I didn't like fucking either, it was always a disaster!'[58] That's more like it!

The Rise and Rise of Revolutionary Feminism

Despite the sexual fulfilment promised from predominantly solipsistic sexual *acts* – a surely somewhat lonely pursuit – an altogether bleaker view had crept into feminist discussion of sexual relationships from the mid seventies onwards. The joys and delights of female sexuality had proved, unsurprisingly, more elusive than many feminist texts had promised. Both heterosexual and lesbian feminists still found that their sexual relationships involved much the same mixtures of pleasure and satisfaction, frustration, ambivalence, and difficult dependencies as they always had.[59] The old optimism that we could simply choose to transform our sexual experiences evaporated.

But it was not the idea of some inner core of genuine, positive, female needs and desires which was rejected, nor the idea of women finding their shared female identity through a discovery of their 'authentic' sexuality. The editorial collective of the socialist feminist magazine *Scarlet Woman* introduced their issue on sexuality in 1981 by reaffirming the belief that 'all women whether lesbian or heterosexual [do] have the same kind of sexuality.' And, they added, 'we also think that there is a real difference between women's sexuality and men's – perhaps related to our different reproductive functions, differences exacerbated by patriarchy.'[60] But there was also, by this time, an equally strong belief that women's own sexuality was 'crippled' and 'denied' by men's imposition of 'compulsory heterosexuality'.[61] A prevailing 'political lesbian' or sexual separatist ideology was growing stronger within the women's movement. Political lesbianism, however, was not the affirmation of a sexual orientation in its own right: sexual desire for and engagement with women was not its defining characteristic. It was defined negatively by its rejection of heterosexuality: a rejection seen as the political solution to the problem of male dominance. (Some lesbian feminists, not surprisingly, were soon to object to such a desexualised, tactical definition in which their sexuality was seen to elect them as a type of moral vanguard.)[62]

The turning point in the adoption of this new feminist analysis of sexuality in Britain was when the Birmingham National Women's Liberation Conference in 1978 passed (against such fierce opposition that it terminated all future national conferences) the motion to make 'the right to define our sexuality' *the* over-riding demand of the women's movement, preceding all other demands. Men's sexual domination of women, which prevented the emergence of women's self-defined sexuality, was now being formally accepted as the pivot of women's oppression. The old feminist message that 'the personal is political' had been inverted to become 'the political is personal', and the personal is sexual. The message had once served to enable feminists to throw off self-blame and self-hatred by being able to see their apparently 'personal' problems as socially produced, a product of all the ways in which women were subordinated – legally, financially, culturally, socially and sexually. It now served more to induce personal guilt and self-blame, where some feminists felt accused of involvement in 'incorrect' sexual and personal relationships.

The clearest statements locating women's oppression in men's sexual practices and 'the institution' of heterosexuality came, in Britain, from a few widely influential revolutionary feminist groups which emerged in the late seventies – ironically, mostly composed of former socialist feminists. But their ideas were not new to feminist politics; they were only a magnification of themes always present in radical feminism. Susan Griffin, for instance, had written back in 1971: 'the basic elements of rape are involved in all heterosexual relationships.'[63] The paper 'Political Lesbianism: The Case Against Heterosexuality', written in 1979, summarised the revolutionary feminist position. It is a simple one. Sex is the problem; avoiding heterosexual contact is the solution. Here, rejecting the significance of class and race, the writers affirmed that it is specifically through sexuality that the fundamental oppression, that of men over women, is maintained.[64] Therefore, 'Giving up fucking for a feminist is about taking your politics seriously.'[65] (They later qualified this statement; women cannot actually give up 'fucking', only 'getting fucked', because: 'We now think it's rubbish to say that women fuck men; what happens is that men fuck women, or women get fucked by men.')[66] Heterosexuality is damned, for, like Original Sin, it inevitably enfeebles a woman ('undermines her confidence and saps her strength') and empowers a man ('makes him stronger, not just over one woman but over all women').

The awesome, all-conquering power attributed to the penis in male – and female – fantasy, as the mighty symbol of men's power to subdue the world, is here presented as literal reality, lived ideology with a vengeance. How could such concrete reductionism, such phallic obsession, have got such a hold on feminism? Partly, I would suggest, because feminists had always tended to write about sex as though it existed autonomously, outside the context of relationships.

One apparent strength of revolutionary feminist writing, apart from its expression of a realistic anger at so many men's violence towards women, was that it correctly challenged the liberal complacency behind earlier feminist appropriations of the prescriptions of sexologists. These had avoided the question of men's power and men's violence (in and out of the bedroom) to concentrate their advice on men's inadequate sexual perform-ance, and the joys of a more masturbatory sexuality, unconnected to any particular type of sexual partner or relationship. But, more frequent and better orgasms did not empower women. By the mid seventies it was obvious that sexual liberation and greater sexual satisfaction, in themselves, did not create or even threaten to create greater power for women. They certainly could not do so if they occurred in isolation from more general social and economic equality. It was this aspect of women's liberation which many men, perhaps mendaciously, often claimed to support, while the media were not slow to depict and apparently endorse a greater sexual assertiveness and bodily enjoyment in the 'new' woman.

But revolutionary feminists avoided other contradictions: some women wanted to improve their sexual relations with men while also wanting to confront the frightening prevalence of men's hostility and violence towards women. Instead revolutionary feminists merely dissolved the contradiction by collapsing all heterosexuality into 'male violence'. They rightly re-examined the notion of 'women gaining control of their own sexuality' and the mistaken sexual politics which equated such a pursuit with undermining the power and privilege of men. But they went further, and accused all sexologists, and those they had influenced, of a conscious and successful conspiracy to undermine and subvert feminist aspirations by pressurising women into subordination through sex.

In a more recent analysis, *The Sexuality Papers*, published in 1984, revolutionary feminists present a historical sketch of the last hundred years as a century in which sexologists from Havelock Ellis to Kinsey and Masters and Johnson have undermined women's struggle for equality.[67] There is, they argue, 'a negative relation' between sexual reform and the stress on women's sexual pleasure in marriage on the one hand, and women's struggle for equality on the other. No evidence is provided in support of their central thesis that the ideology of sexual liberation has caused the containment of feminist aspirations (whatever may have been the professed or hidden intentions of its advocates) other than the temporal overlap of the decline of militant feminism and the development of the sex reform movement in the 1920s. One could more plausibly argue that it was the growth of welfare feminism (the successful 'maternal endowment' campaigns to improve women's maternal and domestic lives) led by Eleanor Rathbone and others in the 1920s which caused the decline of militant feminism. But no single factor propels or explains such historical shifts.

If we accept, as indeed we might, that the conscious goal of Masters and Johnson's sex therapy, and that for which they were originally funded, was to shore up heterosexuality and marriage (and thereby male domination) by forging a bond of pleasure between the sexes, we would have to conclude that they have failed spectacularly. The divorce rate has soared by 400 per cent in Britain over the two decades in which the sex therapists have supposedly fought to preserve marriage, and even more in the US.[68] It seems plausible to me, and the moral right would agree, that women's expectations of sexual pleasure (so often frustrated in marriage) are more likely to threaten than to stabilise marital harmony, at least once women have any possibilities for economic independence.

The Symbolic and the Real

Revolutionary feminist thought still appeals to many feminists, however, because it connects with other aspects of women's sexual experience which the earlier behaviouristic promises of sexual liberation completely ignored. It emphasises the power of the symbolic (the dominant social imagery and language of sex) in shaping our thoughts, desires, and experience of sex. ('No act of penetration can escape its function and its symbolic power.')[69] But there is a more complex interplay between popular symbols of active sexuality as aggressive and male, and our particular sexual experiences. Our personal histories of pleasure, pain, desire and coercion surrounding sexual experience shape our understandings of sex at the same time as popular symbols and meanings shape our experience. Other meanings also become available to us from within feminist thought, alongside images we may have picked up from elsewhere, of strong and sexually assertive women, and gentle and caring men.

But it is true, although not the only truth, that the idea of power and submission is built into the language and imagery of heterosexual encounter. It is also true that sexual fantasy and experience are saturated with the eroticisation of power. But the connection between symbol, fantasy, experience and behaviour is a treacherously complex one (which I will return to in discussing pornography), and has, not surprisingly, served to disquiet a good many feminists. For instance, masochistic fantasy is a common source of sexual arousal in women. (It is also a common source of sexual arousal in men.)[70] Women's sexualised fantasies of submission to men can certainly seem very distressing alongside a feminist project for equality, all the more distressing, of course, if we see our sexuality as the core of our individual identity and the key to social change.

How does a feminist handle the fantasy of desire for sexual mastery from men alongside the day-to-day struggle to combat men's power in every sphere of life? The revolutionary feminist project presents itself as a very immediate way of handling this problem and removing conflict. If heterosexual contact really is a type of sexual violence, then feminists' own 'perverse' masochistic fantasies can seem to make some sense as the only way that women have learned to cope with men's coercive sexuality. They are forced upon women, rather like the nightmares of shell-shocked soldiers who relive the experience of battle to help them cope with it in future.

Justine Jones in the revolutionary feminist anthology *Women Against Violence Against Women* argues that women have been 'influenced to be masochists from a very young age, so that we'll become heterosexual and enjoy it'.[71] Writing of her 'hatred' of her own masochistic fantasies, she chooses to repudiate them as unconnected to her own self-defined sexuality: 'I *hate* them and fight to accept I'm not alone, nor a pervert.'[72] She must repudiate them, for she still believes that the 'stirrings of our own self-defined sexuality challenge male sexuality at its *roots*' (her emphasis).[73]

Clearly, we are not going to challenge patriarchy at its roots by exposing our masochistic fantasies. What is not explained, whatever the coerciveness and conditioning by men or sexologists, is the pleasure some women find in sex with men. Rape is not pleasurable. Women are not confused about this, whatever men or women might fantasise about it. Women's (or men's) experience of sexual arousal to masochistic fantasies of dominance and submission bears not the remotest resemblance to the actual experience of rape; yet it is crucial to the revolutionary feminist argument that sexual fantasies connect *directly* to reality. It would follow that if some women are excited by fantasies of rape, they must enjoy the experience of rape – at least a little bit. This is dangerous nonsense. And if women's sexual fantasies of domination carry over into everyday servility towards men, why do men's well-documented masochistic fantasies not serve the same function? Neither women's nor men's sexual fantasies reflect simply the reality of male dominance and misogyny (although they are influenced by this reality). They draw upon all manner of infantile sexual wishes, active and passive, loving and hating, all the way back to our very earliest feelings of desire and pleasure in childhood.

There is in revolutionary feminism, as there has been in most feminist writing about sex, an unresolved tension over what is meant by 'the sexual'. Revolutionary feminism begins from a clear and repeated rejection of the essentialism and biologism of sexology ('male sexuality is socially constructed not biologically determined') only to return in a circular fashion to essential male sexual needs now redefined as male power needs. It is, they argue, the exercise of male sexuality which creates and determines men's power, and yet it is 'the need to dominate and exercise power in sexual activity' which determines the nature of male sexuality.[74] We are not given any explanation of why men need to control women, or how they succeed, except through sexual activity. Are there not sturdier weapons than the penis? One way or another, and despite insistent assertions to the contrary, we are forced to leave behind the complex historical formation of men's social power – and how this social power confers a symbolic power to the penis as the defining characteristic of the male – to return to a naked sexual capacity which can be, and therefore is, used to control women. In the description of the relentless power of the steely prick, the biological, so forcefully ejected from the front door, swaggers in, cocksure, through the back.

The revolutionary feminist ascendancy at the close of the seventies thus strengthened the return of essentialist thinking in feminism, re-asserting an ahistorical image of sexuality existing outside specific social contexts and relationships. In this respect, revolutionary feminists resemble the sexologists, medical 'experts' and pornographers they so fiercely oppose. They also strengthened, of course, the idea of men's and women's fundamentally opposed sexual natures, reinforcing all the most undialectical, dualistic thinking of 'male' versus 'female', 'active' versus 'passive', 'power' versus 'submission'. Ironically, by the mid eighties revolutionary feminists found it necessary to turn their attention from heterosexuality to the policing of lesbian identities, particularly of lesbian sadomasochism. They accused lesbians who spoke of finding pleasure in sexual fantasies of power and submission, or, more reprehensibly still, enjoyed acting out such roles in consensual sex acts, of internalising 'male' values. Like heterosexual women, some lesbians too were now vilified as supporting men's power and men's violence against women through refusing to change, or else to repress and silence, their sexual fantasies and behaviour.[75]

This whole elaborate declaration of women's Original Innocence, and the need to deny or repress our own sexual experience as 'false' or 'perverted' would be unnecessary if, however, we adopted what I see as a more satisfactory analysis of 'sexuality'. Such an analysis would reject the idea of a unitary and conflict-free sexual essence at the core of women's (or men's) identity, and would also reject the idea of sex as the key to self-expression or the necessary clue to social change. But that would be to challenge one of the most basic assumptions of bourgeois thought – a blow to the heart indeed.

Revolutionary feminist literature which treats *all* sexual contact with men as damaging to women cannot begin to do justice to those groups of women – Black women, working class and immigrant women – whose more general social powerlessness and vulnerability has meant they have suffered most, and often fought hardest, against exploitative sexual behaviour from men. Nor does it mention in its theoretical analysis that Western images of sex are not only sexist but also quintessentially racist. For in the mythology of sex, the 'beast' of male sexuality is also the 'beast of darkness', the 'black beast'. White men's and women's guilt and fears over sex have been projected on to all Black people, creating the myth of the Black male superstud, and the lewd and lascivious Black woman. Black men historically have been and still are more harshly punished than white men for sexual crimes against white women. They are still more likely to be falsely accused of rape, where once they were lynched in the United States and elsewhere for the merest suggestion of a sexual advance to a white woman. Black women, on the other hand, have been sexually exploited with complete impunity by white men. As Angela Davis wrote in 1981, 'The historical knot binding Black women – systematically abused and violated by white men – to Black men maimed and murdered because of the racist manipulation of the rape charge – has just begun to be acknowledged to any significant extent.'[76] And from about 1983, it was the rise of Black feminism and disputes over race which were eventually to muffle, though not resolve, the fierce debates generated by revolutionary feminism and political lesbianism in feminist gatherings and publications.

Feminist Explanations of Rape

Revolutionary feminism was most influential beyond feminist circles in its analysis of rape and violence towards women as acts necessary to maintain the universal system of male domination. All men, they argued, rely upon such practices, whether individually coercive and violent or not. Such an analysis is now often presented as *the* feminist explanation of rape and male violence. It was first widely popularised in 1975 by the North American radical feminist Susan Brownmiller in *Against Our Will*. It was further developed and elaborated by Andrea Dworkin who states with finality that male power 'authentically originates in the penis'.[77]

This explanation of rape, however, ignores the absence of reported rape in some societies, and provides a very strange analysis of power relations in general.[78] For while powerful groups do use force as a last resort against threatened insurrection, in modern societies the everyday practices of domination, in every sphere including the sexual, are not usually maintained by brute physical force.[79] (The use of physical force, in fact, often characterises the behaviour of the relatively powerless.) And indeed, if sexual coercion really were the ultimate and characteristic instrument of men's power, it is hard to see why women would not long ago have acquired the physical skills and equipment to 'disarm' rapists – unless we assume women are both blind and stupid (blinded and stupefied, revolutionary feminists might qualify). Men's power, in my view, is not reducible to direct sexual coercion of women. And tackling the problem of rape means, above all, tackling the dominant mythology which sees rape as an inevitable product of male needs, whether for sexual release or for aggression and dominance.

The fear of rape is certainly a crucial factor in restricting women's freedom, often keeping us, at least in public, sexually passive, hypocritical and submissive to men. It is true that men, both individually and collectively, do rape women to enhance their sense of 'masculinity', and hence of power. As I suggest in the next chapter, rape expresses many 'needs': anger, inadequacy, guilt and fear of women, all linked with men's attempts to affirm their 'masculinity'. The prevalence and problem of rape in our society stems in part from the cultural connections which are made between 'masculinity' and heterosexual performance. As the gay liberation movement has argued, it ties in with the repression and ridicule of 'effeminate' masculinities, and in particular with the policing of 'deviant' sexual identities, such as male homosexuality. The prevalence of rape in our society stems as well from the economic, political and ideological practices which, in creating men's power over women, have allowed men sexually to abuse women with relative impunity.

In combating the menace of rape, feminists should not endorse the inevitability of men's urge to dominate women, but rather attack the way in which our society constructs and condones the idea of a coercive sexuality as 'male'. We need to expose and denounce, relentlessly, all the juridical and popular discourse or perception of rape which sees it as an act which can be precipitated by any indication of active sexuality in women, evidence of any such active sexuality signifying the 'guilt' of the raped victim rather than the rapist.[80] We can still observe this assumption in most rape trials, as we saw it in the grotesque abominations of the 'Ripper' murders in England, where the police, the media and the prosecution all at least partially endorsed Peter Sutcliffe's pathological obsession (if not his tactics) with punishing prostitutes – only the most 'respectable' of his victims being described as 'innocent'. We also need to denounce the fact that men's 'private' violence in the home against women is socially condoned and usually unpunished. Similar violence used against others in the workplace, for example, would be met with instant dismissal, whatever the tolerance for milder forms of sexual harassment at work.

As relentlessly, we need to criticise the way in which rape and male violence is sensationalised, glamourised and made sexually titillating in popular culture. In all cases of rape, violence is the dominant motive, and (despite revolutionary feminist and popular concern with it) phallic penetration quite often does not occur. The usefully educative strategy behind Clare Short's ridiculed and defeated amendment to Winston Churchill's censorship Bill in April 1986, for example, was that she sought to prevent the popular press's habitual juxtaposition of rape stories with semi-nude female pin-ups on Page 3. Sex rather than violence is made the primary factor in media coverage of rape, a distortion which conceals the vengeful, fearful, inadequate and disturbed motives behind rape. But a somewhat similar criticism can be made of some feminist analysis of rape. As bell hooks observes, 'Often feminist activists talk about male abuse of women as if it is an exercise of privilege rather than an expression of moral bankruptcy, insanity and dehumanization.'[81]

In tackling the prevalence of rape, then, it is essential that we are engaged in constructing new definitions and images of women's active sexuality, to which every woman is entitled without courting violence. Similarly, we must be engaged in constructing new images of men's sexuality, seeing that it may be – as well as phallic and assertive – passive, receptive, diffuse and sensual, expressing all manner of joyful and generous as well as twisted and vicious emotions. This means that we must constantly challenge the dominant and obnoxious forms of 'heterosexism' – legal, social and interpersonal – which help maintain rigid and coercive forms of masculinity and a submissive femininity by denying social rights to and condoning physical and sexual violence against all those who fall outside its definitions of the 'normal'. But the central importance of these tasks neither establishes that rape is the single or even the primary way men maintain their power over women, nor that the maintenance of men's collective power is the primary explanation of rape.

Pornography and the Power of Men

It seems likely that it was partly the problems inherent in presenting rape as the root cause of male power which led the radical/revolutionary strand of feminism to a focus on pornography in the 1980s. Men are able to terrorise and dominate women, not simply through the actual performance of rape (a demanding and risky business, whatever its ghastly prevalence); they also terrorise women at all times by surrounding them with the fearful knowledge that, in their eyes, women are nothing other than receptacles for their hatred: by placing women in the swamp of pornography. This is how Andrea Dworkin describes the purpose and effect of pornography: 'The woman's sex is appropriated, her body is possessed, she is used and she is despised: the pornography does it and the pornography proves it.'[82] 'The penis' as a 'symbol of terror', Dworkin tells us, is 'even more significant than the gun, the knife, the bomb, the fist, etc.'[83] Women, she concludes in her lurid book on pornography, 'will know that they are free when the pornography no longer exists.'[84]

In Dworkin's analysis, as well as teaching women their place as whores, pornography also serves as ubiquitous propaganda, spurring on the flagging or wimpish male to ever greater acts of violence against women, while scaring women off from any possible hope of resistance. 'Pornography is the theory. Rape is the practice', Robin Morgan first suggested; and countless feminist graffiti artists have since proclaimed the same idea. The statement is succinct and powerful. A focus on pornography is popular, as popular with men as with women, with the right as with the left. Pornography does typically encapsulate all that is most distressing and depressing in the portrayal of women's bodies in our own culture: women become sexual commodities, usable, disposable, endlessly available for the titillation of men. Yet, in my view, the idea that pornography, as Dworkin suggests, not only depicts but creates the reality of 'the imperial power of men' is not just an exaggeration but a fundamentally flawed argument.

The billion dollar pornography industry has flourished in the West precisely as women's economic *independence* (a far cry, of course, from women's economic equality) has increased, and the power and control of men over women has declined. No longer is it the case, for instance, that women in the West must always remain in brutal and loveless marriages, whatever the handicaps they face on divorce. There is a correlation between women's financial independence and divorce, which, given that it is most often women who initiate divorce, suggests that it is they who are making the decisions. No longer is the unmarried mother excluded from any respectable career or job, as she was only 20 years ago, nor is she faced with inevitable social ostracism and contempt, though these are not always absent. Women can and do choose to have children without men, though for many this will cause inevitable economic hardship.

We can now sometimes laugh (despite the threat it still poses) at the moral right on the rampage, warning us, like Paul Johnson of the *Daily Telegraph*, that 'the one parent family is a kind of social disease and it is spreading fast'. As the right is well aware, marriage as an institution giving men enormous control over their wives and children has been progressively undermined. In the overwhelming majority of households today men are no longer the sole breadwinners, and as their economic power has declined, domestic conflict and strain have increased in a situation where 'working' wives shoulder a double burden of work, usually with little real domestic help from husbands. The contradictions in women's lives have certainly deepened, and progress is uneven, but what we have *not* seen is any straightforward increase in men's immediate power over women.

Patriarchal power has declined and conflict increased in the home at a time when the advice columns and other areas of the mass media encourage women in particular to seek and expect more sexual satisfaction from their marital relationships. Women now judge and expose the inadequacies of men's sexual performance, even in counselling programmes on radio and television before an audience of millions, whereas once the virgin wife had only the choice of 'thralldom' or 'frigidity' in sexual matters. Recent research by Mary Louise Ho on agony aunts tells us something of the changes which have taken place. Traditional columnists like Mary Grant were still extolling selflessness in women 20 years ago:

> It would do you and your marriage a power of good if you turned your thoughts away from your own feelings to your husband's. It's not too late to try to make *him* happy.[85]

But, more recently, columnists like Irma Kurtz have a different view. She constantly urges women to put their own needs, interests and careers before any man's, insisting upon greater self-assertiveness in women:

> Be as angry as you want – rage, storm and throw things if you feel like it. Let him see that you are hurt, betrayed, frightened and angry. Don't be afraid of offending him; hasn't he offended you?[86]

In every sphere, it would seem, men can no longer feel so secure in expecting a lifetime of emotional support and sexual servicing from women. In this situation it would seem to me that one very likely explanation for the increased consumption of pornography by men (apart from the significant factor of the opening up of a very highly profitable market for capital at a time when many others are closing down) is that pornography is a compensatory expression of men's *declining* power. It serves to expose not imperial strength but pathetic weakness – a gargantuan need for reassurance that, at least in fantasy, women can remain eternally objects for men to use and abuse at will. It is the last bark of the stag at bay.

Andy Moye, reflecting as a man on the function and effect of pornography, comes to this conclusion:

> It works by denying the reality which men know and fear to be true. Sex (for men) is not unproblematic but is beset by complications and anxieties – those of sexual isolation, clumsiness, 'inadequacy', the tension attendant on 'doing it right', of not being or feeling sexually desirable. It is in the space between this anxiety and the fantasy realm of a perfect sexual world that pornography achieves its power ...[87]

Pornography, far from being the manifestation of men's power over women, would seem to suggest, as Andy Moye argues, sexual anxiety and paranoia amongst men. It depicts not men's actual sexual control over women, but rather men's neurotic and debilitating obsession with 'the netherworld of phallic failure'.[88] Or again, as Elizabeth Wilson suggests:

> Far from being the celebration of male power, pornography sometimes seems designed to reassure men and allay fears of impotence. Where it is violent, it displays fear and loathing not only of women but also of male passivity ... Some men must degrade women in order to be potent; others must themselves be degraded. Much male sexuality seems compulsive and joyless, plagued by the performance principle, shadowed by deep-seated fears of impotence, inadequacy and failure.[89]

Revolutionary feminists believe that a study of men's 'highly bizarre' sexual fantasies and practices should help us understand how men use their sexual power to retain control over women.[90] In contrast, I would suggest that a study of men's sexual fantasies and obsessions, particularly at their most bizarre, should lead us more to puzzle over how it is still possible for men to retain control over women *despite* their sexuality, not because of it.

I am not, however, trying to suggest that pornography is inoffensive or harmless. It does distress most women, and it has always distressed me. It distresses me first of all because it is so readily incorporated into my own sexual fantasies. Far from being the product of my sexual experiences with men, these fantasies date back to childhood. They seem to me to express an urgent and compelling childhood need to fantasise a type of maternal loving which I was always so desperate to receive: in fantasy, such loving always took the form of the strong, protective and sensual embrace offered as reparation for my own heroic and humiliating suffering. I have always been at best ambivalent about these fantasies, and would love to be able to disown them as inauthentic intrusions, but the projection would seem all too obvious.

Much of pornography angers and disturbs me now, however, not so much because of its titillation (which has worried me less the more I have thought about it) but rather because of its place in the panorama of sexist objectification and stereotyping of women which engulfs us. And it angers and disturbs me also because it is such a tragic testament to the continuing truth about sex in our society: it is still, despite a hundred years of sexology, experienced as basically dirty, forbidden, offensive and wrong. It is still, too often, a source of despair, frustration, guilt, anxiety and rage, rather than of pleasure and fulfilment. This is true particularly in men, where dominant images of male sexuality and male aggression so easily fuse together; sexual performance can serve – is perhaps sometimes *all* that can serve – to shore up a subjective sense of identity and power.

Many feminists now believe that there must be a direct connection, if not between pornography and the creation of men's power over women, at least between pornography and men's violence against women. It is certainly true that a portrayal of women's sexual availability and submission is the basis of much, though by no means all, pornography. And it is equally true that pornography is predominantly prepared by and for men (whether or not women also find it arousing). There is also a small but familiar percentage of pornography which portrays implicit visual connections between representations of women's passionate sexual submission, women's sexual climax, and death.[91] This would seem to reinforce and condone ideas of women's desire for domination by force, or even worse, to establish a connection between eroticised female bodies and death: a connection brought home to us as we read daily of the diabolical cruelty and sex murder some men inflict upon women.

Psychological research and official statistics, designed and collected to test the link between pornography and violence against women, however, are unclear and contradictory. A series of psychological investigations by Mosher in 1971 and Jaffe and others in 1974, though predicting that the effects of viewing 'non-aggressive' pornography would strengthen men's approval of the sexual objectification and sexual exploitation of women, found no increase in men's negative verbal comments or callous attitudes expressed about women.[92] A variation on this study by Donnerstein and Barrett in 1978, using similar material but where the subject was subsequently provoked by a man and a woman acting as the researcher's stooge or 'confederate', found that those who had just viewed the pornography were slightly less aggressive to the female than the male confederate.[93] However, a similar study by Donnerstein in 1980, using 'aggressive' pornographic material with female victims, did lead to men displaying increased aggressive behaviour towards the female confederate who later provoked them.[94] Malamuth and others in 1980 studied the long term effects on men of sexual violence in pornographic magazines, and found that the different ways in which rape was portrayed – that is, whether the victim was presented as either 'enjoying' or else harmed by the rape – affected the subjects' attitudes towards women victims in subsequent depictions of rape narratives. Those who had been shown the victim 'enjoying' the rape were less concerned about harmful effects in subsequent stories.[95]

These behaviourist studies are however of limited use. They adopt such a passive and reflex model of human behaviour, devoid of any account of subjective interpretations of the experimental situation or the stimulus material, as to give us little possibility of generalising their findings.

The statistical surveys which have looked for a causal connection between availability of pornographic material and increase in violent crimes against women, have, however even more methodological problems. It is hard to get an accurate measure of either of the two variables, when definitions of pornography are inevitably vague and contentious, and reported crime rates do not necessarily reveal the actual incidence of attacks against women. The official surveys have, nevertheless, up until now rejected any causal relationship between the two. The US National Commission on Obscenity and Pornography in 1970 concluded that in North America there was no consistent relationship between the availability of pornography and changes in sex crime rates, and that the alleged vast increase in sex crimes had not actually occurred. In Britain the similar Committee on Obscenity and Film Censorship set up in 1979 concluded that 'the rising trend in sexual offences generally, and rape and sexual assaults, started long before it is alleged that sexual materials began to be widely available', and also that 'increases in sexual offences generally, including rape and sexual assaults, have been significantly slower in the last 20 years than that in crime generally.'[96]

Both the psychological studies and the statistical surveys, however, suffer from all the weaknesses of traditional social science research on the effects of the media. They focus on immediate, concrete and measurable effects of media consumption in changing attitudes and behaviour, usually finding limited or inconsistent effects. But media images do not operate simply as one-off triggers of responses; rather they operate as a part of the continuous shaping and reshaping of dominant ideas and frameworks of thought. Dominant pornographic imagery is a problem not because it creates instant rapists – the empirical studies show no consistent link between sex offenders and exposure to pornography – but rather because it is one aspect of the continuous social construction of polarised images of women and men. These images usually confirm women as passive, fetishised objects for male consumption, while denying weakness, passivity and 'femininity' in men. In its perpetual and insistent confirmation of men's difference from women, in the way it endorses men's fears and rejection of passivity, pornography inevitably does play a part in constructing a dominant form of masculinity which fears and abuses women, and a dominant form of femininity which expects mastery from men. So while it is true that there is little evidence linking pornographic consumption, on its own, to violence against women, and while it is also true that societies free from pornography, as we know it, are often far more prone to patriarchal violence than our own, it is equally true that much sexist pornography is the repetitive, ritual confirmation of existing ideas of sexual difference, as well as of the illicit and fetishised nature of sex. It is also clear that most women do not like pornography, however difficult (and often unnecessary) feminists have found it to provide any agreed definition of it.

When it celebrates sexist and dehumanising images of women, pornography is a legitimate target of attack by feminists. But, I would suggest, this should not be through the highly ambiguous and unfocused action of firebombing sex shops. Is it really the black rubber knobbly dildo which is threatening us? Even less should such attacks include counterproductive actions like the disruption of screenings of pornographic films organised by women specifically to analyse and understand their content and appeal. Both the above were actions undertaken by feminists organising against pornography in Women Against Violence Against Women (WAVAW) groups in Britain in the 1980s. Most feminists in Britain have not strongly advocated increased state censorship of pornography, but some members of WAVAW do support it (one member publicly announced her support for Mary Whitehouse in a national BBC television discussion on pornography in the early eighties).[97]

The dangers of supporting censorship legislation against pornography are obvious: the lack of agreement over its definition would almost always strengthen the powers of the moral right to police all it sees as 'deviant' sexualities, and indeed any and all representation of explicit sex. This is precisely what is happening with Winston Churchill's 1986 Bill to 'clean up television'. Although he claims to be concerned about violence against women, it is, for example, the homosexuality of Derek Jarman's films *Sebastiane* and *Jubilee*, not the violence of *Starsky and Hutch*, which he and his supporters have explicitly cited as their target.[98] Anti-pornography legislation has been drafted by Andrea Dworkin and Catherine MacKinnon in the US (supported by Mary Daly, Robin Morgan and other feminists) and passed (though not yet implemented) in Indianapolis. This has fiercely polarised the feminist movement in the US, where other feminists are fighting the legislation in the courts. Those opposing the legislation object to the theoretical analysis behind it, and argue that it reinforces sexist myths about men and women. They point out that women are presented as weak and helpless victims who do not enjoy sex, and that feminist art, erotica, and advice on women's sexuality will be laid open to possible prosecution. The legislation also fails to address sexist representation more generally.[99] That the US judiciary is now deciding the outcome of a dispute within the feminist movement shows how deeply divisive and destructive the debate and tactics over pornography have become.

More appropriate feminist action would seem to me to involve not the demand for state censorship of pornography but the attempt to understand, analyse and publicly discuss the appeal of pornography, commenting upon and at times taking direct action to remove pornographic and sexist images of the use and abuse of women's bodies primarily for men's titillation. (In some workplaces, for example, feminists have successfully demanded that nude calendar pin-ups of women are removed, stressing that it is not explicit sex but the sexual objectification of women which they find offensive.) And we must also demand that men analyse and tell us why so many men like and 'need' pornography, and that they understand why much of it is offensive to most women, and act on this understanding. (Two male shop stewards from a Direct Labour Department near Birmingham, for example, campaigned successfully in 1979 to remove pin-ups, porn pictures and girlie calendars from all their department's workplaces and sites.)[100] But if our comments are to be instructive and our interventions effective we need to look carefully and critically at the total array, context and packaging of images of women, and of men. For, as Rosalind Coward and others have argued, the offensive codes and meanings of pornography appear as prominently in most of our representational practices:

> This is a primary reason why I think that pornography as such is the wrong object of attack. Unless we refine our ways of talking about sexist codes in general, how they operate and produce their meanings, and why they are offensive, we run the risk of being misunderstood ... Our descriptions of 'sexist', 'offensive' and 'degrading' remain curiously underdeveloped.[101]

Sexism in representation is not reducible to portrayals of explicit sex. And were we to reduce it to what is most obviously sexually titillating, romantic fiction, written by and for women, would seem as suitable a target of feminist analysis, critique and understanding as men's pornography. Here too we find a persistent worship of the strong, the powerful, the phallic male. Its effects could indeed be seen as more insidious, because less explicit. But sexism resides in almost every image of almost every media production: they are none of them above suspicion. By sexism I mean the presentation of images of women as less than and inferior to men, existing to titillate and service men.

The clean 'family' entertainment in the Oscar-winning film *Terms of Endearment* is, for instance, thoroughly sexist in its presentation of the selfish, narcissistic, immature woman (played by Shirley MacLaine) who puts her own needs first until finally redeemed by a man; she is compared with the selfless, obedient, sacrificial daughter (played by Debra Winger), who exists for her husband and children.[102] This film is at least as strong a backlash against feminist aspirations for autonomy and sexual freedom as *Dressed to Kill*, a film trashed by WAVAW for portraying women as the victims of men.

If our critique of pornography is to be more than the projection and denial of our own anxiety and confusion about sex, feminists will need (as many now have) to take a broader and deeper look at all forms of representation of women. We must, in fact, abandon any radical or revolutionary feminist position which asserts what we need to reject and rejects what we need to assert. We need to reject the idea of there being some inner sexual essence, healthy in women and unhealthy in men. We need to assert that women, too, are full of contradiction and conflict over sexuality. We need to understand the ways in which the prevalence of men's sexual violence is neither simply the product of inner sex drives, nor inner power drives – realisable through the possession of the penis – but rather a product of men's social power in general. Men's subjective sexual needs, complex and contradictory though they are, are inseparable from all the social pressures which construct particular styles of aggressive masculinity.

A number of recent books on sexuality and desire have begun to adopt such approaches.[103] They argue that all sexual practices, whether heterosexual, lesbian, gay, or of any other type of sexual orientation, act or style, are mediated by the historical meanings they acquire from within our dominant social institutions – legal, familial, religious and medical. The maintenance of heterosexual regimes by these institutions creates a narrowness and rigidity in all our notions of sexuality. But it does not prevent either women or men from engaging in the struggle to transform the context, meaning and power relations typically manifest in heterosexual practice. And it does not prevent the struggle of gay and lesbian people, as well as heterosexuals, to affirm the positive nature of diverse sexualities. As Barbara Ehrenreich has suggested:

> We need to find a way to take gay rights out of the gay ghetto. I want to take it out of being a special interest. I think it is in every person's interest to have their notion of sexuality expanded.[104]

This new North American and British socialist feminist writing of the eighties has begun to focus on the nature of 'desire' and its connections with power, tracing the links back to infancy and our personal histories of pleasure and pain in erotic attachments to others, as well as to the surrounding context and ideologies of male dominance. It argues for an approach which stresses the varieties of sexual pleasure women seek and receive alongside the dangers which stem from many men's violence towards women. Such a perspective rejects any attempt to celebrate one type of sexual practice over others, as more rewarding, more fulfilling, more correct. Undermining the current institutions and social meanings constructing the dominant male and submissive female, as well as the 'natural' and the normal ideologies of heterosexuality, are indeed central struggles for feminist thought and practice today. But, as Jeffrey Weeks has argued, we will need to do this by looking at, and attempting to change, the *context* of sexual relationships, rather than simply focusing on sexual acts themselves.[105]

Although the priority given to rape, pornography and male violence as the explanation of women's subordination has been a dominant public voice of feminism in the eighties, this is only because, as Liz Heron pointed out in 1981, other currents in feminism 'no longer have a voice or a clear identity within the women's movement'.[106] There have been alternative feminist analyses to the radical and revolutionary feminist view of sex, which have been more popular with socialist feminists in Britain and the US. These alternative attempts to explain the connections between sexuality and violence, between sexuality and the assertion of power, draw upon different theoretical frameworks which reject the reductionism and biologism underlying most of the ideas we have looked at in this chapter. The French Lacanian school of thought has been influential within academic feminism, while the American object-relations school of psychoanalytic thought has been absorbed into a more popular form of feminist thought. In their explanation of sexual difference these psychoanalytically guided theories provide new possibilities and present new problems for feminists attempting to understand the politics of personal life.

4.   *Beauty and the Beast II:*

Sex, Gender and Mothering

> When feminist writers were rediscovering sex roles and
> demonstrating their use in the perpetuation of patriarchy,
> they had stressed the need to abolish culturally produced
> differences between men and women as the surest path to
> equality. Now, far from seeking to minimize women's
> differences from men, feminist scholars were asserting
> their importance as a legitimate and even a crucial focus of
> study.
>
> Hester Eisenstein[1]

> The resurgence of feminist interest in motherhood has
> positive and negative implications for the feminist
> movement. On the positive side there is a continual need
> for study and research of female parenting which this
> interest promotes and encourages ... On the negative side,
> romanticizing motherhood, employing the same
> terminology that is used by sexists to suggest that women
> are inherently life-affirming nurturers, feminist activists
> reinforce central tenets of male supremacist ideology.
>
> bell hooks[2]

From Mary Wollstonecraft to the present, feminists have used
psychological theories to understand the differences between
women and men. We need a psychology with which to challenge
prevailing ideas of women's natural inferiority to men, and to
explain women's own attachment to ideas and values which tie
in with their position as the subordinate sex. If only to counter
the common knee-jerk response to feminism – 'women are their
own worst enemy' – feminists have attempted to analyse the
nature of sex differences and to explore the formation and power
of sexual identity. In this chapter I look at different feminist
approaches to psychology, and their links with feminist practice.

   In Chapter One I suggested that feminists in the early
seventies, in contrast with many feminists today, tended to deny

that there were any – or at least many – important differences between women and men; existing differences were more often seen as artificially produced by a 'sexist culture' in order to subordinate women. There was a general acceptance in the early seventies that 'femininity' was an inadequate description of women's psychology, and that it also described characteristics which were, by and large, unhealthy, servile and petty.

In explaining sex differences women's liberationists believed that women and men had been 'conditioned' differently. In our talks and writings of that time, we mostly drew upon the behaviourist social learning theories of psychology to illustrate how women in male dominated societies are conditioned into the emotional and cognitive traits of subordination and dependence. As a popular feminist ballad of the time (still full of nostalgia for me) expressed it:

> Well I tried to be the kind of woman
> > you wanted me to be ...
> Made to please, and not to tease,
> > it's the custom-made woman blues ...
> And I tried to see life your way,
> > and say all the things you wanted me to say
> Loving thoughts, gentle hands,
> > all guaranteed to keep a hold of your man,
> Made to please, and not to tease,
> > it's the custom-made woman blues.[3]

Women's liberation involved throwing off much of this false conditioning: re-learning assertiveness, self-confidence and the whole array of skills which had served men so long and so well – so well indeed, that men could destroy women's active involvement in the shaping of their own destinies.

The Learning of 'Sex Roles'

Once again it was the North American writings of radical feminists like Kate Millett and Shulamith Firestone, and of feminist psychologists like Naomi Weisstein, Judith Bardwick, Martina Horner and Phyllis Chesler, which fired the passions and intellect of feminists in Britain and in the US. In this literature, 'society', through the pressures of role learning, conditioned its little girls into the traits of servility, submissiveness and fear of success, and its little boys in the competitive and cognitive traits necessary for public success, power and achievement. Weisstein in her popular article 'Psychology Constructs the Female, or the Fantasy Life of the Male Psychologist' had concluded that 'the first reason for psychology's failure to understand what people are and how they act is that psychology has looked for inner traits when it should have been looking for social context.'[4] Society, Martina Horner argued, 'has been teaching [women] to fail outside the home.'[5] Judith Bardwick and Elizabeth Douvan described how a girl is 'encouraged to remain dependent' and is 'punished for conspicuous competing achievement' whereas in a boy dependent behaviour is 'prohibited' and he is encouraged to 'value himself for real achievements in terms of objective criteria'.[6] Most passionately of all, Phyllis Chesler declared that on existing cultural expectations, as displayed for instance in the judgements of clinicians, 'It is clear that for a woman to be healthy she must "adjust" to and accept the behavioral norms of her sex even though these kinds of behavior are generally regarded as less than socially desirable.'[7] Men and women were more similar than different, feminists and psychologists alike argued in the early seventies (drawing on the now classic writings of Eleanor Maccoby),[8] except for the differences society imposed on them.

There was certainly no lack of evidence about polarised and stereotyped social expectations of women and men. Ann Oakley's influential book *Sex, Gender and Society* published in Britain in 1972 made a distinction between 'sex' and 'gender', a distinction which many feminists began to use: ' "Sex" is a biological term: "gender" a psychological and cultural one.'[9] She concluded that the role of biology in determining gender identity was 'a minimal one, in that the biological predisposition to a male or female gender identity (if such a condition exists) may be decisively and ineradicably over-ridden by cultural learning.'[10] Feminists set out to explore the variations in 'masculinity' and 'femininity' in different societies, and to uncover how our social notions of gender are learned by boys and girls, men and women. Exciting work began exposing the existence of contrasting ideologies and images of women and men in every cultural medium: in advertising, textbooks, children's readers, popular fiction, music, and anywhere else we choose to look for them.

'Society', in this role learning analysis, however, tended to be seen as a fairly static and monolithic entity, separate from and imposing itself upon the individual. In Ann Oakley's words, 'Gender, like caste, is a matter of social ascription which bears no necessary relation to the individual's own attributes and inherent abilities.'[11] Or, describing how children's readers 'teach widely separate sexual roles', one feminist study group concluded, 'all in all, they form an ideological prison from which the child would be lucky to escape.'[12] Society was rarely broken down into diverse and changing sets of relationships between people, constituting the complex social institutions and practices which vary across class, race, ethnic group and geographical location. These variations in our experience of 'society' throw up different types of conflicts, tensions and strains which undermine any notion of there being a single type of experience, or single set of 'social expectations' surrounding gender. Another problem with the role theory approach was, and remains, the passivity and infinite malleability it attributes to human social behaviour. It leaves little space for appreciating the types of understanding, improvisation, resistance and psychic conflict that individuals bring to the social roles expected of them – apart from acknowledging personality disorders and possible mental illness caused by failure to adjust to social roles.[13] Finally, role theory analysis, which sees people as inevitably conforming to the social expectations surrounding them, cannot adequately explain the over-riding significance we each attach to our sense of gender identity, its force and power over us, despite all the personal confusion and insecurities which surround it.[14]

In wanting to deny the significance of any basic gender identity, women's liberation in the early years played down what was most distinctive about women's lives (here in contrast with traditional role theory, like that of Talcott Parsons). Pregnancy, childbirth and breastfeeding, for example, were less likely to be seen as positive and creative, and more likely to be seen as a hindrance for women. I have suggested that this feature of women's liberation theorising rebounded later, when earlier notions of the 'feminine' as unsatisfactory and inferior were inverted to become the 'feminine' as desirable and superior. Like the early criticism of romantic love and exclusive relationships which contributed to a growing silence over many women's actual sexual desires and practices, criticism of the isolation and frustrations of motherhood and caring for others – although correctly portraying the bitterness and disillusion we heard from so many women – contributed to a silence over many women's pleasure in motherhood and our strong desires to find fulfilment through motherhood and caring for others.

Feminism and the Return to Freud

Freud was fiercely denounced in most early writings on sex roles and women's liberation. Indeed the whole psychoanalytic tradition was seen, with some justification, as a (if not *the*) bastion of male supremacy in our society: a pseudobiological imperative used by clinicians and welfare agencies alike to impose domesticity and inferiority on women. Its phallocentric notion of penis envy as the pivot of feminine identity offended most feminists. Bouncing off this sound of fury, Juliet Mitchell's *Women and Psychoanalysis* published in 1974 was to serve for some feminists as a 'type of second conversion' later in the seventies. Juliet Mitchell had always insisted that feminists were wrong to dismiss Freud, however vulgarised and prescriptive the use and abuse of his discoveries had become.[15] The deeper discontents of women's feminine identity would remain forever unexplored, in her view, without an awareness that this identity was not something women simply acquired (for better or worse) but was intrinsically problematic. This meant understanding what Freud had discovered about the central importance of the unconscious in adult life, and the persistence of infantile desires and conflicts.

As I have indicated in previous chapters, feminists by the mid seventies were facing many new difficulties, not the least of which were the difficulties we found in working together. Mitchell's stress on the inevitable problems of femininity matched the inevitable frustration many of us had begun to feel as our political practice failed to match our ideals for loving, non-competitive relations in our collective work. Similar problems, as we have seen, also befell our attempts to create new and happier personal and sexual relations, with or without men. Many feminists were beginning to look for some less voluntaristic reappraisal of the psychology of women.

At a local discussion group in 1975 I heard the then unpublished novelist Alison Fell speak of the significance for her of Juliet Mitchell's work. Many other women's groups up and down the country at that time were also reflecting upon just how hard it could be for feminists to make any lasting changes in their lives. The constant battle we had been waging to construct our interests and desires towards self-sufficiency and strength seemed so often undermined, not just by the immediate obstacles and prohibitions thrown up by social institutions and the behaviour of men – real as these were in many spheres – but also by our own personal contradictions over how we saw ourselves as women, our own self-doubts and deceptions. Were we always clear about our own objectives, and what it was that most women wanted? Perhaps psychoanalysis could, after all, shed some light on the complexity and confusion of psychic life and sexual identity. Perhaps it could tell us why our dreams and desires might seem to conspire against our plans and perspectives.

Juliet Mitchell's work drew upon the work of the French Freudian school of Jacques Lacan. Lacan was popular with a small group of socialist feminists because he rejected any direct influence of biology on the construction of women's subordination, putting forward a structuralist account of sexual difference. It was the underlying social structure of patriarchy (and not just an array of different social expectations of gender) which was seen as constructing sexual difference. British feminists provided slightly differing interpretations of Lacan, but all began from the orthodox Freudian stress on the importance of the unconscious in adult life, with its layerings of contradictory infantile desire. These layerings of contradictions in our psychic make-up made any notion of a single or unitary self, or fixed and coherent identity, sexual or otherwise, an illusion. Indeed, the illusion of a stable and coherent identity was seen as the central myth which bourgeois culture imposed on its subjects.

Lacanian feminists therefore became the main theorists to oppose the simplicities of the conditioning approach which saw stable identities emerging as a product of social learning.

Lacanians argued that their emphasis on the complexity of subjectivity and the fragility of sexual identity is the primary strength of the psychoanalytic position: 'Feminism's affinity with psychoanalysis rests above all, I would argue, with this recognition that there is a resistance to identity which lies at the very heart of psychic life.'[16]

Together with its emphasis on the inevitability of psychic fragmentation and division hidden behind each person's proclaimed identity, English intellectual appropriations of Lacan's re-reading of Freud stressed the centrality of language in creating human consciousness and constructing the contents of the unconscious. Within language, Lacan had affirmed the pre-eminent and essential role of the phallus (as symbolic of but distinct from the biological organ, the penis) in the social construction of subjectivity: masculinity and femininity. Within patriarchal culture the child can only see itself represented through a sexual differentiation where the phallus is the privileged signifier, and the symbol of the power and law of the father, of patriarchy itself. The phallus is the privileged signifier because it is only with reference to the phallus, the possession or lack of the phallus, that the subject can take up an identity as a sexed being. And it is only in taking up an identity as a sexed being that the child can enter as a subject into language, into the symbolic order.

The status of the phallus as the signifier of difference ensures the femininity is nothing other than the difference from masculinity. The fact that the phallus is the symbol rather than the reality of the law and the place of the father, means that to possess it is as problematic for the boy identifying himself as male as it is impossible for the girl identifying herself as female. There are no fixed and stable identities outside of the symbolic. In Lacanian thought subjectivity is always complex and sexual identity is always precarious.

In any psychoanalytic account, if we want to understand the connection between adult sexual identity (however fragile and fraught) and sexual desire and behaviour, we would begin from the belief that sexual desire is entangled with a whole variety of unconscious hostile and aggressive – as well as dependent and adoring – fantasies and feelings. We would expect much the same mixture of hidden and ambivalent, hostile and tender feelings in women as in men. Adult sexuality, Freud argued, is formed through each person's unique history of desire. But it connects back, most significantly, to the child's experience of the pleasures and pains, the delights and torments, of infantile sexuality. It is in the polymorphously perverse child, where infantile sexual desires are not channelled in any one direction, that different areas of the body become the primary focus for the psychic experience of bodily pleasure, or, very often, for the denial of pleasure.

From 'soon after birth', Freud wrote, the young child both receives sensual pleasure and expresses an active desire for such pleasure. This desire is directed towards those who care for him or her, but in particular, of course, most typically towards the mother. The young child desires and loves its mother. But Freud also wrote of the quite inevitable frustration of such desire, which accompanies the denial, or withdrawal, of pleasure. In the first instance, (and prefiguring all subsequent erotic relations) this is the denial or withdrawal of the breast. Subsequently, in the anal and phallic expressions of sexuality, the child confronts other prohibitions and punishments. The frustration of desire, Freud believed, always had the immediate and powerful effect of unleashing hostile fantasies and feelings, and producing such painful conflict for the child that the hostility is necessarily repressed, to remain a part of the unconscious mental life, hidden away from and therefore untouched by the demands of reality. But these buried hostile impulses, Freud argued, continue to have an effect on adult behaviour, in ways which adults usually cannot recognise and will deny. The important point is that, in this view, such repressed feelings affect us all, not just a select few.

The centrality of importance of the Oedipal drama in orthodox psychoanalytic theory is Freud's belief that men and women are neither simply 'masculine' or 'feminine', but that they acquire their adult identity only through the resolution of childhood incestuous attachments to their parents. Only at this stage, and not before, do boys and girls acquire a sexual identity, and with it a differing relationship to their own sexuality. This begins when, at around the age of three or four, the child first registers the significance of the father in preventing the child's complete possession of the mother. It is then that the boy will experience castration anxiety: the fear of castration as punishment for his sexual feelings towards his mother. The anxiety grows to such an intensity that it eventually subsides only along with the boy's repression of his sexual desire for the mother, and his simultaneous identification with his powerful father who has been seen as so threatening to the boy's incestuous attachment to the mother.

The little girl's incestuous attachment to her mother, however, is repressed only after she comes to realise her own lack of the superior sex organ, the penis, and along with it, her mother's similar lack of this much-valued possession. The realisation begins her transfer of desire from the mother to the father, and from her former active clitoral sexuality to a more passive and receptive desire for love from the father, and for a baby (as a penis substitute) which only the father (or father substitute) can provide. 'Quite different' Freud had written 'are the effects of the castration complex in the female. She acknowledges the fact of her castration, and with it too, the superiority of the male and her own inferiority; but she rebels against this unwelcome state of affairs.'[17]

Freud believed therefore that people are both masculine and feminine in varying degrees: 'pure masculinity and femininity remain theoretical constructions of uncertain content.'[18] But femininity in particular was acquired only with considerable resistance. The pre-Oedipal child had no fixed sexual character until the differentiation brought about at the point of the castration complex. The chief significance of the Lacanian re-reading of this account of psychosexual development and the Oedipus complex is the highly contentious assertion that we can interpret Freud as not really referring to biological organs or biological needs at all, but always only to their psychic apprehension and significance through language.

Any acceptance of Freudian theory clearly has implications for feminist explanation and analysis. The role and significance of unconscious psychic processes connecting all of us back to infantile experience and desire introduces a completely new dimension to our understanding both of sexual identity and of sexuality. In psychoanalytic thought, neither sexual identity nor sexual behaviour is reducible to any type of biological essence (or biological difference), at least not in any of the interpretations which remain true to Freud's own final thoughts on the subject.

But neither are they reducible to any straightforward social conditioning (whether we see this as the imposition of general social expectations of gender, or as strategies men have consciously learned to maintain their power). To understand sexuality and the deeper dynamics of sexual difference we would need instead to study the separate world of the unconscious. The study of this world involves some understanding of the diverse mechanisms of unconscious thought, like those of repression, projection and reaction formation. These are held to be techniques whereby we resolve psychic conflict or anxiety by denying the desire which gave rise to it, projecting such desire on to another person, or replacing it with its opposite. They are mechanisms which Freud said can be most readily perceived in fantasy, dreams, errors, neurotic symptoms and 'perversions'. Both masculinity and femininity, seen from the perspective of infantile desires and the Oedipal experience, are divided in and against themselves, in significant contrast to and continuing conflict with the cultural ideologies and expectations which define them at any particular time and place.

Feminists who wished to develop a progressive sexual politics informed by psychoanalysis felt they needed to explore and understand these conflicts. Their project was to connect the divisions and complexities of the psychic with the patriarchal linguistic structures of the social.

The Potential and Problems of Psychoanalytic Feminism

Such a project, as Juliet Mitchell would agree, was always likely to prove a most precarious one.[19] It was the debate within feminist psychoanalytic theorising which first introduced the word 'femininity' for serious re-examination in the women's liberation movement. This coincided with deeper understandings of and discussions about the link between biological sex and social gender, or biological sex and sexual difference (as the Lacanians preferred to call it). Some of the deeper confusions and conflicts we experienced as women, around motherhood, sexuality and relationships, were beginning to emerge; but at the same time the increased attention some feminists were giving to intellectual work and the theorising of subjectivity was also drawing them further away from feminist activists – those working in the women's refuges or rape crisis centres and elsewhere. It was becoming more and more difficult to have a dialogue between the two camps.

This was partly because the application of Lacanian perspectives, unlike earlier feminist enterprises, attached less importance to women's individual and collective exploration of their own experience. This inevitably seemed to distance the Lacanians from any direct engagement with the political practice of feminism. The Dalston Women's Study Group were the first to outline their negative response to the Patriarchy Conference organised in London in 1976, where many feminists had found the two papers using Lacanian perspectives 'intimidating and mystifying':

> It felt ironical, then, to arrive at a women's conference and feel defined negatively in relation to it; to listen to papers being read about women's silence and women having no social language, which itself made us passive and silent.[20]

The papers, they complained, did not attempt to connect with the experiences or issues which had been raised in the women's movement; they did not even (unlike Juliet Mitchell's original work) engage critically with alternative perspectives like those of Laing and Reich which had been a strong influence on feminism. (In fact the two papers of which they complained have been of lasting interest and value in explaining the new Lacanian perspectives, but their impact at the time on an open group of feminists was contentious.)[21]

It was not just the new and difficult theoretical language of Lacanian feminism which was a problem for some feminists. Once we did try to understand Lacanian feminism, it was also hard to see how to connect its analysis of the inevitability of women's negative entry into the symbolic order (i.e. into language) with any possible political project for change. We could do little, it seemed, but sit passively waiting for the end of patriarchy. Juliet Mitchell, Ros Coward and others were indeed promising us, in what seems to me the least convincing sections of their analysis, that this desired end might be somewhere in sight. This was because the iron laws of Capital (the need for profit) no longer required the iron laws of Patriarchy (the incest taboo, and the nuclear family as the unit of reproduction).[22] But there didn't seem to be very much feminists could do to hasten this final clash between the two structures. Such optimism was all the more confusing and discouraging when they also wrote of the 'relative autonomy' of patriarchy from the mode of production. Elizabeth Wilson, for example, objected to what she saw as 'this new orthodoxy':

> The last thing feminists need is a theory which teaches them only
> to marvel anew at the constant re-creation of the subjective
> reality of subordination and which reasserts male domination
> more securely than ever within theoretical discourse.[23]

But, in a powerful and lucid reply to such criticisms, Jacqueline Rose was to reiterate the importance of psychoanalysis for feminism, despite its theoretical difficulty and its lack of any immediate 'blueprint for political action'.[24]

My own view is that Jacqueline Rose is right to insist that psychoanalysis is useful for feminists. It is useful in its descriptions of the inevitable psychic conflict and difficulty of developing a feminine identity in the context of male power (as experienced subjectively through the symbol of the phallus): 'most women do not painlessly slip into their roles as women, if indeed they do at all.'[25] And I also see no reason why a more complex notion of psychic conflict, fragmentation and instability in sexual identity need undermine or deny women's conscious and collective opposition to the many sites of men's power: in the home, the workplace and all our ideological, cultural and political structures. Only in psychosis does psychic division prohibit purposive social action. The belief that infantile experience and unconscious forces add enormous complexity to our inner psychic reality – a complexity of which we may often have little immediate knowledge – does not necessarily preclude women coming together to share an everyday awareness of the habitual domination of men in our lives, nor our determination to struggle against it. It should only be at odds with the idea of there being some single type of conflict-free female essence, which all women share, but which patriarchy has denied, crushed or distorted, the idea which prevails in radical and revolutionary feminist accounts of the essentially autonomous, gentle and pure sexuality of women when uncorrupted by heterosexual imperatives.

The overall impact of the Lacanian reworking of orthodox Freudianism on feminism, however, remains problematic and contentious. Clearly it is important to assert and to study the complexity of a psychic reality which is not reducible to any immediate social reality. It also seems likely that it is the need to acquire a sexual identity (in our own and all known cultures) which disrupts the early infantile attachment of both the boy and the girl to the mother. Psychoanalytic insights can also be particularly useful in analysing the meaning of fantasy, and can illuminate, for example, the contradictory titillation and disgust women, and probably men too, experience towards pornography. In an interesting article on fantasy using psychoanalytic insights, Elizabeth Cowie points out that fantasy does not depict objects as they are desired in reality (they could well be anathema in reality) but rather it provides the stage or backdrop to allow for the possibilities of playing out different forms of infantile desire.[26] This is why daydreams and fantasies are so often intensely embarrassing to us, and a complete denial of our everyday reality. It is also why the revolutionary feminist reduction of fantasy to reality is so misleading.

Ironically, Susan Griffin herself uses a psychoanalytic form of reasoning to explain 'the pornographic imagination'. She suggests that women's bodies can arouse in men the helpless rage and impotence of childhood in relation to the all-powerful mother; hence men's need to portray women as utterly possessed, controlled, submissive and humiliated in adult pornographic fantasy.[27] Pornography thus incorporates and refers back to the fantasies of childhood. Griffin, however, with stunning nonchalance, chooses to ignore the situation of the infant girl, who, on the very same reasoning, should also share men's sadistic fantasies from her own experience of powerlessness and loss in relation to her own early desire for the mother. If cruelty and aggression are also a component of women's infantile fantasies, we need to speculate on what happens to these repressed childhood fantasies, to wonder if and where they find their substitute gratifications.

It seems likely that the huge appeal of romantic fiction, read regularly by one in three women in Britain, might hold some clue. Tania Modleski argues from her study of Harlequin Romances, for example, that the stories indeed allow for some gratification of anxiety, anger and aggression in the construction of their fantasies: 'A great deal of satisfaction in reading these novels comes, I am convinced, from the elements of a revenge fantasy, from the conviction that the woman is bringing the man to his knees and that all the while he is so hateful, he is internally grovelling, grovelling, grovelling ...'[28] And she continues:

> It is crucial to understand the double-edged nature of women's revenge fantasies. As long as resentment is accompanied by self-denigration, Harlequin Romances can hardly be said to perform a liberating function. However, once it becomes clear how much of women's anger and hostility is reflected in (albeit allayed by) these seemingy simple 'love stories', all notions about women 'cherishing the chains of their bondage' become untenable.[29]

Rosalind Coward similarly reveals how popular romance allows for the full indulgence of infantile fantasy, the adoration for the powerful parent before adolescent disillusion and the struggle for autonomy. It exposes 'the push for power in female fantasy' as the heroine secures for herself alone the omnipotent power of the beloved, and has the pleasure of humbling and overpowering him in the process, seeing him the helpless victim of his own uncontrollable passion for her.[30]

Women's enjoyment of romance, on this analysis, is not just 'a product of male conditioning'[31] as Susan Brownmiller says (and most radical and revolutionary feminists would agree with her) but one way that women try to come to terms with their own anger and aggression towards men – and towards other women. (Though they are fantasies played out only within the narrow and conventional context of familial heterosexuality.) It is crucial to understand this disjuncture between fantasy and adult reality if we are not to be led widely astray. For example, women's consumption of romance, like public displays of pornography, has dramatically increased over the last 20 years: that is, it has increased along with the growth and influence of feminism and greater financial independence and autonomy for women. I have heard many feminists argue that, behind women's apparent increased autonomy, they are really worse off, citing the increase in pornographic representation of women as the proof. Once we have a more sophisticated awareness of the nature and use of fantasy in representation, we might be less likely to write off so cavalierly the role and significance of women's struggles and achievements.

There is, then, a usefulness for feminism in the psychoanalytic exploration of psychic structure in its own terms. But the specific focus of Lacanian psychoanalysis on the structure of language, and its use of the inflexible determinism of a controversial and unconvincing Saussurean linguistics (which sees the structure of language as unilaterally determining the way we see the world), have produced an extreme form of theoretical abstraction which in practice has left little space for political engagement. Certainly it seems quite at odds with the former feminist focus on the importance of building up our knowledge of women's lives and struggles from attending to women's own experience. For here women are merely 'subjects', and subjects are denied autonomy, trapped within the operation of linguistic structures and laws.

In non-structuralist psychoanalysis we might possibly suggest that changes in the patterns and power relations of family life would impinge upon and disrupt the particular Oedipal scenario which Freud described. However uncharacteristic it might be to mention the material basis of family life in Freudian writing, we might even suggest, as some people have, that while the Oedipus complex has tended to characterise our own nuclear family patterns, it is neither universal, nor necessary, for human development. But a Lacanian analysis, based on the inevitable structures of language, would make such disruption impossible, at least before the total abolition of patriarchy. We could suggest that changes in the patterns and power relations of family life would begin to interact with and change the structures of language, but this notion of the interaction of language with other social forces would disrupt the primacy given to language in Lacanian thought.

A type of rationalised pessimism rather than any form of political optimism seems the most natural companion of psychoanalytic structuralism. It seems to have encouraged a more detached, elitist and less committed attitude among some feminists rather than engagement with, or even interest in the more mundane struggles in the lives of most women. It has thus reinforced the polarisation of feminist ideas: academic feminists stressing the contradictions of subjectivity and feminist activists influenced by revolutionary feminism stressing essentialist contrasts between the power-seeking and violent natures of males as against the co-operative and nurturing nature of females.

However, Lacanian feminism rejects biological essentialism only to replace it by a new type of psychic essentialism. Where language, with the phallus as its necessarily privileged signifier of sexed identity, is homologous with, that is, corresponds exactly with, reality, 'feminine' identity is everywhere and inevitably (under patriarchy) constructed as the negation of and inferior to 'masculine' identity. For this reason some post-Lacanian feminists have embarked upon the project of asserting the nature of the 'feminine' and subverting 'masculinist' or 'phallogocentric' modes of thinking.

The French feminists Julia Kristeva and Luce Irigaray have each, in different ways, attempted to oppose masculinist thinking, that is, the symbolic discourse which places 'man' at the centre of the universe. To do this women must return to *jouissance*: 'the direct re-experience of the physical pleasures of infancy'.[32] (But must we always return to infancy, forsaking adult strategies?) Irigaray writes of the fundamental physical differences between male and female sexuality. Because women's 'sexe' is formed 'of two lips in continual contact', her sexuality, always at least double, is actually plural: in Irigaray's description *'women have sex organs more or less everywhere'*.[33] Women's sexual pleasure compared to men's is thus 'far more diversified, more multiple in its differences, more complex, more subtle, than is commonly imagined ...'[34] Most significantly, Irigaray argues, it cannot express itself through masculine logic, where 'the male imaginary' has suppressed 'the female imaginary'. Kristeva and Irigaray are searching for a new 'antiphallogocentric' language, one which for Irigaray can express a female imaginary based upon the morphology of the female body, and which for Kristeva can express the child's pre-Oedipal experience with the mother, and therefore challenge phallogocentrism.

Irigaray's writing seems to suggest that it is through finding the words to express the female body, rather than through the analysis of social forces or cultural meanings, that we can understand and represent female identity. For both Irigaray and Kristeva, subverting male oppression is not so much a matter of material change as of finding a route back to a language which can once again express the sexual pleasures of infancy. This pre-phallocentric language is seen as more rhythmic, more fluid, gestural, open and non-linear, calling upon the pre-linguistic erotic energy Kristeva calls the 'semiotic'. It is, for Irigaray, a language yet to be invented. Irigaray does write of the necessity to analyse all the systems which oppress women, although her own project is for women to rediscover a language which will allow them to 'speak of their sex'.

Such a project has been exciting and important to some feminists in exploring how the male is always represented as normal and the female, especially female sexuality, is represented, when at all, with contempt and disparagement in all phallocentric discourse. The approach has inspired women's creative efforts to find new ways of expressing women's consciousness and sexuality in both literary and visual texts.[35] But, in the controversy which has surrounded Irigaray's work, I would agree with the criticism that her project is limited by its idealism and essentialism. As with the Lacanian construction of sexed identity, its account of sexual experience in the female imaginary is one which exists outside the changing social institutions like the family, which interpret and mould it. We have yet to see even the recognition of the need to theorise the formation of the unconscious within differing types of social and familial groupings. And there has been no attention in either Lacanian or post-Lacanian writing to questions of class or race in the construction of female subjectivity, where gender is isolated from historical context. As Cora Kaplan suggests in critical support of this work:

> semiotic and psychoanalytic perspectives have yet to be integrated with social, economic and political analysis. Critics tend to privilege one element or the other, even when they acknowledge the importance of both and the need to relate them.[36]

The writings of Irigaray are most readily interpreted as strengthening and celebrating traditional gender ideologies of fundamental biological difference between women and men.

They play down the differences between the lives and struggles of different groups of women, and are distanced from any call for collective political action. Kristeva does reject rather than celebrate the fundamental opposition between 'masculinity' and 'femininity' and the emphasis on female morphology in Irigaray's writing, but she now adopts an intransigent idealism, asserting that subverting the symbolic defines the project of political resistance.[37] And she has moved away from former radical commitments to assert the now-fashionable foolishness, 'We try not to be political'.[38] She succeeds in being disappointingly reactionary – particularly in the light of her forthright homophobia.[39]

Lacanian and feminist post-Lacanian explanations of the construction of gendered subjectivity have been important in feminist cultural analysis, but for a narrowly defined intellectual audience. Advocacy of the need for change in social practices other than in cultural aesthetics or intellectual discourse lies outside their terrain. But if Lacanian theory has had a limited impact on more popular feminist strategies and engagements, the influence of feminist appropriations of other developments of psychoanalytic thought has been different. In particular those psychoanalytic developments which ignore the father and the phallus, and focus instead almost exclusively on the mother-child, mother-daughter relationship have taken a popular hold within feminism.

Object-Relations Feminism and the Construction of Gender

The object-relations school of psychoanalysis is concerned first and foremost with the young child's early, or 'pre-Oedipal', relationship with its mother. It begins from a belief in the centrality of a primary unfolding ego or self in search of relationships with others. This contrasts with the classic Freudian account which begins from the centrality of a primary or unfolding libido, or sexual drive for sensual gratification, which expresses itself as psychic desire. Michael Balint, a leading analyst of the object-relations school, argued that infants are object-directed from birth, and that the later distortions and repressions of sexuality arise from the thwarted or distorted object relations which can occur in the earliest years.[40] Infants desire first of all to relate to others, and this desire is mediated through sensual contact. It is this fact which gives infantile sexuality its lasting importance in adult life, not any primary sex drive itself.

For feminists, however, it was Nancy Chodorow's writing which popularised this approach, and was closely studied. It served to challenge the more orthodox Freudian account of 'gender development' (the term Chodorow, as a sociologist, preferred to 'sexual difference') and to suggest new ideas on sexuality and mothering.

It is easy to see why Chodorow's book *The Reproduction of Mothering*, published in 1978, was exciting and important to many feminists. Chodorow built upon the work of Dorothy Dinnerstein and Adrienne Rich to focus on the issue which is so central and significant in the lives and identities of most women: the causes and consequences of women's role as mothers.[41] Feminists in the early seventies had, understandably, tended to stress the isolation, conflict and economic dependence most women faced as full-time mothers, or else the weary exhaustion of working mothers. These were the complaints feminist researchers like Lee Comer had heard from mothers on almost every doorstep.[42] And so we had pursued a variety of strategies for better childcare provision and for men's involvement in childcare. And we had also insisted that no woman should be forced to bear children when accidentally pregnant or unable to give them the love and care they would need. It is not true, however often we hear it repeated, that feminists then were unconcerned about mothers and their children, but it is true that Dinnerstein, Rich and Chodorow began to write of mothering in a different way: to attempt to grapple with the full psychological complexity of women's desire to mother, and the full political significance of the institution of mothering.

The writing of Adrienne Rich, Nancy Chodorow and others both reflected and reinforced a shift which had been developing within the women's movement itself. There had always been women who were mothers, and had chosen to be, in the women's movement. But an increasing number of women's liberationists were in their thirties rather than their twenties by the latter half of the seventies, and therefore facing a new urgency over the choice of motherhood. In this period the defence of women's rights to abortion, and activity in NAC, was more often accompanied by feminists reflecting upon their 'mixed feelings' about pregnancy and abortion.[43] Many feminists were beginning to reassess motherhood and to observe infancy in new ways. This can be seen, for example, in the Lacanian-inspired *Post-Partum Document* of Mary Kelly, a feminist art work which was exhibited widely in the late seventies. She documented the experience of childbirth and childcare, focusing on the development of the child's consciousness, and the effects of the mother-child relationship on the mother's sense of her own femininity. In Mary Kelly's words, 'It is not only the infant whose future personality is formed at this crucial moment, but also the mother whose "feminine" psychology is sealed by the sexual division of labour in childcare.'[44] Feminists began not just to question men's absence from childcare, but to ask why it often proved so difficult for men to nurture others adequately.

So Nancy Chodorow's work, which was the most theoretically elaborated of the new writing on mothering, and on which I therefore focus, came out of this particular political climate within the women's movement. There is now an ever-growing feminist literature on mothering and mother-daughter relationships, as popular in Britain as in the US, where much of it originated. Indeed mothers and daughters became the other principal preoccupation of feminists in the late seventies, alongside rape and male violence: an equal measure of hope and despair.

To answer the question of why women mother, Chodorow argued, neither a biological nor a role-training model will suffice. We need instead to apply certain psychoanalytic understandings to explain women's capacity and desire to mother, as well as to explain how mothering maintains women's continuing social subordination. In Chodorow's analysis, it all begins from the fact that it is women, and not men, who mother. This is the key to understanding the contrasting or 'assymetrical' ego structures and interpersonal or relational capacities in women and men. Women's relations with their daughters and their sons, in a society where women are devalued, cannot but develop in contrasting ways.

Mothers, Chodorow said, will experience their daughters as less separate from themselves, and will form closer and more narcissistic bonds with them. Girls in turn will forever retain their early and intense attachment to and identification with the mother, the first object of their love. Because fathers are physically and emotionally much less available to their young daughters as caretakers, girls will tend never to make any total transfer of affection to their fathers, but will remain always closely bound up with their early pre-Oedipal relation to their mothers. Although men most often do become the primary erotic object of women, they remain emotionally secondary in women's lives. As a consequence, girls' sense of self is weaker and less differentiated than boys' (they have looser, frailer ego boundaries), but they have a greater capacity for empathy and sensitivity towards others.

Feminine identity and the desire to mother are therefore straightforward and almost inevitable for girls. Difficulties only arise later, through women's weaker sense of autonomy and their identification with a negatively-valued gender category:

> As long as women mother, we can expect that a girl's pre-Oedipal period will be longer than that of a boy and that women, more than men, will be more open to and preoccupied with those very relational issues that go into mothering – feelings of primary identification, lack of separateness or differentiation, ego and body-ego boundary issues ...[45]

Chodorow rejects the idea that penis envy ever comes to permeate or dominate women's lives and sees its existence as multi-determined; it expresses desire for autonomy from the mother, awareness of the mother's differential and preferential love for those with the penis, desire to make love to the mother as does the father and, of course, the girl's awareness of the social privilege which the penis symbolises.

Mothers' love for their sons is different from their love for their daughters, in Chodorow's account. It is less 'narcissistic' and more 'anaclictic', that is, a love for someone perceived as other than or different from oneself. Nevertheless the boy's pre-Oedipal attachment to the mother does create great difficulties for the development of his sense of masculinity: for he, like the girl, longs for total 'mergence' with this first object of his love. Masculinity, while being overvalued in society, is less available and accessible to boys in a world where fathers are largely absent from childcare. On this view, then, masculinity is a problem for boys in a way femininity never is for girls. To acquire his masculine identity the boy must both reject and deny, totally and drastically, his former dependencies, attachment and identification with the mother: 'A boy represses those qualities he takes to be feminine inside himself, and rejects and devalues women and whatever he considers to be feminine in the social world.'[46] Men thus emerge from their pre-Oedipal attachment with a weaker, more fragile sense of masculine identity, as well as a lasting devaluation and fear of women and incapacity to fulfil women's emotional needs: 'the very fact of being mothered by a woman generates in men conflicts over masculinity, a psychology of male dominance, and a need to be superior to women'.[47] It creates, in short, nothing less than 'the psychology and ideology of male dominance'.[48]

One way in which object-relations feminism differs dramatically from Lacanian feminism and connects practically and usefully with the general aims of feminism is in its far greater stress on the therapeutic: the desire to bring about immediate change and improvement to the personal lives of women. It offers a cheaper, more accessible form of therapy than psychoanalysis. It has directly informed the practice of 'feminist therapy', and challenged the prevailing notions of mental disorder and psychological distress in women. In Britain the Women's Therapy Centre was opened in London in 1976 by Susie Orbach and Luise Eichenbaum, with the aim of uniting feminism and therapy to heal the damage done to women growing up female in a male-dominated world. They were later to write, 'We see "Feminist Therapy" as a progressive development from psychoanalysis and feminist politics'[49] and to express the hope that it could serve to help overcome the divisions, now so apparent, within feminism itself: divisions produced, they believed, by the competition, envy and mistrust women's basic insecurities arouse.

Thousands of women, of whom I was one, flocked to the Centre. There they received enormous encouragement and support from the growing team of feminist therapists who, despite poor financial compensation, have devoted considerable time and energy both to building the feminist therapy movement in this country and to building – through extensive love and commitment – the individual strength and confidence of many of their clients. As Luise Eichenbaum and Susie Orbach explain in their books, their feminist therapy is in accord with the work of Nancy Chodorow and object-relations theory.

Eichenbaum and Orbach also focus on the mother-daughter relationship as central to women's lives. Women's lives are bereft because men are incapable of nurturing them as adults, and they are bereft because they are the needy little girls of mothers who, inevitably, taught them to put their own needs second. Mothers identify with daughters because of their shared gender, and project on to them their feelings about themselves. Consciously and unconsciously mothers teach their daughters to curb their own needs for emotional care and attention, leaving little girls 'with feelings of deprivation, unworthiness and rejection'.[50] Little girls thus remain forever emotionally needy, but repress the expression of this neediness. Daughters' unmet needs provide the well from which they give to others. In this way women's ego structure comes to reflect their social position. Boys, in contrast, while taught to repress all expression of their own emotional dependency, are more likely to be taken care of by women. Men's dependency thus remains the best-kept secret, the terrifying taboo, of masculinity, as boys experience and expect nurturing simply as 'part of the fabric of life'.[51]

This theoretical approach has proved a powerful and compelling practical guide for feminist therapists in this country. They have successfully relied upon its highly concrete formula connecting social and psychic reality, its confidence that the female therapist and client can, working together in mutual trust, rebuild the client's 'sense of self' and confirm that she needs and deserves to be taken care of and will – through the 'repair work' of therapy – begin to grow in strength and autonomy. 'The taking-in of caring from the therapist both heals the hurt of the little girl and also provides a woman with a chance to embody the goodness of the therapist, to feel that goodness inside herself.'[52] Therapeutic efficacy, however, does not establish theoretical adequacy, beyond the therapeutic relationship. And there are many conceptual problems with this approach.

The primary problem with the theoretical analysis of Eichenbaum and Orbach (as with that of Chodorow) is the extent to which their generalisations about individual psychologies simply mirror the generalisations they make about social phenomena. Do all women carry out their social roles exactly as they are meant to? And, if they do, is it true that daughters inevitably follow in their footsteps? It seems to me that what is radical about psychoanalytic understandings of individual psychology is rather different: it suggests a more autonomous and more conflict-ridden dynamic to the psychic than that of mere conformity to social pressures. And what is radical about any progressive marxist or critical theory of society is also rather different: it rejects a mechanistic and functional view of social institutions, social roles and relations to suggest a more complex, contradictory and conflict-ridden view of society.

My own mother worked her twelve-hour professional day within a week of my birth. Cooking, cleaning, empathic skills — she has none, though she is an excellent surgeon and acclaimed gynaecologist. And, as I have sought sympathy for my own 'unnatural' childhood, I have found everywhere evidence of the amazing diversity buried within the ideology of the familial: fathers who were present and caring, 'working' mothers who were strong and powerful within the home, daughters who bonded tightly with fathers or older brothers, mothers who could not love their sons, mothers who never accepted their daughters, mothers who identified with their sons, and so on. As Liz Heron comments in her fascinating collection of women recalling their childhood in the fifties: 'Each story belongs somewhere inside that general pattern [the public image of 'the family'], yet none of them quite fits ...'[53] The twelve autobiographies each offer a unique experience of family life in the fifties, when 'the family' was presumed at its most stable, and ideas of the separate roles of women and of men were at their most polarised and sanctified. Carolyn Steedman has written the story of her mother raising two daughters in the fifties. The economic and social circumstances of her mother's life and the resentment and envy they produced meant that ambivalence, anger and resentment, not self-sacrifice and love, were the 'maternal' emotions her daughters received.[54]

Mothers do not always embody conventional 'feminine' styles and behaviour for their children. The parallel between the social and the psychic is too tightly drawn in most of the fast-accumulating mother-daughter literature, with little consideration of all the external and internal factors which impinge upon and disrupt the 'ideal mother, ideal family' scenario. Chodorow, Eichenbaum and Orbach, and most of the other literature on mothering, fail to discuss how class and race, for example, impinge upon family life. Indeed, as bell hooks argues, they assume a bourgeois family lifestyle in the types of maternal care and attention they describe; it is 'a form of parental care that is difficult for any working class parents to offer (for better or for worse) when they return home from work tired and exhausted.'[55] We find in the literature on women and mothering a somewhat similar type of reductionism from the ideal to the real as we found in the revolutionary feminist literature on men and sexuality.

I also cannot accept what we are told about daughters. Is it really so easy, as Eichenbaum and Orbach suggest, for mothers to wean their daughters 'very early on from relying, at an emotional level, upon having [their] dependency needs met'? At least at the unconscious level, surely, the daughters rebel: we should expect infantile rage and resistance to such denial. As Jean Bethke Elshtain has argued in criticism of Chodorow: 'The human subject as a desiring, fantasizing, self-defining agent is lost'.[56] And the human subject as a desiring agent can and does identify with other objects of desire which, on psychoanalytic evidence itself, are not necessarily restricted to members of one's own sex — as Freud's famous study of the Rat Man can testify.[57]

Nancy Chodorow is herself ambiguous on gender identity. She asserts that 'gender difference is not absolute, abstract or irreducible; it does not involve an essence of gender'. Indeed she cautions us to reject the shift in feminism towards seeing women and men as fundamentally different, as well as the notion of women's special nature as guaranteeing the emergence of a future and better world: 'Feminist theories and feminist enquiry based on the notion of essential difference, or focused on demonstrating difference, are doing feminism a disservice.'[58] Yet, in contrast with such sentiments, Chodorow does believe that there is a basic and stable male and female gender identity and difference, though they are historically produced and changeable: 'female identification and the assumption of core gender identity are straightforward', while male gender identity is defined more negatively 'in terms of that which is not female, or not mother'.[59] And despite her own cautions, Chodorow's work has appealed to those feminists (increasingly numerous) who do wish to focus upon and to celebrate essential difference between women and men. For what some feminists have abstracted from Chodorow's account is the idea that 'femininity' is the valuable and better identity, 'masculinity' the source of coerciveness, intolerance, insensitivity and brutality. Women have richer, more complex, more caring, less compulsive and narrow psychologies than men. What is more, these superior characteristics of women are universal, since they derive from the transhistorical and global reality of female mothering.

A New Psychic Essentialism

So we have come full circle. We are back with a fundamental and essentialist theory of gender difference, although we made a detour through a universal truth of the social. The problem is not one of Chodorow's alone, and I do not wish to devalue the interest she and other feminists have generated in studying mothering as an institution, or the lifelong significance of mother-daughter bonding for the girl and of the rejection of that early bonding for the boy. But any theory which pays only lip service to the actual variations, complexities, dialectics and history of social relations inevitably becomes the raw material for essentialist analysis and politics. Because of her lack of historical analysis, Chodorow's genuine cautions cannot save her work from the same fate.

All psychological theories attempting to explain what they see as universal sexual or gender difference share this problem. For instance, Chodorow argues that it is the specifically bad things about contemporary late capitalist or state bureaucratic societies which female parenting generates:

> Thus the 'fetishism of commodities', the excessive rationalism of technological thought, the rigid self/other distinctions of capitalism or of bureaucratic mass societies all have genetic and psychological roots in the structure of parenting and of male development, not just in the requirements of production.[60]

Yet Chodorow has told us that 'women's mothering is one of the few universal and enduring elements of the sexual division of labour'. So was there some strange mismatch between the institution of mothering and the psychologies of men in pre-industrial society? Was the potential male bureaucrat and commodity fetishist out a-hunting and a-gathering waiting in frustration for his historical moment to arrive? Of course you could suggest that female parenting has been the motor force of human history, propelling it on towards capitalism, commodity fetishism, state bureaucracy and beyond. But it is not the most convincing of suppositions.

There surely is an intractable problem for all those who attempt to locate the origins of male dominance in personality structures produced by what they see as a historically universal feature of child rearing, yet which correspond precisely to 'femininity' and 'masculinity' as we conceive of them now. How do they explain the historical and cultural variation in forms of masculinity and femininity, and in systems of male dominance? It is true, at the very least, that we know of cultures where men are far more expressive and emotional than in Anglo-Saxon culture – even under capitalism. And machismo even in our time takes many forms. It does not seem to be the personality characteristics of men which remain the same, but rather the continuing existence of differing power relations which privilege men. Over the last two decades, for example, social attitudes and images of masculinity have loosened up in Britain. Men are expected to show more interest in fashion, in childbirth, in their children, are encouraged to express their emotions and to pay more attention to women's needs. The soft and gentle man is not such a rare creature. But power relations between men and women have not shown a corresponding decline, indeed they have tightened up rather than loosened within the workplace during those decades as more women have been drawn into the growing part time and casual work areas of the labour market.

Nor would it seem to be simply the psychologies of women which propel them towards domesticity and motherhood, free from doubt, conflict and anxiety. Reading about women's lives in the fifties, recalling the lives of our mothers, is often grim and painful – tales of bitterness, resentment, and regret. Not only was our women's movement based upon young women's very determined resistance to such lives, but even outside feminism many women who have had the opportunity have chosen, over the last 20 years in particular, to have a child or children only after they have established their own careers. Many more women are now having their first children in their thirties, even in their late thirties and early forties. Mothering, it would seem, can wait. Has the maternal bonding been weakening, or was it, as I would argue, never so straightforward as Chodorow and others have suggested?

A further problem with an analysis which suggests that women's mothering creates the psychology and ideology of male dominance and sexual difference is that it presupposes a male-dominated society where women are already subordinated and masculinity is already more highly valued.[61] There is a circularity in the reasoning, which may well reflect a circularity in reality, but nevertheless we need to be wary of abstracting women's mothering as a primary causal factor, separated off from other aspects of male dominance. Some of the more interesting recent work in socialist feminist theory for instance (as I argued in Chapter 2), though less popular than the work on mothering, has shown how sexual hierarchy is also created in the workplace, through men's small physical advantages, in size and strength, combining with differential access to training and technology to keep women in subordinate positions in the workforce. Clearly feminists cannot pay equal attention to every area at once, but any emphasis on single-cause theories of women's oppression is inevitably incomplete and may serve to mislead us. Writing of what she sees as a blind spot in socialist feminist theory, Cynthia Cockburn's compelling analysis of men in the printing trade leads her to conclude that 'the construction of gender difference and hierarchy is created at work as well as at home – and that the effect on women (less physical and technical capability, lack of confidence, lower pay) may well cast a shadow on the sex-relations of domestic life'.[62]

It is true that Chodorow does warn us of this problem: 'In short, I argue that the sex-gender system is a social, psychological, and cultural totality. We cannot identify one sphere as uniquely causal or constitutive of others.' But in the same paragraph she goes on to reaffirm, 'Our sexuality and engendering take a particular form because we grow up in families where women mother.'[63] Somehow the fact that we grow up in societies where women are underpaid, men are in control of technology, and so on, slips from focus, as a secondary phenomenon. And this is all the more true in the extensive literature on mothering which has been described as a type of 'maternal revivalism' or maternal triumphalism, celebrating the eternal bonds of women outside and beyond phallic penetrations. This time it is Adrienne Rich who best encapsulates the enchantment for many feminists of the mothering literature:

> The daughters never were
> true brides of the father
> the daughters were to begin with
> brides of the mother
> then brides of each other
> under a different law.[64]

A world without men.

The Exaggeration of Sexual Difference

We need to understand where this maternal revivalism has come from. It is good that more feminists today, while hopefully still fighting the coercive ideology of motherhood (women are mothers or they are nothing of value) and criticising the social institution of mothering (the isolation of mothers and young children), feel a less equivocal confidence and joy in choosing to mother – in pregnancy, in childbirth and in childcare. And it is in particular the eloquent poetry and prose of Adrienne Rich, as well as of other feminists writing in this area, which has captured and spread feminists' determination to celebrate this aspect of the lives of women. But we do not need to deny the joys of motherhood in order to suggest that there is a danger of traditional sexist stereotypes of women and men being reaffirmed in this literature. In my view, the revivalism has come also from feminists' disappointment that our aspirations to engage in creative and rewarding work, to struggle for social change, to build warm and supporting communal spaces and friendship networks – as well as to choose to have children – have proved so often difficult, stressful or transitory. Decent work, committed politics, and real community are not easy to find or sustain in the public world of a market economy.

It is these difficulties which make the supposedly 'private' world of family life a more optimistic terrain for feminist theorising (especially for middle class feminists with the time and financial backing to create reasonable conditions for their own mothering). And that is at least partly why Chodorow's work, together with Sara Ruddick's notion of 'maternal thinking', have become so popular in American feminism. It is also popular precisely because it has enabled the return to and re-emphasis of the familiar certainties of 'common sense': the return to conventional ideas of fundamental and comprehensive cognitive, emotional and moral difference between women and men. Rose Lamb Coser, for instance, says she is taking Chodorow's argument 'one step further' when she writes of basic cognitive differences between women and men: 'If women tend to be more field-dependent conceptually [they respond to a whole stimulus field rather than breaking it down into its parts] after age 13, it seems to me, following Chodorow, that they are so because as girls they have been less able to detach themselves from the mother-child field.'[65] This explains, she argues, girls' lesser ability to restructure problem-solving situations, and hence their weakness in abstract and mathematical reasoning.

More ambitiously still, Carol Gilligan, voted Woman of the Year by *MS* magazine in 1984, argues in her book *In a Different Voice* that women's moral development is distinctly different from that of men.[66] Women remain less confident and dogmatic in their moral judgements, employ more concrete, less abstract categories of moral reasoning, and hence show a concern for the individual over any great cause or principle. They display greater compassion and empathy: notions of a more concrete 'responsibility and care' will always remain central in women's conceptions of morality. Always? We can but wonder what women were up to pinning white feathers on faint-hearted fighters throughout the First World War; the behaviour of hundreds of thousands of Italian women, who joyfully donated their gold wedding rings to Mussolini in the 1930s to be melted down for armaments and proudly sacrificed their sons to die for the fatherland, becomes quite incomprehensible on this analysis. There is of course nothing new about the belief in women's moral superiority and unique sensibility, central as it was to the

Victorian ideology of womanhood. Just as there is nothing new in my pointing out, as Gilligan does not, how well this ideology of the 'good' woman serves to perpetuate male dominance. Women's sensibilities are seen as disqualifying them for the 'nasty' world of economic and political power, but equipping them for the socially ill-rewarded work of childcare and, of course, the general servicing of men.

Looking more closely at Gilligan's research it is hard not to see there a methodology designed to exaggerate difference and to disregard similarity between women and men. And this represents a return to the type of psychological research on sex differences which occurred before the late sixties. For example, the major piece of research Gilligan undertakes to establish how women construct and resolve moral dilemmas concerning self and others is her abortion-decision study, where 29 pregnant women discuss their attitudes towards choosing to have an abortion. Clearly we cannot compare this with how men would act in a similar situation, since Gilligan has chosen one of the very few conditions which biologically excludes men; any speculation on possible differences here are quite inappropriate.

Unlike Chodorow's sociologically guided psychoanalytic reflection, Gilligan's work, though explicitly indebted to Chodorow, is based upon empirical observation guided by Kohlberg's theory, derived from Piaget, of individual cognitive and moral development. Gilligan is absolutely correct to criticise Kohlberg and most other psychologists for basing their theories and research conclusions on observations which consistently take male subjects as the norm. But she also adopts all the weaknesses of Kohlberg himself, and most other psychologists in the US, who characteristically ignore every detail of social context. Her own carefully selected comparisons of male and female moral reasoning provide us with no information at all on her subjects (no social background – race, class, religion) or even personal detail (age, education, employment, interests, politics) except for their sex. There is no discussion of the extent of the differences among women, or among men; we must just accept them as unitary categories. We are therefore, because of the methodology she employs, unable to question Gilligan's attribution of all difference to one of gender.

Gilligan does say in her introduction that differences in moral sensibility 'arise in a social context where factors of social status and power combine with reproductive biology' to shape experience, but it is an observation to which she never returns, showing no interest whatsoever in studying the nature of this social context. Difference therefore reduces to some sort of basic internal personality trait, which is a far more static concept than one which would see it as existing within specific social practices and social experiences. Gilligan is interested in using her work to stress the importance of recognising gender difference. And she does believe, however implicitly, in the superiority of women's moral sensibilities: 'Women's development delineates the path not only to a less violent life but also to a maturity realised through interdependence and taking care.'[67]

Ignoring social factors as Gilligan does, however, it is not clear whether or how women's moral superiority and difference might be linked with women's general social subordination. Perhaps this moral sensibility would disappear, for instance, if women were as socially valued and privileged as men. It is well known that those with less social power and confidence are more likely to develop a greater attentiveness, watchfulness, and desire to please in their relations with others. These are typical characteristics of all subordinated people – at least, as Frantz Fanon would say, until the point of resistance. Such capacities are a necessary protection against the greater vulnerability to discrimination and abuse which the less powerful face in most social contexts. The failure to confront the possible connections between women's special qualities and women's subordination becomes a problem for much of the literature focusing on mothering.

I have been arguing that in the mothering literature, and all the work it has inspired, there is an exaggerated focus on difference between women and men. This has meant a minimal interest in conflicts and contradictions as they are experienced within feminine identity, a false universalising of our own gender categories and a disregard for other social practices (outside mother-daughter bonding) as they impinge upon gender identity. There is also an idealisation of 'maternal' and 'feminine' ways of behaving. For instance, as Jane Flax argues in criticism of Sara Ruddick's now very popular concept of 'maternal thinking', the mother's sexuality, aggression and need and desire for an autonomous life are all ignored: 'Important things like rage, frustration, aggression, sexuality, irrational intense love and hate, re-experiencing of one's own childhood, blurring of body boundaries, conflict between the demands of a child, one's mate, other children and other work are missing.'[68]

While this mothering literature is more popular in North America than in Britain, its reverberations are also felt strongly here. It is seen in the popularity of the work of Eichenbaum and Orbach in this country, and it has found cultural expression in the mass media (here directly influenced by feminism) which in soap operas, film and literature has picked up on and reflected the interest in mother-daughter relationships.

It is of course popular partly because it is true that, despite exceptions and qualifications, we *can* expect women to display a greater sensitivity and solicitousness than men towards others. And certainly one possible explanation of this difference is girls' closeness to and identification with their mothers. But there are many other possible explanations, all converging towards the same end and all contingent upon women's secondary place in society generally and the more limited options open to women. However, by far the most important factor in determining what is seen as women's distinctive sensibilities would seem to me to be the nature of mothering itself, rather than the fact that it is women who mother.

Mothering is not determined by consciousness, but consciousness by mothering, to paraphrase Marx and Engels.[69] Young children's characteristic joy and delight in the world, their laughter and tears, the great love they offer the person or persons who 'mother' them, their vulnerability, their dependence, the great demands they make on us, could hardly fail to affect our consciousness and conduct dramatically. But not all mothers will have the time, inclination and capacity to respond to the desires and fears of children in ways which enable the children to flourish as happy, creative, confident and caring human beings. Many women do not display the characteristics of 'maternal thinking' (idealised or not) until they begin to mother. And even then, they may not.

Masculinity and its Discontents

Object-relations feminism has also appealed to both socialist feminists and anti-sexist men because it can be used to explain many of the most troubling aspects of men's behaviour, and suggest strategies for change. So, for instance, the compulsiveness and coerciveness apparent in much of men's sexual behaviour has been explained by Ethel Spector Person and other feminists as the result of the shakiness of male gender identity: 'relative gender fragility in men fosters excessive reliance on sexuality'.[70] Genital heterosexuality, she argues, comes to serve many functions for men: it symbolises the domination masculinity is supposed to confer, it enables the disguised expression of dependency needs, it relieves castration anxiety and helps overcome or stamp out men's primary female identification.

The idea that sexuality in men can be used in the service of non-sexual needs, and that the symbolically laden activity of genital heterosexuality can simultaneously serve both to confirm a sense of power over women and affirm 'true masculinity', is a convincing and useful one. And research on men provides some evidence that the greater the distance between men's ideas of 'proper' masculine behaviour and their perceptions of their own power and status at any particular time, the greater the likelihood that they will behave violently towards women, and violently in general.[71] So the connections between sex and violence in men's behaviour can be understood by combining the object-relations approach with a stress on the importance of the social meanings acquired, of course, within the more general ideology and social practices of male dominance, and in a culture where sex is seen as pivotal to identity. (Such a stress on social meanings is found in the 'symbolic-interactionist' explanation of human action within the social sciences.) But the feminist object-relations account, because of its assumption of a more precarious gender identity in men suggests more than the possibility of men's use of sex acts to confirm masculinity and power. It is this 'gender fragility' which makes men's sexuality driven and not liberated, and which leads to rape and male violence – almost like a type of compensation for men's basic insecurity.

There is now a growing men's literature which endorses this

type of analysis. It is written by and for anti-sexist men, influenced by feminism, who want to understand their own feelings better and to change and improve their relations with women. One such work, *The Sexuality of Men* (probably the best collection of anti-sexist men's writing available in Britain), largely relies upon the work of Dinnerstein, Chodorow, Eichenbaum and Orbach, and Person, and not, interestingly, upon the theorising or descriptions of male writers. It reads, as well, rather like the feminist complaints of being denied access to one's own authentic sexuality, and so has important symmetries with popular feminism. Men are seen as forced to rely upon sexuality to confirm their own weaker masculine identities, whereas women are thought to have other ways of consolidating their feminine identity. *The Sexuality of Men* quotes Person to suggest that 'many women have the capacity to abstain from sex without negative psychological consequences'.[72] But so, of course, do many men – unless we assume that all priests are liars or neurotics. And many women of my generation throbbed along to Bessie Smith's *Lonesome Bed Blues, Organ Grinder* or Lil Johnson's *Press my Button, Ring my Bell*, apparently experiencing a sexual longing not unlike the boys working on their mojos! I find the notion of men's greater gender fragility and also of women's lesser need and desire for sexual expression unconvincing, indeed rather dangerously misleading, reminiscent of all conservative thinking on sex.

The problem stems from the fact that feminist object-relations theory looks at only one aspect of the formation of masculinity – infantile attachment to the mother. The young boy's need to repress his earliest attachment to the mother, to assert his difference from her if he is to acquire a masculine identity, may well be traumatic and difficult. But that is not all we need to know about the construction of men's gender identity. Indeed there is a crucial weakness even within the pre-Oedipal attachment accounts of gender difference. There is nothing within the mother's apparently unique love for her son, however different that may be from her love for her daughter, which could in itself inform the son that he is loved differently because of his masculinity. Why shouldn't the small boy feel that he is loved in precisely the way he is just because of his own sweet self?[73] The awareness of difference must come from elsewhere.

And indeed it does: it comes from an enormously diverse array of social practices. Masculinity, like femininity, is systematically produced throughout a whole lifetime, and for boys connects with the physical strength built up through competitive sport, the skills acquired through education and the use of tools and other technology, the ideologies of sexual performance, the segregation of the workforce, the experience of family life, and the inescapable weight of cultural image and definitions that ubiquitously enclose us. All this must be added to any psychoanalytic analysis based on the boy's experience and repression of infantile desire.

The sociologist Bob Connell has criticised much of the anti-sexist men's literature, arguing that 'masculinity' is securely embedded or 'naturalised' in the body through long years of participation in various social practices.[74] In this way most men do become secure in their masculine identity (indeed, many women may feel, all too secure), whatever anxieties accompany that early awareness of difference and separation from the mother. Connell continues that the problem with most forms of masculinity is not that they are impoverished, insecure and alienated from men's inner needs and desires (they may not be), but rather that these identities as they operate through existing social relations are so very frequently oppressive to women, and, quite often, to other men as well. In particular of course they are oppressive to gay men, or men who deviate from the dominant styles of masculinity of their class, age or ethnic group. For as Andrew Tolson and Bob Connell both suggest there is more than one style of masculinity; it takes different forms across class and other divisions.[75]

Focusing only upon pre-Oedipal attachment ignores the multiplicity of social practices which separate boys off from girls, from an early age, and through which boys develop a sense of themselves. These social practices, from football to computer games, are not necessarily fraught and difficult for boys to participate in, and nor are they in any sense purely negative – although boys and men participate in them to varying degrees, and with varying conflicts and difficulties. It seems bizarre therefore to suggest that boys simply acquire their masculinity negatively, in the rejection of their mothers' embrace, when they are embraced and boosted up constantly (with or without their fathers' presence in childcare) by a myriad of social practices which will continue to place boys and men in positions of power over girls and women. The fears which will accompany the boy's struggle to distance himself from his mother – often with her encouragement and assistance – have many positive compensations. They are compensations which will continue to privilege him in relation to women throughout his life.

It is certainly true that the assumption that masculinity should confer lifelong mastery, authority and privilege on men in relation to women, an assumption central to all ideologies of masculinity, makes some men more prone to sexual coercion and violence. This is all the more likely from individuals or groups of men for whom much of their daily lives confirms only failure and impotence. *But men's violence towards women, I would suggest, comes from the inequalities of power between men and women as much as from any internal psychic dynamic in men.* Men are simply more likely to get away with abusing women than venting their aggression or frustration on most other targets. Black and other ethnic groups which can also be attacked with relative impunity in our racist society, are also targets of verbal abuse and physical attack (the former and sometimes the latter coming from women as well as men). All power relations enable a more overt expression of aggression from the powerful, while ensuring its greater suppression in the powerless, who may direct their aggression against themselves (accounting in part for the higher levels of depression in women) or express it in relatively powerless ways – such as 'nagging' or self-righteousness.

Men's habitual and petty acts of dominance, like sexual harassment, are the straightforward expression of their power in relation to women, a power which is often described by men simply as a form of friendliness but which nevertheless serves to keep women 'in their place'. While not the cause of men's power, such acts of dominance confirm men's place in the world, and make it harder to challenge. No one finds it easy to give up power. Behind rape and battery of women, which are not habitual to most men, there is a particular history to uncover. It is a history tied in with the cultural reality described by object-relations feminists, where sexual performance in men is one very important way of confirming 'masculinity', mixed up with guilt and anxiety over sex, and resentment towards and fear of women. Men who rape are frequently manifesting a contemptible inadequacy and weakness, if not mental disturbance, but I see no reason to accept that the prevalence of rape and violence from men confirms a general fragility of identity in all men.

I equally see no reason to accept that because women show less interest in the public provision of sex outlets for men – prostitution, pornography and sex aids – they are less obsessed or engaged with the sexual. This is now widely believed, even by many feminists. There is, as I have already suggested, no way to understand the huge appeal of romantic literature to women other than as some form of vicarious titillation and wish fulfilment. Ann Snitow, for example, analyses the appeal of Harlequin Romances as suggesting a constant state of potential sexuality in women: 'Harlequins revitalise daily routines by insisting that a woman combing her hair, a woman reaching up to put a plate on a high shelf (so that her knees show beneath the hem, if only there were a viewer), a woman doing what women do all day, is in a constant state of potential sexuality.'[76] Women go to great lengths to make themselves sexually desirable. The fact that there is less explicit public expression of or provision for women's sexual longings and desires is surely not surprising when the display of active sexuality in women is still seen to legitimate sexual violence from men. Women's sexuality is certainly everywhere more confined and controlled than that of men, but it seems unwise to endorse the cultural stereotypes of femininity which suggest that women are freer from sexual desire itself.

If nothing in our own experience as jaded feminists suggests an ardent sexuality in women, a glance at young women's magazines, or at Top of the Pops, should convince us that young women today are more assertive and confident in the expression of their sexuality. As Janice Winship argues from her careful analysis of the new young women's magazines of the eighties:

> It is the young women who flash their bodies, and with their gaze and pose coolly confident, they express less the customary passive sexuality of women than an assertive strength. Maybe it isn't a sexuality which wholly breaks from the oppressive codes of women as sexual commodities but neither does it straightforwardly reproduce them. The conventions of gender and sexuality are, it seems to me, being actively tampered with.[77]

Feminists need to be wary of focusing only upon women's vulnerability or lesser interest in sex, just when younger women have been able to draw upon the confidence and resistance which the years of feminist struggle have helped to produce for women. Winship continues:

> If there hadn't been fifteen years of the women's movement and organized feminism there wouldn't be this cultural space to play with gender and heterosexuality. If there hadn't been those years of pushing feminist ideals and high principles it wouldn't be possible in the eighties for 'the street-wise' to engage more pragmatically (and realistically?) with the contradictions of femininity ... or to laugh at 'schmaltzy, chocolate box romance' whilst also enjoying it ...[78]

Today it is older feminists who need to learn from the contradictions and pleasures in the lives of younger women how to enrich our own politics. My heart drops to my boots when feminists and anti-sexist men talk of there being 'common ground' between feminism and the moral right over our mutual 'concern' to 'protect' young women. This occurred in Britain in 1985 when Victoria Gillick, from the moral right, won her court case preventing doctors from prescribing contraceptives to girls under sixteen without their parents' consent. (The decision was later reversed.) It appeared, for example, in the patronising, and yes, sexist, sentiment of Martin Durham who wrote, 'When Victoria Gillick ... speaks of the dangers of the pill or of male and commercial pressures on young women, she clearly is on common ground with feminism.'[79] Clearly? This is as clear to me as the 'common ground' of north and south. Victoria Gillick is campaigning to *deny* young women the sex education and resources to understand their own sexuality and control their fertility, which might enable them to enjoy sex with men without fear of pregnancy or to resist the pressures of heterosexist culture. Feminism should be fighting for their expansion, for men's joint responsibility for contraception, improved contraception and abortion techniques, and the affirmation of lesbian and egalitarian sexual relations. A gallop back into Victorian sexual sentimentality, in defiance of what has been most progressive about recent expressions of women's active sexuality (whatever its contradictions), is not the way forward.

Shared Parenting and the Limits of the Psychological

The literature on mothering does not have to serve as an endorsement of the reactionary gender ideologies of a male-dominated society. It can be used in a progressive way to suggest that men as well as women need to develop the empathic and caring capacities which are necessary for good parental care, or any other type of caring responsibility or sensitivity towards others. And this indeed has been the object of most of the feminist writers in this area. They also suggest very definite strategic priorities for feminism. Chodorow in the US, Eichenbaum and Orbach in Britain, and most of the other writers in this field argue passionately that the way to create gender equality directly, and a better world contingently, is to involve men as well as women in the care of young children. I would agree that this is an important strategy for gender equality, although one which does not follow very smoothly from their own arguments, which stress that men lack the relational capacities to mother. However, I think their emphasis on the psychological underestimates the obstacles in the way of such a strategy, and exaggerates the extent to which it could, on its own, either overturn conventional gender relations or transform 'the sorry state of things entire'.

Chodorow, Eichenbaum and Orbach are most concerned to discuss the psychological factors which hold men back from sharing childcare. For Chodorow it is the 'heterosexual asymmetries' in men's and women's needs and capacities. For Eichenbaum and Orbach it is 'unconscious attitudes' to parenting. Neither approach places much weight on the gigantic economic restructuring it would entail: nothing less, in short, than the transformation of 'work' in the form we know it. Certainly men's disinclination to share childcare and housework is a problem. Men whose wives work full-time do little more in the home than other married men.[80] But this is not the only problem. Men who would like to spend more time in the home, as many men do now tell us (particularly when their children are young), find that it is precisely when they are most needed at home that economic constraints are greatest and shorter hours at work impossible.[81] Employers, for economic reasons, are notoriously resistant to any agreements for shorter working time, other than the ridiculously exploitative, and hence now popular introduction of part time work, which often carries no job security, protection, holiday pay, etc. It seems to be unmindful of the economic constraints most people face to assert without comment, as Eichenbaum and Orbach do, 'Other couples, heterosexual and homosexual, have decided to share parenting, [and] to seek employment that makes that possible.'[82]

Where it does prove possible for men and women to share childcare is, ironically, either in upper professional jobs or among the jobless. But there is now some evidence that, though probably beneficial for parents and children, the effects of men's involvement in childcare are not as dramatic as one might have wished and hoped. As some feminists have learned with bitterness and regret, 'The odds are that the sharers will start off their existence as parents on a disparate material footing; an imbalance readily exploitable in any later collapse of the goodwill which sustained the original sharing.'[83]

Diane Ehrensaft also reports on the differences in the way men and women relate to children in the small groups where shared parenting now occurs. As other studies now corroborate, women are still doing more of the concrete servicing work in the home, like washing and cleaning up, as well as showing a greater concern with their children's peer relations, while fathers are more likely to be reading to children and taking them out, less involved in cleaning activities and peer and sibling conflicts.[84] Nevertheless Ehrensaft concludes that shared parenting does alter the power relations between parents and children, and between men and women, and can provide a richer and more egalitarian world for children. Both Chodorow and Eichenbaum and Orbach, it is fair to say, argued that the way in which men and women relate to children would not change within one generation.

However, there are more fundamental limitations to the effectiveness of shared parenting in undermining the power relations between men and women. Shared parenting cannot in itself overturn the power and status of men in wider economic, political and cultural spheres. In the short term women may easily find themselves with less power in the home, the one place we were more likely to have power, while of course we are still undervalued and underpaid outside it. Not really surprisingly, one important reason why many shared childcare arrangements have broken down has been the difficulty biological mothers have in sharing the parenting of their children with others, whether with the father, or other women and men in their lives. As Ruth Wallsgrove writes in a sad and moving account of her own loss of the non-biological children she had been parenting, mothers do not as a rule try to offload the labour or joys of parenting, not even the dead-of-night demands for attention. And she explains why:

> I know something about what you get back for doing that; and part of what I know is that you get a sense of power, strangely. Not just over the child, though I do think there's nothing adults can do about the fact that children are relatively helpless and dependent on countless decisions we make for them, but also in relation to other adults. Mothers are oppressed by male-dominated society in so many ways, as are non-mothers. But I suggest that many feminists who are now choosing to have children want to have some area of life, childcare, where they'll have the last word, where the importance of their position – as the one and only Mum – is assured.[85]

Writing of the passing of her own youthful idealism about new ways of bringing up children, Wallsgrove concludes that in a male-dominated society where motherhood does give women both status and power, it is hard to prevent 'endless tension between mothers who feel unsupported and non-mothers who feel betrayed.'[86]

In terms of immediate feminist tactics and strategy there are therefore many problems with the demand for shared parenting as any type of over-riding priority for feminists. First of all, it entails enormous changes in the control employers have always had over their workforce, where time off for domestic responsibilities has never been a part of the bargain between labour and capital, and where men's entrenchment in the key positions of the workforce makes any greater domestic involvement an economic as well as a psychological problem for most households. Men's involvement in childcare is an important goal to move towards, but it is hard to see how it could be fully realised by more than the privileged few, or the unemployed many, short of the abolition of the present capitalist market economy. There is also the problem that the project for shared parenting does not necessarily challenge the ideology of the private nature of caring work (whatever the levels of care which are needed). It does not, in itself, promote the crucial struggle for greater public commitment to and improved state resources for caring for all dependent people, many of whom may not have couples to care for them. The relation between private and public caring still needs much more thought and discussion.

There is a danger, particularly in these days of recession, that an overemphasis on the importance and significance of shared parenting can overshadow the impact of the earlier feminist critique and rejection of the assumed 'privacy' of family life. It is this ideology of privacy which keeps hidden and taboo the reality that in many households with children the quality and nature of caring are a direct product of the level of social support available: of child benefit levels and other state benefits, of nursery provision, playcentres and youth clubs. The emphasis on shared parenting also assumes that children have two parents who can be present: it is of no use to the increasing number of single parents, among whom, as Black feminists have pointed out, there is a higher number of West Indian households.[87] Many of its implications are therefore unintentionally both classist and racist.

There are important strategies which trade unionists can pursue towards enabling men and women to have a greater involvement in childcare and paid work. Some trade unions, particularly whitecollar unions with more bargaining power, like the NUJ, NALGO and NATFHE, have fought for and won paternity leave settlements. The London branches of NALGO have also won time off for sick dependants for their male and female members. The other important struggle here is for shorter working hours, a demand which clearly looks attractive in these days of high unemployment. But we cannot overlook the difficulties we face in the tenaciousness with which employers have opposed such demands.

I am not suggesting that it is unimportant to involve men in childcare, nor that such involvement prevents struggle on other fronts. But I would endorse the doubt so forcefully elaborated by

Denise Riley: 'What tends to happen in practice, given the utterly miserable outlook for social provision for childcare to be extended or maintained under present conservative policy, is a loss of heart for reform in the public domain.'[88] And this loss of heart can find its consolation in the false promise that we can sidestep more public political engagements (so often ill-rewarded) by overstressing the transformative nature of our own more radical parenting arrangements. The mothering literature, although not that of Chodorow or Eichenbaum and Orbach, is sometimes ambivalent on the question of nurseries and public provision for childcare. In the introduction to her own book on mothering Adrienne Rich, for example, has criticised the call for state-controlled childcare. She rejects it in part for the very reasons many women have fought for it: that it has been used to 'introduce large numbers of women into the labour force'.[89] Such a possibility is at odds with Rich's belief that women can achieve liberation only through learning to 'think with the body' – a type of thinking which connects to women developing to the full their own unique mothering capacities. It is understandable, though I think regrettable, that Rich should take this position. The lasting strength of the mothering literature is its powerful assertion of the contrast between the overwhelming importance of women's commitment to mothering and other types of caring, compared with the social undervaluing of such commitment. But this paradox of how to affirm the real value of women's mothering, while seeing how it also serves to perpetuate women's oppression, can also lead to a decreasing emphasis on the public responsibility for the adequate care of all dependent people.

Eichenbaum and Orbach conclude both their books with the expression of immensely positive possibilities for the future, due to the changes in family life which are already taking place. 'Rethinking sexual relations and childrearing practices', they believe, will change the social relations between men and women. And in rethinking childrearing practices 'a pivotal point is equal and shared parenting by both men and women'.[90] Their scenario for a new world of gender equality is one where father and mother, both rearing their son and daughter (in that order) each work part time. Here the daughter will be strong and creative as well as nurturant, while the son will be nurturant as well as strong and creative. What is more, these changes in family life will have changed the world, for paid work will be satisfying (not even a utopian like André Gorz goes this far) while domestic life will be a joy. Nobody will feel insecure ever again.[91] The authors are hopeful about their scenario, as well they might be, since all it seems to involve is a little more effort from Daddy in the home.

Such writing is important in suggesting one possible, and more egalitarian and desirable, domestic arrangement for the future. But it is also a problem in its indifference to strategy, which makes it seem as though all we need is a change in individual aspirations around parenting. Their optimism that shared parenting is a part of an already ongoing 'social revolution' ('albeit one that is happening slowly') is blind to many of the forces which are keeping men out of the kitchen and nursery. Susie Orbach suggests that the current 'restructuring of employment' has begun to create a greater chance of equal parenting.[92] But this restructuring has not been pointing in that direction, certainly not yet. Instead it has been strengthening the segregation of the workforce, with a smaller core of well-paid skilled workers, and a larger group seen as marginal to 'production', or unemployed. Women are in fact being more firmly located within the part time, marginal workforce. The focus on women's position inside the family has led to some shaky analysis of women's position outside it.

There will need to be many more sites of feminist struggle than are dreamed of in the shared parenting perspective, however perceptive it has been in locating one source of gender fragility and compulsion in men, and however correct in emphasising the importance of greater equality between women and men in the home.

5. Beauty and the Beast III:

Men, Women and War

At Greenham, women's anger finds a clear and sensible target; the male dominated machinery of war.

Ann Snitow[1]

The hard truth for feminists seeking to construct a theory of women and war is this: despite the paeans to the day when the beautiful Souls all get together to curb the primitive beasts and usher in the reign of harmony and peace, no sane person really believes in this outcome. It does seem rather late in the day for facile romanticism.

Jean Bethke Elshtain[2]

War is not so much the construction of a new and virulent form of masculinity, as the recovery for masculine identity of that relational form of identity constructed within the family. It is, in this sense, the return of the feminine.

Ross Poole[3]

Some feminists have focused on men's sexual behaviour to characterise the essence of masculinity and the soul of man, and more significantly to explain men's control of women. Other feminists have focused on men's absence from childcare to characterise masculinity and explain male domination. Both these themes enter into a third focus of contemporary feminism, the concern with peace. This has grown along with the great resurgence of the peace movement itself in Britain and other Western capitalist countries from the close of the seventies. Opposition to nuclear arms production and deployment has mobilised the political energies of hundreds of thousands of women, and provided the motivation for action and commitment for many feminists throughout the eighties. Here too feminist theorising hovers ambivalently around the identification of a basic biological or at least some essential psychological difference between women and men.

Greenham Common and the Women's Peace Movement

In August 1981, 36 women (with four men and a few children) marched from Cardiff in Wales to the US airbase at Greenham Common to protest at the siting of Cruise missiles there. Women have protested day and night at that spot ever since. The women's peace camp which emerged at Greenham Common has served as the model and inspiration for an international movement of women against the threat of nuclear war and the siting of nuclear missiles. It is a threat which most feminist analysis has located, with varying degrees of complexity and relevance, in the behaviour and psychology of men. As the feminist group Women Oppose the Nuclear Threat (WONT) stated in 1980, 'Many of us see war as male activity, from which women suffer, and over which we have no control.'[4] 'The military is the most obvious product of patriarchy', a Greenham Common newsletter declares.[5] Cruise missiles have become a symbol of male domination as well as of nuclear threat and imperialist exploitation.

The idea of Cruise as the symbol of a 'male principle' of domination and destruction opposed by a 'female principle' of co-operation and conservation is an enormously powerful one. Petra Kelly, one of the founders and leaders of the influential German Green Party, believes that because the male principle ('masculine materialism, waste, alienation, domination, possession') has become the predominant principle, it now threatens men, women and nature.[6] Similar ideas are expressed in much North American and British ecological feminist writing today.[7] In creating a women's space as a force for peace at Greenham Common women have been able to celebrate the value they place upon nurturance, co-operation and care as a way of life (and on non-violent resistance as a form of protest) as opposed to the value they feel men place on competition, aggression and the use of military force.

Greenham Common and the women's peace movement have generated considerable debate among feminists which, while never as fierce and bitter as the debates over sexuality, and creating different alignments of supporters and critics, raise many of the same issues. A small group of radical feminists in Britain argue, along with Lilian Mohin in the denunciatory pamphlet *Breaching the Peace*, that 'The women's peace movement, Greenham is co-option on a mammoth scale, a *real threat* to the women's liberation movement' (my emphasis).[8] They feel that Greenham has diverted women's energies from the real struggle against male power and male violence in all its chronic and mundane varieties. But the majority of feminists in Britain, however specifically they might identify themselves, share a more sympathetic attitude to Greenham. Ruth Wallsgrove, for example, also writing as a radical feminist, expresses her own critical support in an interesting and informative reflection on the women at Greenham Common: 'I can't believe that any of us can afford to dismiss them, or even avoid some admiration for their energy, even if we disagree with some of what they do.'[9]

Such faint praise, however, stands in marked contrast to the deep and passionate support most feminists around the world feel for Greenham Common. After visiting the camp several times, North American socialist feminist writer Ann Snitow movingly recalled her experiences there:

> What I discovered has stirred my political imagination more than any activism since the first, intense feminist surge 15 years ago. Though I still have many critical questions about Greenham, I see it as a rich source of fresh thinking about how to be joyously, effectively political in a conservative, dangerous time.[10]

Greenham is important to many feminists because it has proved capable of drawing so many women into political protest and action against militarism and the arms race, the most obvious face of destructiveness and waste in our society. But it is also important and memorable because it exemplifies all the strengths (and weaknesses) at the very heart of feminist thought and practice. Alice Cook and Gwyn Kirk explain this in their book on Greenham:

> As well as being a round-the-clock protest against Cruise missiles, it is also a resource – a women's space in which to try to live our ideals of feminism and non-violence, a focus for information and ideas, a meeting place, and a vital place for women to express their beliefs and feelings.[11]

The two books on Greenham which are written by the Greenham women themselves stress above all else its importance in enabling women to take control of their own lives, in their own space, with maximum support from other women.[12] It exemplifies the feminist ideal of egalitarian collectivity. No hierarchies or leaders are recognised in Greenham's community of women. Decisions must be taken on a consensus basis and every woman is encouraged to participate. Actions must be non-violent. In this new 'female space' women at Greenham see themselves as building for a new world while attempting to expose and remove the most dangerous and terrifying armour of the old. In the beliefs shared at Greenham 'we are starting from scratch, developing attitudes and methods that make domination and acting out impossible ... we are teaching each other in an intense way.'[13] The excitement, pain and difficulty of collective action in such a situation, the levels of intensity and joy between women, alongside simply surviving in the cold and mud of Greenham, create a continuously expressed comradeship and solidarity.

A little like the first years of our women's movement, women have discovered at Greenham a sense of individual and collective power, how to love and respect one another, and most important of all, they have found a new meaning for themselves as women. Again and again women write of such feelings aroused by their visits to Greenham. One said,

> The idea of being a woman really thrilled me for the first time.
> We can do anything ... and we care about each other while we're doing it ... it's like coming alive.[14]

Women at Greenham can feel strong, brave, creative, and also see themselves as changing the world − all experiences most frequently confined to men. At Greenham 'the future rests on women'. Ironically the most obvious parallel I can think of in men's lives is the solidarity which keeps men together under fire in times of war. Strangely this is captured in the words of one Greenham woman: 'In the past men have left home to go to war. Now women are leaving home for peace.' Women at Greenham responded to the rising tide of anxiety over nuclear weapons, talked of the urgent need for action, and showed that no one need be passive or feel unable to confront the issues at stake and the threat of nuclear holocaust.

Such is, or was, the amazing power of living at or visiting Greenham. It is why so many women around Britain and the world have raised money and worked in affinity groups to support Greenham, have attended the mass actions there, and have linked up with other women organising for international peace, co-operation and the greater influence of women. Greenham has provided an inspiration for peace for men as well as women throughout the world. It is without doubt the Greenham Common peace camp and the European-wide women's peace movement which have most dramatically drawn attention to the wider anti-nuclear movement. Their protest has also alarmed the NATO alliance. The women's peace movement is one of the strongest progressive forces in the 1980s. Its activism and resistance are essential in an escalating cold war climate where the British government has supported – has applauded – the increasing use of military force by the US to protect its own economic interests and political power in the Third World. In April 1986 the British government, against the wishes of two thirds of its population, was the only nation in Europe to allow US bases in its country to be used to launch the US bombing of Libya in an assassination attempt on Colonel Gadafy. Once again Britain endorsed the most blatant military aggression from America, and the reassertion of US power both in relation to the Third World and to Europe.

In such times as these it would be foolish not to support and value the success and determination of the women's peace movement in mobilising public opinion, and especially women's opinion, against the placing of American nuclear missiles in Britain and the rest of Europe. Opinion polls inform us that it is women, today, who most strongly oppose Cruise missiles in this country. And it is impressive that it is most obviously women who are prepared to devote so much of their lives and energies to the struggle to prevent nuclear destruction. On visits I have made to Greenham, especially during weeks of mass action in 1983 and 1984, I was uplifted by the sense of purpose and confidence Greenham has given to so many women. This was particularly noticeable in the great numbers of older women and very young women living at or regularly visiting Greenham. The courage and determination of so many women does serve as a kind of hope for the future.

The strength of the Greenham Common Peace camp undoubtedly derives from the fact that it is organised only by and for women. It is perfectly obvious that many women are silenced within the more formal structures of most mixed groups, and cannot experience the control, confidence and solidarity they more often share with one another. The imagination, wit, creativity and humour women have used to confront the vast and grotesque physical monstrosity of the US Greenham Common airbase is truly awe-inspiring. On the one side women camp in green and leafy woods; on the other, US soldiers crouch in and patrol behind layer after layer of barbed wire in a bleak and barren wasteland, with the assistance of the British police and the British army. The traditional tactics of protest used in the radical institutions that men have always dominated could never have taken the form of the stirring life-against-death symbolism Greenham actions have used to maximum effect. Whether linking together 300,000 women to 'embrace the base' or entering time after time, through the lethal-looking fence of the base, to plant snowdrops, have a picnic, dance on the silos, occupy a sentry box or a traffic control tower, or paint peace signs on a US spy plane; whether tearing down mile after mile of fencing and padlocking the gates, dressing up as witches or taking two hours to walk 200 yards, women at Greenham have been able for years to mock at and disrupt the efficiency, security and routine of a key military installation of the most powerful country in the world.

A minority of feminists have argued that women's liberation is more important than nuclear disarmament, and that the peace movement has drained away women's energy from their own liberation. One contributor to *Breaching the Peace*, for instance, believes that 'stopping the holocaust is easier than liberating women'.[15] But many more feminists have made convincing connections between the two struggles (and others which I think are less convincing). The money poured into military spending could be diverted into welfare spending, thus creating the public resources necessary to transform much of the work women do in and outside the home, and facilitating the sharing by both women and men of waged and non-waged work. The society most feminists are struggling to build would need to divert technology, resources and energy away from an aggressive and acquisitive militaristic economy towards one based upon creating useful work and meeting human need. It is obvious that there is a near-total clash between most military aims, which are rarely simply those of strict defence, and any daily commitment to caring and responsibility for others.

It is also easy for feminists to see that men's role in armed combat and their control of military technology and strategy are important components of the ideology and ritual, as well as the concrete reality, of men's power in society. The formal military training of men in the professional use of violence is indeed likely to spill over into a greater use of violence by men in their personal lives; work with battered army wives would seem to support this.[16] The exaggeration of sexual differences, on which military values rely, feeds the general misogyny of our culture. The Greenham women are right to connect the ideologies and practices of militarism and those of 'masculinity'. There is nothing strange in feminists linking the struggle for peace to the struggle for a better future and a better world for women. Indeed, it is a strange feminism which does not.

But at least two aspects of the feminist analysis of warfare and disarmament characterise for me the worrying face of contemporary feminism. It is not their women-centred tactics nor their focus and goal. I am troubled by the belief in some intrinsic or inevitably greater pacifism in women than men, and how this fits our preconceptions as well as media attitudes which sensationalise and simplify the issues. And, related to this, I am troubled by a rejection of what I see as any adequate analysis of modern militarism and the arms race for one which reduces it to an issue of individual psychology and immediate interpersonal relations.

Women and War

I have said that there is a connection to be made between feminism and anti-militarism. Feminists have made it before. The catastrophic carnage of the First World War, coming as it did at the height of the first women's movement, provided an urgent and dramatic challenge to that movement. Some feminists then worked bravely and tirelessly to end the slaughter. Crystal

Eastman, the American feminist and socialist, was convinced of the link between feminism and anti-militarism. Defining a feminist as 'one who believes in breaking down sex barriers so that women and men can work and play and build the world together',[17] she knew her own vision of freedom and a better world for all could only be built upon the basis of international peace. Crystal Eastman and Jane Addams founded the Women's Peace Party in the US in 1915. With war already raging across Europe, the Women's Peace Party joined with other anti-war feminists from Holland, Belgium, Germany and Britain to accomplish the extraordinary feat of holding a Women's International Congress for peace in The Hague in Holland in 1915. The equally extraordinary resolution of this congress was for women to embark immediately on the task of persuading all heads of neutral governments to enter negotiations to end the war.

The white South African feminist and socialist Olive Schreiner had written passionately and compellingly even before the First World War of women's rejection and horror of war. She described war's untimely waste and the loss of what so many women struggled 'alone with a three-in-the-morning courage' to create: 'so many mother's sons'. Only women could prevent war, Schreiner believed, for only a woman 'knows the history of human flesh; she knows its cost; he [man] does not.'[18] Women as mothers, many feminists agreed, cannot ignore the pain and futility of war. Olive Schreiner, together with Sylvia Pankhurst, was among the 180 women delegates from Britain who were prevented by the British government from attending the congress in The Hague. Schreiner's sentiments were the same sentiments which had, as feminist historian Jill Liddington puts it, 'fuelled the towering optimism' of Dr Aletta Jacobs, the original instigator of the Hague Conference. Like Schreiner, Jacobs believed:

> Woman suffrage and permanent peace will go together ... Yes, the women will do it. They don't feel as men do about war. Men think of the economic results; women think of the grief and pain.[19]

Inspired by such sentiment, women who supported the Hague Conference, though obviously defeated in their immediate campaign, created the nucleus of an international women's peace movement which continues to this day.

The English delegation was prevented from reaching The Hague, but between two and three thousand members of the British section of the Women's International League organised against conscription throughout the war. Together with other internationalist socialist groups they tried to shelter and support the men opposed to war, they spoke out bravely for peace and organised marches for peace. Their courage and tenacity were amazing, as the suffragette Gwen Coleman later recalled:

> Working for peace during the war wasn't easy, it was harder, much harder than working for the suffrage movement, that was child's play compared with what one put up with during the war. I mean you were a traitor to your country, you should have been shot at dawn.[20]

Alice Wheeldon, for example, a working class suffragette, socialist and pacifist from the Midlands who provided shelter in her home for conscientious objectors on the run, was given a ten-year jail sentence in 1917, accused by police spies (almost certainly falsely) of plotting to poison Lloyd George.[21]

But the peculiar knowledge of women, in which Schreiner and so many other feminists put their faith, could not end the first Great War. Indeed, it did not prevent the majority of women from actually supporting war – as it has not done before or since. While some feminists then (most of whom were also socialists) linked their fight for women's freedom and a better world with a total opposition to war, other feminists supported the war with patriotic passion and pleasure.

The first women's movement was torn apart by the war. Sylvia Pankhurst organised for peace; Christabel and Emmeline Pankhurst, who had never supported Sylvia's socialist commitments, travelled Britain and beyond recruiting for war. In 1915 the English Women's Social and Political union (known as the W.S.P.U.), the militant wing of the suffragettes, under the charismatic but autocratic leadership of Christabel Pankhurst, switched the name of its paper from *The Suffragette* to *The Britannia*. Women, as many leaders and followers in the W.S.P.U. were quick to see, could and did benefit, and benefit considerably, from their support for Britain at war.

Women achieved a lot more than eventual suffrage from their participation in the First World War. Virginia Woolf, Vera Brittain and many other feminists and pacifists, recalling those days of war, were well aware that many women loved the war. They had excellent reasons for loving it: it liberated many women for the first time from the isolation and stifling shackles of the home. War became women's passport into the experiences and world of men. For many women as well as for many men there remained a definite nostalgia for both the Great Wars, when so many people had been united by the call for action, loyalty and sacrifice, and by a common purpose which – at least momentarily – could transcend the normal more individualistic concerns of peacetime. If we are to avoid a psychological reductionism on men's and women's relation to war, it is important to understand how women's aspirations could connect with the patriotic demands of wartime.

The British government was at first reluctant to rally the resources of women, and women were equally reluctant to volunteer their services. But after introducing universal male conscription in 1916, the government was forced to enlist women's services for a huge variety of professions and crafts from which they had previously been excluded (and would in peacetime be excluded once again). Women gained money and prestige during the war – though they also faced new types of exploitation and received rates of pay vastly below those of men. Sandra Gilbert has detailed some of the ways in which the First World War liberated women, drawing upon the writings of women involved.[22] Photographs which remain of women from that time reveal their newly found pleasure and confidence, leading Gilbert to conclude:

> Liberated from parlors and petticoats alike, trousered 'war girls' beam as they shovel coals, shoe horses, fight fires, drive buses, chop down trees, make shells, dig graves.[23]

Nor was it only work on the home front which added zest and vitality to women's lives. Many women were also to experience the contradictory exhilaration, thrills, anguish and despair of the front lines of battle. As despatch riders on motorcycles, driving ambulances, or nursing in the hospitals, there were women who were later to recall and to regret the passing of the excitement of those days. The novelist May Sinclair, who served with the Field Ambulance Corps of the British Red Cross in Belgium, was later to exalt over her life on the front lines: 'What a fool I would have been if I hadn't come. I wouldn't have missed this run for the world.'[24] And Vita Sackville-West, though later denouncing war, also described the 'wild spirits' war unleashed.[25] Other women encouraged men by word and by deed to enlist – and, as they were to do again in the Second World War, used white feathers to humiliate those who appeared to be resisting the call to arms.[26]

The fullest and most famous woman's account of that war is in Vera Brittain's haunting *Testament of Youth*, first published in 1933. She described it as 'history's greatest disaster' and an 'indictment of civilisation', with the waste, pain, cruelty and disillusionment it caused affecting most of her generation:

> For me, as for all the world, the war was a tragedy and a vast stupidity, a waste of youth and time; it betrayed my faith, mocked my love, and irredeemably spoilt my career ...[27]

And yet even as the war made Vera Brittain a lifelong and committed pacifist, she was aware of and troubled by the momentary 'glamour' and 'magic' of combat:

> It is, I think, this glamour, this magic, this incomparable keying up of the spirit in a time of mortal conflict, which constitute the pacifist's real problem – a problem still incompletely imagined, and still quite unresolved. The causes of war are always falsely represented; its honour is dishonest and its glory meretricious, but the challenge to spiritual endurance, the intense sharpening of all the senses, the vitalising consciousness of common peril for a common end, remain to allure those boys and girls who have just reached the age when love and friendship and adventure call more persistently than at any later time. The glamour may be a mere delirium of fever ... but while it lasts no emotion known to man seems as yet to have quite the compelling power of this enlarged vitality.[28]

This was not, however, a glorious or glamorous war for most of its soldiers. Many men immobile in their trenches beside the rotting corpses of their comrades might well have echoed Wilfred Owen's desperate words on 'The pity of war, the pity war distilled', and testified to the hideous truths his poems exposed: the 'unnaturalness of weapons', the 'madness', 'heroic lies', 'inhumanity', 'horrible beastliness', 'insupportability' and 'foolishness' of war.[29] It was a war which did not always arouse bellicosity in its male soldiers. As Vera Brittain reported, many soldiers on both sides knew they did not hate the men they fought, and felt only sorrow for the 'enemy' who died.[30] It was not only Yeats's *Irish Airman* who in foreseeing his death declared 'Those that I fight I do not hate/Those that I guard I do not love'.[31]

After the Armistice in 1918 many more women began to organise for peace. The Women's International League for Peace and Freedom was set up in 1919 to work for an end to all future wars. It was originally proposed by those same pioneering feminists who had formed the earlier Women's International Congress and met (or tried to meet) at The Hague in 1915.[32] Throughout the 1920s, the 50 branches of the League in Britain joined with other pacifist groups to campaign for peace and disarmament. As the Second World War drew ever more obviously and more ominously close, these women's organisations collected millions of signatures for international disarmament. In 1938 Virginia Woolf published *Three Guineas*, perhaps the most powerful feminist polemic yet written against war. In it she argued that the cultural and political exaggeration of the differences and divisions between men and women helped pave the way for the growth of the authoritarian politics of fascism and the menace of war. The fiercely competitive and busy lives of professional men in the public world, separating them off from their children and other human relations, she wrote, means men 'lose their sense of proportion – the relation between one thing and another! Humanity goes.'[33] But *Three Guineas* is mostly quoted and remembered by feminists for its closing section on how women might put an end to war by remaining 'outside' men's world and rejecting men's imperialism, patriotism and dominance:

> Therefore if you insist on fighting to protect me, or 'our' country, let it be understood, soberly and rationally between us, that you are fighting to gratify a sex instinct which I cannot share; to procure benefit which I have not shared and probably will not share; but not to gratify my instincts, or to protect myself or my country. 'For', the outsider will say, 'in fact, as a woman, I have

no country. As a woman I want no country. As a woman my country is the whole world'.[34]

In the same year, Emmeline Pethick-Lawrence had published her account of standing in Manchester in the 1918 elections as the peace candidate for a just settlement after war. (She was defeated.) Her recollections starkly challenge Woolf's hope that women, though living in the same world as men, see it 'through different eyes':

> I realized at once that my supporters were not the women ... they were all for 'going over the top' to avenge their husbands and their sons. *My supporters were the soldiers themselves.* They spoke from my platform, they canvassed the constituency, and those who were abroad sent letters to be read at my meetings ... It was a strange experience for one who had given eight years of life as I had, in the endeavour to win votes for women, to watch working class mothers, with their babies and small children, eagerly going to the poll to record their votes against me. But no more strange than that soldiers should vote for a pacifist.[35]

And when war did come, once again women offered their services – in the home, in the munitions factories, under fire. The only military service from which women were in principle rigidly excluded was that of directly killing people. But the maintenance of this particular boundary of exclusion was more symbolic than real, more hypocritical than humane, as Di Parkin's research on women in the Second World War has revealed. It was also resented by many women. British women soldiers in 'Ack Ack' battalions during the Second World War, for instance, were instructed to direct searchlights and guns to locate enemy planes, and so were directly under fire, but were forbidden to pull the triggers of the guns which they were aiming.[36] The taboo on women firing weapons was, and is still, designed not to protect women but to protect the mythology, morale, motivation, prestige and privileges of the male soldier, to uphold the idea of the inevitable masculinity of combat. And the taboo was, and is still, necessary to uphold the idea of the essential femininity of those who must 'be protected', those who give birth, those who cannot kill – the women for whom men must fight, and men must die. As both Di Parkin and Cynthia Enloe have argued, women must be seen as helpless, nurturing and dependent to reinforce the discipline, coercion and threat of execution which keeps male soldiers on a battlefield.[37]

Di Parkin's evidence suggests that 'the opposition to women being allowed to shoot was from men rather than from women'.[38] In 1942 Edith Summerskill, then a Labour MP and a campaigner for women's rights, formed the Women's Home Defence which by the end of that year had trained 10,000 women in the handling and use of rifles and machine guns in London alone.[39] The War Office, however, remained implacably hostile to Summerskill's activities (and many women's wishes) and continued to deny women access to the official Home Guard except as auxiliaries. Similar practices existed in the Air Force. Women were trained as pilots to fly bomber planes, and were used to transport these planes to strategic locations, but were forbidden to fly missions.

Though forbidden to use the bullet and the bomb, women once again were liberated from the isolation of the home by this war, and able to enter most of the more skilled, highly valued and better paid jobs usually denied to them. Women did not and could not stay behind simply to 'keep the home fires burning', whatever comfort the singing of such sentiment may have offered the boys on the battlefield. Angus Calder in *The People's War* describes women's varied experience of work during the war: it ranged from the intense boredom, long hours and unhealthy conditions of factory work to the easier conditions of middle class women with older children in part time work. Of the latter group the Mass Observation studies of the time noted: 'The chance of spending her day outside her own home, of making fresh contacts and seeing people, is occasionally welcomed by such women with something approaching ecstasy, which neither strain nor fatigue can spoil.'[40]

Masculinity, Violence and War

The ideology of women's essential difference from men, of women as peacekeepers and homemakers, has served to inspire some women to resist war. But it has also served, as Virginia Woolf argued so forcefully, to encourage men to fight, and to maintain military discipline. As every army training officer knows, the fear of appearing 'cowardly' and 'unmanly' provides the strongest motivation for men to fight and act tough. But the usefulness of our ideas about sexual difference in the service of war does not, of course, in itself establish either their truth or their falsity. So while it may be true that the majority of women have always supported 'men's wars', and not apparently with reluctance, it could still be argued that it is not women who initiate and encourage war. (Although we would have to admit that women's exclusion from political power makes this a more difficult initiative for them – except in the cases where, like Margaret Thatcher, Indira Gandhi, Golda Meir or Mrs Bandaranaike, stateswomen have shown themseves to be just as bellicose as their male peers.)

A kind of homegrown radical feminist sociobiology has in fact emerged around the issue of male violence and war. Sounding remarkably like the sociobiologists (who attribute human behaviour to some fixed biological inheritance), and despite her criticism of them, Andrea Dworkin tells us: 'male aggression is rapacious. It spills over not accidentally, but purposefully. There is war. Older men create wars.'[41] This form of radical feminism which sees men, again in Dworkin's words, as 'distinguished from women by their commitment to do violence rather than be victimised by it', does emphasise the role of culture – in particular the role of pornography – in inculcating male violence. But the role of culture for Dworkin, as for the sociobiologists, is one where it interacts with male biology in some inevitable and immutable way: 'For men, the right to abuse women is elemental, the first principle, with no beginning unless one is willing to trace origins back to God and with no end plausibly in sight.'[42]

However, there is no way that culture can interact with or transform the biological basis of maleness in an invariable and timeless way unless we assume an underlying fixed biological or natural predisposition in the male sex, after the fashion of sociobiology. In any non-reductionist biology, which places the biological firmly *within* the diverse and changing practices of the social, we could never so neatly collapse social phenomena into any fixed biological category, like that of 'male'. In Chapter 4, I mentioned the many social relations, social practices and definitions through which men build up their sense of masculinity, and acquire (to whatever extent) the more characteristically 'masculine' strength, confidence, assertiveness and positions of power. These diverse processes could not possibly produce any single, uniform, unchanging behaviour pattern in *all* men. Even the most intransigent separatists know that it does not. (Irritatingly, these writers often list their own men friends and companions as the sole exceptions to their own rules – leaving other women's male companions, and hence other women themselves, as suspect!)[43]

In the early days of contemporary feminism, some radical feminists in the US, Jill Johnstone among them, described man as 'the biological aggressor'; but this was a minority view.[44] A slightly more popular view was that of Shulamith Firestone which saw women's subordination tied inevitably to their reproductive biology.[45] Turning Firestone's argument on its head, Brian Easlea and others today have argued that it is men's lack of the 'magical power' of giving birth and suckling infants which creates men's terrifying vulnerabilities and insecurities. They must find substitutes for the babies they cannot bear: men therefore 'give birth' to science, to weapons, to atom bombs – to assuage their insecurities.[46] Easlea's analysis is influenced by the type of essentialism now more prominent in feminist writing. We have seen its apotheosis in Andrea Dworkin's intense despair, 'violence is male and the male is the penis', alongside Mary Daly's romantic delight, 'the source of wholeness [of rootedness in the earth] is within women'.[47] All these sentiments are continually expressed by most of the women in the two books from Greenham.

The 50 Greenham women whose voices are heard in *Women at the Wire*, published in 1984, are nearly all agreed that 'you don't achieve disarmament unless you remove the desire and need for men to fight'.[48] Men are 'out of contact with Life'; only women remain connected to the forces of life. A religious celebration of women's spiritual strength is expressed frequently in the two books on Greenham, while the idea that the problem of nuclear missiles *is* the problem of male violence 'from rape of individual women to the rape of the planet' is pervasive. As women from Greenham wisely link up their own struggle with the international struggle against nuclear missiles, they less wisely see this as enabling them to 'build up a picture of male violence all over the world'.[49] A vulgar feminism, or sex reductionism, prevails, where 'patriarchy', men's control over women, explains anything and everything: 'I know why there is militarism and imperialism and racism and sexism. I know why all the negative "isms" exist. It is because of patriarchy – male rule.'[50]

More cautiously, but along similar lines, Alice Cook and Gwyn Kirk summarise the sentiments which keep women at Greenham in *Greenham Women Everywhere*, published in 1983:

> Some think of this role in a more mystical sense, a belief in women's spiritual insight and connectedness to the forces of life. This strand has roots in the earliest matriarchal religion ... Some see the campaign against cruise missiles as part of their wider opposition to all forms of male violence. Some believe that women have innate good qualities and are better qualified than men to take up this issue. Others feel that women are less aggressive and more caring on account of their conditioning rather than any innate biological characteristics.[51]

Providing an eloquent and moving description of the horror of women's lives in Holloway Prison whilst herself in jail after a Greenham protest, Carole Harwood in *Women at the Wire* saw a common link behind the plight of all the women prisoners: 'The common link had a gender, it was male.'[52] Carole Harwood is a socialist feminist, and yet the common links of class and race oppression the majority of women prisoners share dissolved before the Greenham gaze.

The Greenham filter is right to perceive that military values are 'manly' values. They promote the 'rational' use of force, skill and technology to establish power over others. Military institutions, at least in their most visible form, exist to preserve and train men in the use of violence: to kill, maim and otherwise coerce, discipline and harm other people on orders, as requested, without explanation. They are, it would seem, the quintessence of male power. But such a feminist filter fails to perceive much that is also important to any understanding of modern warfare, nuclear missiles and the arms race. Descriptions of the 'needs' and 'mentality' of men leave us with no analysis of modern militarism and its current threat. Wars do not occur because men are eager to fight; on the contrary, military aggression always requires carefully controlled and systematic propaganda, at state level, which plays upon public fears, vulnerabilities, pride and prejudice. As Martha Gellhorn concludes from her 50 years as a war correspondent:

> There is no record of hordes of citizens, on their own, mobbing the seat of government to clamour for war. They must be infected with hate and fear before they catch war fever. They have to be taught that they are endangered by an enemy, and that the vital interests of their state are threatened.[53]

The military has never, and now less than ever, been able to rely upon men's supposed needs and mentality to obtain the number and quality of recruits it would like, without the help of 'economic conscription' through unemployment. The male image of militarism, jealously guarded, also serves to deny or obscure women's relation to nationalism and militarism.

Uses and Abuses of Biological Reasoning

Yet the belief that the human male has evolved with, and because of, genetically programmed hunting and killing instincts is remarkably widespread. It is constantly propped up by popular science, in and outside academic institutions. '*Man is man*', Robert Ardrey, Lionel Tiger, Robin Fox and others inform us, '*because for millions upon millions of years we [sic] killed for a living.*'[54] It is a heritage which is hotly disputed, despite its instant fascination for the twentieth-century urban male. Other research suggests that early humans were not aggressive hunters at all, but rather seed eaters and foragers as well as hunters, sharing their food in ways quite unlike other primate groups.[55] Richard Leakey argues that 'sharing, not hunting or gathering as such, is what made us human'.[56]

And were a 'killing instinct' a part of *man*'s heritage, we would have to conclude that modern man is remarkably ambivalent about his legacy. Boxing and wrestling may have their fans, and some men may still enjoy the violence and aggression of direct combat, but killing is not popular. John Keegan, who lectures in War Studies at Britain's elite military college, Sandhurst, points out that

> Killing people, *qua* killing and *qua* people, is not an activity
> which seems to carry widespread approval ... it is worthy of note
> that the one sort of front line soldier who has some choice over
> whether he will kill or not – the officer – has ... consistently and
> steadily withdrawn himself from the act itself.[57]

And he later adds: 'Battle, always unpleasant for a minority of the
participants, has increasingly become an intolerable experience
for the majority.'[58] But such reports of real men in real wars sit
colourlessly beside the eagerly appropriate man-as-ape stories
which have never done justice even to apes, but which confirm
our conventional mythologies of sex and society.

Of all the biological mythologies that surround human
behaviour and social arrangements, the one that 'man' is
inevitably aggressive, whereas 'woman' is not, is the most
tenacious. Throughout this book I have repeatedly encountered
and criticised the appeal of biological reductionism. Here, where
it appears in its most intractable form, I want for the last time to
re-examine in some detail the arguments for and against it. One
common criticism which has been made of biological
reductionism is that it has been used primarily to justify male
dominance and to condemn any attempt at change. Lynda Birke
and Jonathan Silvertown, for example, suggest that if male
domination is a product of male biology, 'Feminist hopes for a
better future would, then, be in vain'.[59] Certainly, as I too have
argued in my criticism of cultural feminism, it is a pessimistic
view: it implies that we feminists cannot expect men, even lovers
and comrades, to join us in the struggle to change themselves and
sexist practices generally. But it would not necessarily preclude
all possibility of change; part of the attraction of biological
reductionism is that it can be used as a way of engineering and
organising for social change. It can also serve to heighten the
criticism of things as they are, when other ideas involving the
complexity and contradictions of changing social practices
suggest only a slow and difficult progress.

The reappearance of a more essentialist and separatist
feminism suggests that such reductionism can serve as a
motivating force for change, at least of a sort. The biological,
however purely conceived as biological, can be altered,
controlled, manipulated, perhaps avoided or eliminated. It may
even be simpler to conceive of types of biological intervention

and avoidance than of social transformation, even of obviously social problems. For example, apart from a feminist strategy of avoiding all contact with what is biologically male, it is not impossible to conceive of women gaining control of reproductive technology to eliminate the majority of men – as many a feminist utopia has hinted at.[60] Or, we could simply feed men regular doses of oestrogen, or perhaps merely the huge quantities of valium which women are currently swallowing to curb men's aggression. However great the obstacles in the way, it is now a perfectly possible and practicable goal for feminists to work towards the elimination or control of the Y sex chromosome, if we believe that it is this that is responsible for human destructiveness. Biological reductionism then, far from precluding change, provides a very clear route towards it. It is important to emphasise that what is wrong with biological reductionism is not its conservative acceptance of things as they are, but rather its strategic unacceptability and theoretical limitations. Politically, if taken seriously, it tends towards the fascistic and authoritarian (for conservatives, radicals and feminists alike), and, conceptually, it relies upon a flawed biology.

Robert Ardrey and Desmond Morris have used research on animals they see as closest to man to conclude that 'human nature' is inevitably territorial, hierarchical, aggressive and sexually differentiated in ways that promote dominance and sexual promiscuity in males, and dependence and sexual passivity and nurturance in females. The massive popularity of their writing, however, is only a magnification of ideas already invested with all the authority of the scientific establishment. It is an authority which has been in ascendance ever since the acceptance of Darwin's theory of evolution helped displace the former authority of religion and belief in God's creation of man as the centre of the universe.

Professor Konrad Lorenz, described by Sir Julian Huxley as 'the father of modern ethology, the study of animals in their natural setting, that rapidly growing branch of science which is destined to provide a strong foundation for the science of human behaviour and psychology', first published his 'scholarly' and popular *On Aggression* in 1963.[61] There he concluded that all animals are 'status seekers' and all are therefore innately aggressive. Lorenz believed that the human invention of modern weapons of warfare may mean that 'man's innate killing inhibitions' were now insufficient to control his 'innate aggression':

> No selection pressure arose in the pre-history of mankind to breed inhibitory mechanisms preventing the killing of conspecifics [one's own species] until, all of a sudden, the invention of artificial weapons upset the equilibrium of killing potential and social inhibitions. When it did, man's position was very nearly that of a dove which, by some unnatural trick of nature, has suddenly acquired the beak of a raven.[62]

Lorenz also believed that 'in prehistoric times intra-specific selection bred into man a measure of aggression drive for which in the social order of today he finds no adequate outlet'.[63] With other ethologists Lorenz described the inevitability of greater aggression and dominance in males as compared to females: 'there is an expression, taken from animal behaviour, for the contemptible, really submissive man: he is called henpecked, a metaphor that well illustrates the *abnormality* of male submissiveness, for a real cock does not let himself be pecked by any hen, not even his favourite.'[64] And so the courteous professor contemplates his cockish legacy (adding 'Incidentally, cocks lack the inhibition against fighting hens'!)

Lorenz saw most aspects of human conduct, whether sport, friendship, loyalty, or militant enthusiasm as all signs of innate aggression: 'We do not know how many important behaviour patterns of man include aggression as a motivating factor, but I believe it occurs in a great many.'[65] Lorenz's belief is hardly surprising, when almost anything which men habitually do in their positions as the most powerful group in society is included in Lorenz's ill-defined and imprecise definition of 'aggression'. And it is true, and a confusing aspect of all our reflections on 'aggression', that the word may be used to mean many different things. They may not be negative, destructive or physically combative; they may be assertive, creative and intellectually stimulating. In ethological research, however, 'aggression' is mostly used synonymously with 'dominance'.

It was back in 1922 that a 'pecking order' was first reported and widely publicised in farmyard chickens.[66] In the next few decades ethology grew rapidly. Hierarchies of 'dominance' were soon 'observed' in nearly every animal group, vertebrate and invertebrate. However, what was being described as 'dominance' behaviour varied enormously, and, as Hinde critically responded to fellow ethologists, even within one species correlations between different measures of 'dominance' in the very same animal were low.[67]

The problem with most of the ethological studies is their obvious projection of characteristics of particular value and significance to humans back on to animals, where they can then be 'discovered' and used to explain human society. This practice is known as anthropomorphism. And so we read of 'baboon harems, propaganda-making ants, prostitution in humming birds or gang rape in mallard ducks', as Steven Rose illustrates the process.[68] To preserve this anthropomorphism, differences between animal societies and human societies, indeed between one animal group and another, even one type of ape and another are played down. As the biologist Washburn concludes: 'Animal behaviour is extraordinarily diversified, and almost any thesis may be defended if an author is free to select the behaviour of any animal that supports the contention of the moment.'[69] Other biologists, like de Vore and Reynolds, have made it clear that, for example, ape societies vary considerably: some like orangutangs do not form groups at all, while chimpanzee groups are more open and less structured than baboon groups, and even male baboons are less aggressive and territorial in the wild than in captivity. The same is true for non-human primate patterns of sex and parenting, which 'may vary from near-promiscuity to consort relations of varying duration, to lifelong pair bonds'.[70]

So whatever biological characteristics one might want to attribute to both apes and humans, these are not uniquely determining of any particular type of social or sexual arrangements – even in apes. It is not that there are no similarities between the behaviour of apes and that of human beings, or that any similarities are irrelevant (though we could never leap from an observed similarity to infer a common cause). But it is the case that the differences between apes and men, ape males and human males, to put it for the moment as simply as possible, far outweigh the similarities – however appealing it is to play ape. And yet, as Rosalind Coward wittily comments in

The Sex Life of Stick Insects, we are bombarded daily in our living rooms with the perennially popular nature programmes obsessively concerned to 'reveal' a natural world of male dominance and the inevitability of sexual difference.[71]

In the mid seventies sociobiology emerged within the natural sciences, promising new methodological sophistication and a new formula for uncovering the biological imperatives underlying all human and animal behaviour. Heralding also a new conservative climate both within and outside the social sciences, the publication of E.O. Wilson's *Sociobiology, the New Synthesis* in 1975 initiated a renewed scientific interest in and respectability for biological reductionism. This new formula connected population genetics and evolutionary theory. (E.O. Wilson was, like Alfred Kinsey, an entomologist, and convinced that 'the same principles of population biology and comparative zoology' which explained the rigid 'social systems' of insects also explained the social systems of humans. Is there something in the study of insects, the most ubiquitous group of animals on earth, which feeds the all-encompassing theoretical ambitions of their taxonomists?) The essence of sociobiology is the importance it places on genetic determinism. For E.O. Wilson genetic determination 'is decisive'.[72]

Sociobiology argues that Darwin's evolutionary theory of the survival of the fittest operates at a 'kin' rather than a purely individual level. This means that any behaviour which confers a reproductive advantage, that is, encourages the maximum transfer of the genes which individuals share with their closest relatives, will be genetically favoured and survive. Altruistic behaviour therefore occurs because in helping close relatives individuals are, genetically speaking, helping themselves. The less close the genetic relationship, however, the greater the hostility and aggression between individuals. The evidence for these 'laws' of genetics, sociobiologists believe, can be found in the universal importance attached to kinship systems and the universal prohibition on incest, as well as the larger size of the male, greater male promiscuity and aggression alongside female commitment to monogamy and prolonged childrearing. These practices all secure reproductive advantage.

So there is, Wilson and others now assert, a genetic basis to kinship patterns and incest taboos. But neither contemporary understanding of genetics nor the findings of any other social science support this view. Advances in genetic theory now reject the equation of single genes with specific behaviour patterns made by sociobiologists, while anthropologists like Marshall Sahlins and Mervin Harris make nonsense of the idea that any kinship systems or incest prohibitions follow, or even remotely resemble, what one would expect on genetically determined principles of kin selection.[73] As the feminist anthropologist Gayle Rubin has observed: 'A kinship system is not a list of biological relatives. It is a system of categories and statuses which often contradict actual genetic relationships.'[74] (In different cultures, 'father', 'mother', 'sister', and 'brother', may all be used to refer to people with whom there is no biological connection.) When sociobiology cannot explain the very social phenomena supposed to supply its basic evidence, the wider sweep of its social speculations becomes thoroughly unconvincing.

'Throughout history,' Wilson asserts, incorrectly, 'warfare, representing only the most organised technique of aggression, has been endemic to every form of society ...'[75] (In fact there are many societies, for example the Eskimos, which do not engage in warfare.) In line with his genetic theories, Wilson believes that 'the force behind most warlike policies is ethnocentrism, the irrationally exaggerated allegiance of individuals to their kin and fellow tribesmen.' This in turn rests upon a 'hypertrophied biological predisposition'.[76] Human identity is of course tightly bound to the specific culture in which it arises, but we do not need to deny a certain fear and suspiciousness towards those we see as culturally different to insist that the uneven and inconsistent frequency of human warfare bears no relation to any underlying principle of innate aggression towards strangers. Conceiving of warfare as the organised expression of 'innately aggressive' tendencies tells us nothing useful about when and why wars have occurred.

Sociobiologists retort that while genes and biological predispositions are important in determining social behaviour and social structure, these do interact with the environment. This, Wilson argues, 'should satisfy both camps in the venerable nature-nurture controversy'.[77] But satisfaction is not thereby provided. The conception of the biological in sociobiology is as inadequate and impoverished as in any other form of biological reductionism.

The starting point for a non-reductionist biology, as I suggested in my opening chapter, is that it is not possible to separate the biological from the social. It is not that the biological is absent from human behaviour; we wax and wane like every other living thing, but our biological states are always transformed by the social practices surrounding them, and experienced through the social meanings attached to them. The biological alone is therefore never wholly determining of experience and behaviour. For example, all people must eat, but what we eat, how, when and where we eat, the phenomena of vegetarianism, dieting, dietary rules, obesity, anorexia, indeed any human practice or problem surrounding eating cannot even be adquately conceived of, let alone understood, only by talk of biological propensities.

Social practices and meanings do not merely interact with biological conditions in some additive way, as psychologists have traditionally assumed, attempting, like Hans Eysenck, to calculate the relative percentages of 'nature' and 'nurture'. They constitute them: in the view of the biologist Steven Rose 'everything is at the same time biological *and* social'.[78] Commenting on the genetically inexplicable dramatic increase in the average Japanese IQ over the last few decades, for example, Rose points out that the properties we attribute to individuals develop only within historical and social contexts. We could say, he concludes, that

> Whatever human nature is *now*, it is not the same as human nature was a hundred years ago, or five hundred, or a thousand years ago ... It is the constant transcendence of our nature by ourselves which is the unique human biological quality.[79]

These are the assumptions of a 'liberatory biology' today. It is one which would see that our very notion of 'aggression', with its complex, varied and perhaps subtle manifestations, is itself a human construction derived from a human context. For instance, it may seem superficially rational to connect up such diverse social phenomena as competitive sport, physical assault, the arms race and warfare with some inner propensity for aggression, but such a connection really serves to obscure rather than to clarify how such practices emerge, who engages in them, with what type of satisfaction, and how we might individually and collectively, as women and men, support or reject them. It also tells us nothing at all about the nature of modern warfare and arms production.

Gender Ideologies and Military Technologies and Training

There are two aspects of modern warfare that feminists in particular need to analyse: the essential role of ideologies of sexual difference in the preparations and productions for war and the continuing and increasing relation of women to the technologies of war.

The 'masculine' nature of the military has to be both fostered and protected by military institutions and the state. Military training for men is designed to promote a particular type of aggressive 'masculinity': 'woman', 'cunt' and 'queer' are the most frequent insults hurled at each new recruit by obediently sadistic drill sergeants.[80] Rigid maintenance of our sexualised dichotomies of male and female, strong and weak, active and passive, keeps homosexuality illegal in the armed services (despite its partial decriminalisation in Britain in 1967). Heterosexuality is conspicuously promoted via pornography, and the use of women prostitutes by male soldiers is either tolerated or encouraged. The toughening up of the male combat recruit is not only a preparation for military practices, but also necessary to maintain the image of 'military manhood' as the pinnacle of manly daring, the image necessary to attract new recruits eager to prove themselves 'proper men'. The image helps sustain the morale and self-esteem of the men already in uniform, most of whom, much of the time, will lead lives of relentless subservience, obedience and passive dependence – characteristics more typically attributed to 'women'.

We do not need to play down the cruelties and atrocities of men at war, many of them against women, like the 500 cases of *convicted* rape a month in the US army in Berlin in 1945, to accept that all men do not automatically love war.[81] Armies must work hard to prepare men for war. Richard Holmes in *Firing Line* reaches the pessimistic conclusion that harsh army training which systematically degrades groups of young men to 'their lowest common denominator' is still effective in preparing men for the brutality of military combat. But he also reveals that today's armies (like the US in Vietnam) are not very good at maintaining military morale. In Vietnam, men who showed themselves too eager for action, the Rambos, risked 'fragging' (murder by their own comrades): 'As many as 20 per cent of US officers killed in the war may have died at the hands of their own men.'[82]

Combat soldiers, however, form only a small segment of the mechanised giant created by modern military-industrial technologies. Inside modern armies, over 70 per cent of enlisted manpower is involved in non-combat jobs.[83] Aggression and violence are not characteristics suitable for such jobs. Outside the armed forces, in Britain and the US in particular, many leading industrial companies are involved in military-related production. Many non-military civilians are a vital part of our institutions of war. And both inside and outside military institutions, modern warfare relies increasingly on women's labour.

As we have seen in the two Great Wars, women have always served in times of war: as nurses and in other jobs in the front line of battle, or as wives and prostitutes sustaining male combatants and easing them back into battle. But the courage and suffering of the army nurse have been only shabbily acknowledged by the nations they have served, in order to separate women off from the 'real' work of war: 'men's work'. And the servicing by prostitutes and wives has been seen as little more than a necessary evil requiring varieties of regulation of women's conduct in the former case, and surveillance of their duties towards the army in the latter. Today, however, the continued production and sale of arms and constant global policing to preserve Western capitalist and Soviet bloc interests around the world require a whole new military involvement of women in what we know as 'peacetime'.

Women now compose nearly ten per cent of the American armed forces, and nearly five per cent of the British. Difficulties in recruiting manpower at the educational levels necessary in modern armies and falling birth rates in industrial nations mean that those numbers are likely to rise. There is continuing pressure on military institutions to enlist more women.

The threat this poses to military strategists is not that women fall short as good and useful military recruits, not at all, as we should know from the role of women in guerrilla and liberation armies around the world. It is rather that women's presence in the established armed forces of the state threatens the maintenance of that 'masculine' image of military life essential for the morale and incentive of men. Men need to believe that their job is necessary for the protection of women, and a job they alone can do, as Cynthia Enloe has described so well in *Does Khaki Become You?* In the words of General Barrow on the problem of women in the army, quoted by Enloe: 'It tramples the male ego. When you get right down to it, you've got to protect the manliness of war.'[84]

But the manliness of war is not so easily protected nowadays, when the British army and navy have finally agreed to train women in the use of handguns (on a voluntary basis only) and when women operate the control panels of nuclear missile warheads in American bases around the world.[85] Even if the front line combat soldier remains a male soldier, as is likely, the women at the 'rear' are engaged in jobs far more deadly. Long range weapons in fact mean that there is no meaningful war zone, no rear, no tail, no way the soldier boys at the 'front' could function to protect 'their' women 'back home'.

Much of the microelectronic assembly line production of modern armaments is also work traditionally seen as women's work. This means that it is of course low paid, and is also fiddly and monotonous, requiring manual dexterity and causing eye strain and many other health hazards. Exploited not only in Britain and America, but far more so in Hong Kong, Singapore, South Korea, the Philippines and elsewhere throughout the Third World, women workers are becoming the backbone of huge multinational electronics 'defence' industries. Women's jobs around the world are increasingly dependent upon the production of armaments; and women need jobs.

The expansion of jobs, particularly for women, is a component of the expansion of 'defence' spending and arms production. So much is this so that the upping of defence spending in the US was justified, for example by Secretary of Defence Caspar Weinberger, in terms of job creation. It seems to me important that feminists, and peace activists generally, attempt to understand what rational, or apparently rational, economic, political and ideological forces lie behind militarism and the arms race, and what real stake people have in them, if we are to successfully organise against their deeper irrationality.

Arms production today is so integrated with commercial industrial production, at least in advanced industrial economies, that it has been described by peace theoreticians like Mary Kaldor and E.P. Thompson as having its own autonomous, internal, economic logic and dynamic, quite unconnected to any external threat or opponent. Certainly between East and West, the US and the USSR, there is not at the moment any real competition for resources; nor has any genuine territorial dispute provoked the current unprecedented US arms expansion. Once established, Thompson argues, the new 'Satanic Mills' of destruction have their own momentum. They cannot be closed down, or slowed down, without threatening surrounding employment and the economy more generally.

Long before each new and monstrous weapon system is completed (often to be scrapped), its manufacturers will already have planned some bigger, 'better' follow-on. The baroque weapons themselves, Mary Kaldor argues, like the 100 billion dollar MX missile system and the untransportable Trident submarine (too large to remove from the channel where it was built), are militarily vulnerable and inefficient, despite their gargantuan destructive potential.[86] Reagan's 'Star Wars' project, though requiring a gigantic increase in arms expenditure and threatening to curtail the former strategy of mutual 'deterrence' between the superpowers by making a first-strike nuclear attack survivable, has little chance of achieving its goal: intercepting 'enemy' nuclear missiles. (Britain, however, has hastened to accept the technological contracts already flowing from it.) Already over 600 billion dollars is spent annually on military expenditure, while in the US about 30 per cent of all scientists and engineers, and 10 per cent of *all* production workers, service the weapons industry.[87] And in Britain a staggering 50 per cent of all government-funded research and development money (£2.1 billion in 1985) is spent on defence, and is responsible for the disastrous under-investment in new technology in British industry generally.[88] Nor is it easy, as workers at Vickers in Britain have found, to switch from military production (where costs do not matter so much) to commercial production which is subject to the competition of the market-place.[89] Entirely internal, economic considerations are therefore important in the production of weapons; men and women each have some stake in this production. As women workers at British Aerospace commented when the Falklands war brought home to them more fully the lethal nature of their work, they could not afford to lose their jobs. Indeed many of them saw CND as threatening to take away their livelihood.[90]

Arms Production and the State

Before 1945 the traditional marxist explanation of militarism was in terms of the economic needs of capitalist states for imperialist expansion to obtain raw materials and access to new markets. Major wars occurred between competing imperialist powers. After 1945 the analysis was extended to stress the military force needed to retain control over colonial or former colonial territories. The successful anti-imperialist struggles occurring in the Third World usually received some support from the Soviet bloc. Militarism was thus seen as necessary for capitalism, and escalating post-war arms spending as functional for capitalism as a whole. The 'permanent arms economy' theory advanced by several marxists in the late sixties even argued that it was arms spending which had stabilised post-war capitalism.[91] But while it is true that arms spending has been used, for instance by the US in the 1940s and 1980s, to ward off recession, there is other evidence that arms spending also involves economic costs.

Among the major Western countries the US and UK spend the highest proportion of national income on the military, and they have the two slowest growing economies in the West, while low military spenders like Japan and West Germany have done well.[92] Military investment creates fewer jobs than other forms of industrial investment, while diverting urgently needed resources away from them. Indeed it is the weakening of post-war US economic dominance, in some degree due to their military costs in Vietnam and elsewhere, which has strengthened European and Japanese capital, making it more competitive with the US.[93] Reagan's renewed militaristic and Cold War offensive derives in part from the threat to US economic and political dominance from other Western economies. On their own, neither the search for internal economic growth nor external economic gain can any longer explain the ever-increasing military spending and military interventions of the major world power, the US. The costs of Vietnam grossly exceeded any possible economic gain, as did the (still mounting) costs of the Falklands war for Britain.

Recently, more sophisticated marxist analysis has rejected a strictly economic analysis to emphasise the political and cultural basis of militarism. After 1945, US world dominance was as much geared towards preserving the political and cultural relations of other capitalist states (many of them, like West Germany, Japan, Italy, Greece, shaken up or collapsing immediately after the war) as towards securing the immediate economic gains of open markets for US goods, cheap labour and raw materials. Three predominant threats to Western capitalism lie behind the post-war tenfold increase in US military spending: the ideological (rather than military) threat of an alternative economic system in Eastern Europe and China; the economic and ideological threat of successful liberation movements in the Third World; internal class conflict and other movements of resistance at home.[94]

The political and cultural role of militarism in preserving internal social relations within nation states (whether capitalist or state bureaucratic) is a significant one. In both Britain and the US in the 1980s the Cold War rhetoric of external danger has served to justify increasing attacks upon the labour movement, the freedom of the press, and civil liberties generally. As we saw during the miners' strike in Britain, the notion of 'the enemy within', resuscitated from the days of McCarthy, has been used to justify attacks on all those in conflict with the interests of current ruling groups and to ally them with 'the enemy without' – the Soviet Union. The armed forces also function to inculcate the values of discipline, hierarchy and national interest, most importantly into young working class men deciding to enlist rather than face the misery of permanent unemployment. Patriotic militarism helps to divert struggles against class, race, sex, age and regional hierarchies into the shared warm glow of national identity, pride and patriotism. More obviously, the army, like the police, keeps internal order when used for strike-breaking or against spontaneous insurrections (drawing, in Britain, upon the tactics learnt for controlling the Republican movement in Northern Ireland).

Modern military institutions thus exist to preserve the interests of individual nation states – externally within a system of nation states, as in US attempts to preserve their 'influence' throughout most of the world, or Britain's craven US bootlicking to preserve its own image as a 'world power', and, internally, maintaining the nation's political, social and economic relations.

Women as much as men are committed to what they see as the 'national interest'. We all saw the wives and 'sweethearts' who waved their 'boys' off into a ludicrous, faraway battle by air, land and sea against teenage Argentine conscripts, to defend a few sheep farms, and to be 'winners'. They warn us of the folly in the faith so fondly expressed by Nottingham WONT feminists: 'women have less vested interests in the present system, and are more easily able to criticise it.'[95] More telling by far is Stuart Hall's trenchant reminder that 200 years of British imperialist conquest has meant that 'imperial splendour penetrated into the bone and marrow of the national culture'.[96] Women exist within and share that culture. Britain's imperial heritage helped Thatcher to win a genuinely popular (not simply male) support for her vision of a stronger, more powerful, technologically streamlined, more capitalist British nation. A little more sacrifice from the poor and the weak, a little more support for American militarism, now that the US has imposed the God-given justice of its own period of world dominance, and Britain can be Great again. Such was the fantasy of many British women and men, at least for a while following the Falklands war.

Militarism and arms production in the UK are thus about strengthening – or, more accurately, creating the illusion of strengthening – the existing British state to maintain its influence over other nations. Those who design and produce our nuclear weapons systems are not mad or monstrous, however mad and monstrous their products. They believe that it is right and necessary to advance the interests of their own nation and their own systems, and nowhere is this clearer than in the rigid hierarchies and ideologies of its military institutions.

Women have no power or authority within any state army, including the Israeli army. There is not a single woman in the

NATO command structure. But, neither the power of men in relation to women in all our state institutions – reaching its pinnacle in the army – nor the internal or external coercive and repressive role of the army undermines the appeal of nationalism to most women. The state and its army are not the self-evident enemy of women. Indeed state violence, in its most obvious form, would appear to be used most often against men, on strike, or rioting in the streets, or resisting British-backed Loyalist dominance and discrimination in Northern Ireland.

Whatever men's power in the state, a sense of national identity is not of significance only to men. We all need a sense of belonging, to overcome our human anxiety about existence and mortality. Outside our idea of the family, which at birth we do not choose to enter but to which we nevertheless belong, and for which – particularly as women – we sacrifice ourselves, the nation provides a collective identity to which we also belong, again beyond personal choice, and for which we are expected to make sacrifices. Nationalism thus meets existential needs in both women and men. For women as for men the nation seems to hold a key to the significance and meaning of life beyond individual effort and self-interest: a key to the future for our children, the purpose of our labour, the promise of a type of immortality. The primary significance of war in relation to the nation is, as Australian philosopher Ross Poole has argued, 'not so much as an outlet for primeval (male) destructiveness, but rather to provide an arena for self-sacrifice'.[97] Such self-sacrifice establishes that there is something which can transcend, and hence justify, individual existence. When surviving soldiers recall their wartime experience, what they exult in is the intense comradeship, self-sacrifice and love they felt, a love which had 'no limits, not even death'.[98] What is celebrated in the ritual commemorations of war is the sacrifice required of a loyalty and love beyond individual existence:

> War is not so much the construction of a new and virulent form of masculinity, as the recovery for masculine identity of that relational form of identity constructed within the family. It is, in this sense, the return of the feminine.[99]

Trying to understand the appeal of nationalism can give us some clues on how to combat militarism and arms production.

We need to do more than condemn the weapons of war, and their symbolic link to masculinity. We have to tackle the twin sides of nationalism: to see how it is used by dominant elites to promote their economic and political interests over other nation states and to deny internal conflict, while also serving to provide a collective identity which can inspire sacrifice and service to others – appealing to both women and men. British nationalism in the first half of the eighties is harnessed to the Thatcherite rhetoric of 'the rebirth of Britain', the idea that Britain must and can assert itself as a dominant power in the world. In fact Britain's power in the world today, as Reagan repeatedly reminds us, derives *solely* from Britain's uncritical support for US global dominance and aggression. But while ruling groups of any nation have always used nationalism to deny the reality of unequal, racist, sexist and class-divided societies, and have constructed national enemies to enable the expansion of their own power base internationally, national identities are also constructed from other, rival histories which involve comradeship, and opposition to exploitation and the denial of individual rights and needs.

Co-operative, caring and egalitarian ideals are also part of every nation's history: in Britain, they were asserted in the socialist vision of many working-class struggles from the Owenites to the present, as they are asserted in the feminist vision of an end to male dominance. They inform us that we can at least conceive of a different Britain: a Britain where democratic and collective control over the means of production and the resources available for meeting social needs creates useful work and richer and more fulfilling personal lives and relationships. This vision has been a part of the British imagination from the Diggers' struggle in St George's Hill in 1949 to the Docklands struggle today, where local residents, led by women, are fighting for control over the planning and use of their community.[100] Combating militarism and the arms race is part of building this new Britain: a Britain which finally, once and for all, sheds its brutal imperial past for a socialist Britain free from race and sex exploitation.

Can Women Prevent War?

I do not dismiss the very real hopes of many women and men

that it is women who will, in the last resort, do most to save us from the ultimate catastrophe to which militarism and the arms race seem headed: the intentional or unintentional extermination of life on earth. We may be forced to agree that women share in the patriotism and commitment to national interest which sustains militarism and condones war. We may have to agree that neither men's biology nor men's psychology, in themselves, explain the entrenchment of arms production in capitalist and state bureaucratic societies. We may even agree that it is feminist rejection, rather than affirmation, of notions of the separate and different nature and greater vulnerability of women which most threatens the morale of men at arms and the motivation for militaristic thinking. We may agree on all these things, and yet we may still appeal to women's values, to maternal values, to save humanity. However much the supposed peacefulness of women may have failed anti-war feminists in the past, might it not this time be easier for women to see and to challenge the global destruction which so mocks their reproductive and nurturing role?

Jean Bethke Elshtain, for example, uses the notion of 'maternal thinking' to argue that the context of satisfactory mothering provides women with a 'way of knowing' which more readily connects the everyday and the concrete with the larger issue of war. Mothers desire preservation and growth. It is these qualities of maternal thinking which feminists must shift out into the wider political arena. They must not therefore reject 'traditional femininity and motherhood' as a means of challenging 'the militaristic state and militaristic policies and thinking'.[101] Elshtain draws upon the work of Sara Ruddick, who has argued that feminists should demand that women join armed combat units, in order 'to pacify the forces'. Women have learned from their mothers 'the activity of preservative love and the maternal thinking that arises from it', and are therefore more peaceful than men.[102]

Ruddick's argument is less convincing than it need be. This is because she relies upon a fixed role theory model of mothering (which, ironically, Elshtain has, in other articles, and towards other goals, demolished) and because she makes peculiar use of Carol Gilligan's model of women's cognitive and moral development. 'Daughterly peacefulness begins in early experiences of preservative love expected from and bestowed by mothers and other female caretakers';[103] mothers, and others, nurture according to the dictates of ideology. Surprisingly, Ruddick argues that:

> it is increasingly clear that a tendency to abstract is integrally connected to our desire and capacity to wage war. Willing warriors are loyal to abstract causes; they develop a generalised hatred for an abstract 'enemy' that allows them to kill.[104]

This makes no sense to me. I find its opposite equally, or even more, plausible. We might as convincingly argue that 'it is increasingly clear that a tendency to abstract is integrally connected to our desire and capacity to pursue *peace*. Willing warriors are loyal to *concrete* causes, they develop a generalised hatred for a *concrete* "enemy" that allows them to kill.' Abstraction could be seen as a characteristic necessary for us to *connect* ourselves, through love and co-operation, with the whole of humanity. And 'enemies' are usually described in very immediate and concrete terms: 'slit-eyes', 'wops' and 'commies' bring extremely concrete images to mind. 'The Ayatollah sucks' (spray-painted across the USA) doesn't sound too abstract to me, nor does Reagan's rhetoric of the 'Mad Dog' Gadafy, which US journalists syndicated around the country before the bombing of Libya in 1986. I see no reason why women's supposedly greater 'concrete-mindedness' and 'field-dependence' (ideas which Ruddick borrows from Gilligan) establish women's greater peacefulness. (At the risk of repetition, I must also add that empirical studies suggest that these traits which supposedly differentiate women from men vary more within the sexes than they differentiate between them.)

Ruddick's final argument is no more successful in establishing her case. She argues that 'female sexuality' tends more to 'eroticize submission than conquest', and this is not a sexuality or eroticism appropriate for battle. Again, I cannot agree. The motivation most typically required of men on the battlefield *is* to a very considerable extent a submissive and masochistic one, a willingness to die. What does Ruddick make of one of the most compelling battle chants of all times?

> Forward, the Light Brigade!
> Was there a man dismay'd?
> Not tho' the soldier knew

Some one had blunder'd:
Theirs not to make reply,
Theirs not to reason why,
Theirs but to do and die:
Into the valley of Death
Rode the six hundred ...
Into the jaws of Death,
Into the mouth of Hell ...

It would be hard to beat that for eroticised masochism, a dangerous passion to encourage in man or woman, in or out of the armed forces!

The weakness of Ruddick's arguments notwithstanding, the idea persists that at least this time round it must be womanly ways and maternal values that provide our last hope against the holocaust. 'Shall there be womanly times, or shall we die?' asks Ian McEwan's oratorio.[105] For Petra Kelly, as for Susan Griffin and Adrienne Rich and many other feminists today, the connection between women and peace is some sort of 'given' of female nature. 'Woman', Kelly argues, must lead the way to peace, for only she 'can go back to her womb, her roots, her natural rhythms, her inner search for harmony and peace ...'[106] By contrast, Elshtain and Ruddick reject any natural 'given' for the social context of mothering. But either way, if this were really our last hope, we would have cause for considerable alarm.

When, soon after the Falklands war, Hilary Wainwright interviewed the women who wire up the weapons for the big arms industries, including those working on nuclear weapons systems at Marconi, Ferranti, Lucas and British Aerospace, she found they expressed the contradictory extremes of both patriotism and humanitarian revulsion from war:

> Our attitude was that although it was unfortunate we were involved [in the war], once it was upon us we had to get on and do everything to back our boys. People were very willing to work overtime and do whatever was necessary, whether you've got a son involved or not, when it's the English, it's your boys, isn't it? I mean it could be your boy next time. I've got two sons and one of them would have been prepared to go. So you look at them as if they were your boys.[107]

Both extremes were justified in terms of a very concrete 'maternal thinking'.

In August 1985, Greenwich Council named a riverside walk by the Thames 'Hiroshima Parade' in memory of the victims and survivors of that first nuclear cataclysm. Local men and women objected fiercely. One woman appeared on the BBC news that evening expressing her outrage: 'After what they did to our boys, they should have dropped more bombs'. Another woman could be seen sneering at the local CND woman who was pleading for no more burnt and blasted children. A recent survey in the US by Virginia Sapiro of women's attitudes to welfare and legislation to improve the social and economic position of Black people and other minority groups in Illinois found that the mothers interviewed were slightly less favourable towards equality measures than the childless. Whatever sympathy some women have towards greater care and protection for the weak, the poor and the oppressed does not, then, seem to derive primarily from their status as mothers.[108]

The popular faith in women persists, however, because it is also true that women's values and maternal thinking *can* serve, at least some of the time, and in certain contexts, to inspire women to resist destructive and oppressive forces, especially on behalf of others. Nearly all feminists today are more likely to stress the importance of 'women-centred values' (nurturing values), by whatever complex route and at whatever cost women may have acquired (or failed to acquire) the virtues which accompany such values. Some of us would more readily admit, however, the possible contradictions within those values, like the many contradictions of women's consciousness itself.

The same values can have radical or conservative implications, depending upon political and historical context. Women's domestic and motherly habits of sharing, caring and loving (or at least our ideas about them) compared with what we often observe as men's more habitual public pursuit of individual achievement, wealth and power, have served as a basis for radical and conservative collective endeavours of women. It seems unwise, for the sake of some form of female chauvinism, to blur the distinctions between the two, even though there will always be contradictions within the lives and aspirations of individual women. Sheila Rowbotham, for example, has described how the women of the Women's Co-operative Guild could draw upon their own experiences in the home to place a greater emphasis on the values of gentleness, co-operation and caring in the trade union movement of the early twentieth century.[109] Yet these same values, she also points out, were those which had served to consolidate the oppressive restrictions on so many Victorian women. As Virginia Woolf had earlier argued, the notion of women's separate sphere not only meant women were 'locked in the private house'[110] but it also provided the essential and necessary justification for men's uninhibited pursuit of wealth, for the men who must 'bully and shove for their wives and families' in the other sphere, the ruthless world of the market-place.[111] The 'separate' spheres were and are conceptually and materially dependent on each other. Michèle Mattelart has pointed out, for example, that in the early 1970s it was through appealing to the symbols and values of women as mothers and housewives that women of the Chilean right played the decisive role inside Chile preparing for the fascist coup of General Pinochet in 1973, overthrowing the democratically elected socialist government of Salvador Allende.[112]

A politics of gender which stresses the importance of women's ways and female values can therefore either transcend or consolidate the social relations and social meanings of the male-dominated world which gives rise to them. Such a politics cannot, however, exist outside or be unaffected by dominant 'male-centred' values. Within the context of a radical and progressive movement concerned with the welfare and freedom of all humanity, such values can inspire strong and committed struggle against the forces of destruction and repression. The anti-nuclear movement in this Cold War climate provides just such a progressive context. Should more reactionary times overwhelm us (as they did women in Hitler's Germany and Mussolini's Italy, or as they do now in today's reactionary movements of the New Right), these very same values could inspire defensive, self-protective, puritanical repressiveness.

The many different women's groups who work for the New Right in the US, the UK, Australia and elsewhere, are usually composed of those who feel most threatened by women's irreversible (if financially precarious) moves towards greater independence and autonomy through access to jobs and control over fertility. One study of the 'pro-life' movement in the US found that the women involved were nearly all housewives who had married young, had non-professional husbands, relatively large families and fewer educational qualifications than the women they opposed.[113] It is in the name of *women*'s interests and the values of motherhood and homemaking that these groups of right-wing women not only oppose free contraception, divorce, abortion facilities, nursery services, homosexual rights, equal pay and equal training for women, but they almost all fully endorse the militarism of Thatcher and Reagan. Phyllis Schaffly, who led the successful battle to destroy the Equal Rights Amendment to the US Constitution, and who has inspired pro-life and pro-family groups worldwide, has told us that the nuclear bomb is 'a marvellous gift that was given to our country by a wise God'.[114] Yet Lynne Spender, in a recent anthology of feminist and anti-feminist aspirations and perspectives, assures us that 'The divisions between "radical" women and "conservative" women (all of whom see themselves as primarily concerned with women's options and status) need not be destructive ones.'[115] This claim was made at a time when some right-wing women had begun fire-bombing abortion clinics in the US! Her sister Dale Spender, and their editor on this occasion, Robyn Rowland, endorse this idea, and thereby evade the reality that right-wing women *do* want to destroy the gains women have made towards controlling their sexuality and fertility, and increasing their freedom to choose how they want to live and work.

Women's commitment to the welfare of their children and those they love may be important in bringing them into the battle against extermination. But neither an innate peacefulness nor any type of 'special nature' contingent upon women's mothering is our guarantee for human survival. What guarantees we have, I would argue, come from women's and men's engagement in a whole variety of political campaigns against militarism and arms production, and more. Certainly, feminists should support the women's peace movement, the peace camps, CND and other campaigns against the arms trade. But our political analysis and programme will need to do more than oppose nuclear missiles. We have to grapple with the grim reality that, despite the fast growth of anti-nuclear campaigns in Britain and Europe, American missiles have been installed throughout Europe, and the US nuclear programme has escalated (in spite of

Soviet offers of a moratorium on nuclear testing), culminating in Reagan's rejection in 1986 of existing arms limitation agreements under SALT II.

New political, economic and ideological initiatives are needed before any British government could, even if persuaded that it should, confront the renewed American determination to use military force against Nicaragua and most other liberation struggles in the Third World. This means that the women's peace movement should support transnational strategies like that of European Nuclear Disarmament (END), organising to dismantle superpower divisions through a Europe-wide programme for a nuclear-free Europe by dislodging American control of NATO or withdrawing from NATO. It means facing the difficulties of economic planning to convert military industries to other forms of production (when cutbacks in defence spending would cause major dislocation of much of British industry) and formulating a programme for major restructuring of the economy away from military production. It means the constant search for mass media outlets to counter the current wartime atmosphere being generated in the US by Reagan's Cold War rhetoric and manipulation of public opinion over the threat of terrorism. And it means attacking, as feminists always have, the public celebration of forms of aggressive masculinity which can be mobilised in the pursuit of violence. Winning real support for such strategies within the labour movement or any major political party will be achieved only through the united and determined efforts of the whole peace movement.

The two books written by the women from Greenham are now a few years old. Today, although the old sentiment 'women give life, men make death' is still popular, many peace women feel that Greenham politics has moved on and changed. The local groups which support Greenham have made contact with other women in struggle both nationally and internationally. In particular, throughout 1984 many Greenham supporters worked with the local Women Against Pit Closures groups during the miners' strike, and helped to organise several 'Mines Not Missiles' marches. Barbara Norden, for example, has argued that there has been a change of focus among peace women: 'the sort of feminism that saw the nuclear arms race as a direct expression of patriarchy has tended to give way to a more diverse brand of socialist feminism which has enabled "Greenham" to make links.'[116] As yet there is little feminist writing which presents this new and broader non-essentialist theoretical analysis linking a feminist, socialist, anti-imperialist and anti-nuclear politics, but the seeds are there in both the peace movement and the ecology movement.

The women who camped at Greenham Common exposed many of the contradictions of gender, often despite their own more traditional rhetoric of male vice and female virtue. They have shown that women can and must reject the type of 'protection' they have been told they need – whether from men, or from the state. They have lived collectively with other women, given up the domesticity and privacy of women's separate sphere. They have fought not simply for their own families and children, but for all. They have shown that quite new ways of living as women are possible, just as new ways of living for men have always been possible.[117] It was, interestingly, while patrolling the peace women at Greenham Common that one army officer recalls, in Tony Parker's recent collection of interviews with soldiers, that 'a number of soldiers who were usually the jolliest and noisiest were at Greenham very quiet and seemed to have been preoccupied with their own thoughts.'[118] The interviews tell us that many of the soldiers felt not only respect and even sympathy for the peace women, but were also led to question their own role as soldiers. But then, we will need to do more than soften the hearts of men, even of men soldiers, to prevent the huge escalation of arms technology already in operation to promote Reagan's Star Wars project.

6. Neither Foes Nor Loving Friends:

Feminism, the Left and the Future

> By the time we came to the milieu of women's politics, in
> the late seventies, it was already quite an uncomfortable
> place to be ... What we lack is a strategy for these times,
> and a means by which to put it into practice.
>
> Melissa Benn[1]

> Feminism *is* and *must* be a transformational politics which
> address every aspect of life. It is not simply a laundry list of
> so-called women's issues such as childcare and equal pay.
> While these issues are important, feminism is not a new
> ghetto where women are confined, to be concerned about
> only a select list of topics separated from the overall social
> and economic context of our lives. Similarly, feminism is
> not just an 'add women and stir' into existing institutions,
> ideologies, or political parties as they are.
>
> Charlotte Bunch[2]

As I sit here in the mid-eighties, pinning my hopes for the future
on the potential of socialist feminism to encourage engagement,
through autonomy and alliance, in the institutions and
movements of the left, another ample tome makes its
transatlantic crossing, pinning its hopes for the future on the
potential of a matricentric morality to defeat the curse of two
thousand years of patriarchy. Marilyn French's *Beyond Power*
calls upon the female procreative capacity and the female
pleasure principle to 'feminize the world' and thus save it from
destruction.[3] Is this so different from what I am saying?

I think it is. French explicitly rejects the belief (one she
bizarrely attributes to 'capitalist and socialist thinkers alike') that
the conditions of our lives determine consciousness.[4] She defines
patriarchy as a morality which worships power, and one which
has been dominant in nearly all societies for thousands of years,
affecting all people, both women and men. The grip of

patriarchal morality has determined social arrangements and wellbeing, and also means that the prospects for the success of feminism, which she defines as 'a revolutionary moral movement intending to use political power to transform society', are inevitably grim. So she tells us: 'The feminist vision of the world will not be realised in our lifetime, our century, or this millennium.'[5] Nor can feminists safely develop any sort of immediate political programme:

> Although some feminist groups consciously work towards immediate political goals, feminism as a philosophy does not include a political program for the construction of a more humane world. However gratifying such a programe might be in some ways, it would contradict feminist principles, for programs require uniformity and rigidity. In addition, any program devised in the present would be inadequate for future generations, because the minds of all of us currently alive are permeated with patriarchal values, categories, and methods.[6]

When social change does not in itself shift consciousness, when feminist priorities and strategies are suspect, when the 'feminine principle', French admits, is attributed to women by patriarchal thought, when the morality of power worship 'is contagious', it seems impossible to see what could ever shift patriarchy:

> If a worshipper of power decides to extend his power over your society, your choices are between surrendering and mounting an equal and opposite power. In either case, the power worshipper wins – he has converted your society into a people who understand that power is the highest good.[7]

No hope there!

No hope, because if we want to see how we as women can choose to change our lives we must jettison all our notions of unchanging predetermining forces which seal our fate: whether written in the stars or stemming from the fixed values of men. We need instead to focus our attention on the possibilities and significance of the here and now. For it is only in locating the changing and contradictory forces of the present moment, seen for instance in the uneven and unequal progress in the lives of women, that we find the pressure points which suggest how we might work for further change.

Feminism and the Wider Political Context

It is not possible, for instance, to separate the development and significance of feminist thought and action over the last 16 years from political change generally. Feminism re-emerged as a movement as part of the widespread political confidence at the close of the sixties, in trade union militancy, in an internationally oriented left radicalism, in grassroots 'community' activism and, new on the political horizon, in the assertion of the power of women and the demand for transformed personal and sexual politics. Old footage of any Vietnam mobilisation bears witness to the hopes and buoyance of that time, when the student-led demonstrators will be heard to enthuse: 'It is the duty of everyone to change things, to change everything'. The radical New Left was certain that no one could have any illusions about any kind of socialist Labour Party, not with Harold Wilson's support for American 'genocide' in Vietnam. A false feeling of strength was reinforced by the vacillation and final defeat of Edward Heath's Tory government in 1974. The government was brought down by the trade union movement, supported by every type of radical grouping, holding out against a wage freeze. Hopes were high. Different sections of the left, and the various groupings of the 'oppressed', the largest of them the women's liberation movement, could work for political change, it seemed, in the organisations they themselves created, loosely uniting with others when and as they chose.

Times change, and we change with them. The old vanguards, whether leninist organisations hoping to bring socialism to the labour movement, or anti-leninist libertarians hoping to inspire others by the demonstrations of alternative co-operative practices and to encourage the participation of those usually excluded from political power and decision-making, have had to think again.

No radical group today can afford to ignore party politics (apart from the pure anarchists, for whom 'whoever you vote for, the government gets in'). Too much of what we all took for granted has been tampered with and weakened: civil rights, welfare services, employment, even the hallowed institutions of representative democracy itself. But the more feminists become aware of the need for alliances in these bleak times, of the necessity for engagement with the institutions of the labour movement and the Labour Party (if only for defensive purposes), the harder it becomes to find the time and space to explore and develop our own politics, to sort through the complexities of 'feminism'. And the less space there is for open feminist debate and discussion over feminist ideas and strategy, the greater the pull of a more traditional and essentialist politics which ignores the contradictions within women's lives and feminist politics for the simpler notions of common sense: men and women are different, things would change if only women's differences were recognised and valued.

As I move towards some concluding thoughts on contemporary feminism I am nagged by feelings that it is all too late – too late to be clear what the problems, possibilities and priorities for feminism are. 'Feminism' as a concept is so nebulous, now that any sense of a united or coherent women's movement is so long gone. Many women think it uncool, old-fashioned, simplistic, or politically irrelevant to label oneself a feminist at all. Some see no use for feminism from the worldly viewpoint of the streetwise young woman individually struggling to survive and enjoy herself in more difficult times. Some reject all labels and overarching theories from the cognisant and sophisticated viewpoint of post-modernism. Some see feminists' major preoccupations and achievements as white and middle class. So much then for any nitpicking over distinctions between different types of feminism. But however nebulous the concept, however fragmented and weakened the movement, the terrain of 'feminist thought' remains so popular (and commercially successful) that teasing out its diverse implications seems to me all the more necessary, however hazardous and uncomfortable the enterprise.

Hester Eisenstein in her book *Contemporary Feminist Thought* traces the development of an early rejection of natural differences between women and men to a later celebration of them within popular radical feminist writing in the US. She suggests that the basic continuity and central weakness throughout this shift was 'a hostility to the political left and to marxism', combined with a focus on psychology and a false universalism.[8] This hostility to marxism, typified for example in Adrienne Rich's description of 'the deadendedness – for women – of marxism in our time', meant a retreat from political engagement and radicalism, in Eisenstein's view. However, others would accuse socialist feminists of an exclusive preoccupation with the issues of the left, and of therefore neglecting the need to create and sustain a flourishing women's culture. Beatrix Campbell, for instance, says that socialist feminism 'has disengaged from the life of the women's movement'.[9] But has either the rejection of the left or the search for alliance with it been quite so relevant as Eisenstein or Campbell suggest to the life and preoccupations of contemporary feminism?

Melissa Benn, encountering feminist politics in the late seventies, said, 'The first thing I remember having to grapple with was the concept of "political lesbianism". It wasn't not sleeping with men I couldn't deal with, it was identifying women that did it as the enemy.'[10] The sharp conflicts between radical feminists, in particular radical feminist separatists, and socialist feminists were not only over potential allies, or the compatibility or otherwise of socialism with feminism. The conflicts were as much over the perspectives and priorities of feminism itself, over whether we saw the sphere of the sexual and the problem of male violence as the root of women's oppression. And, as I suggested in Chapter 2, socialist feminism was itself in disarray by this time, with accusations of ethnocentrism and theoretical elitism causing conflict and division. And here the context in which feminists were developing their perspectives was crucial. By the end of the seventies, after the collapse of national women's conferences, there was less chance of any open dialogue within feminism. Many feminists were not so much giving up on or embracing the left, as burrowing deeper into more specialised areas – whether that was Women's Aid, Rape Crisis, or projects concerning health, housing, unemployment or women's cultural productions. This was the reason that the book *Beyond the Fragments* was initially popular as an idea with many feminists, despite the reality that a loose alliance of all the 'fragments' proved organisationally unworkable.[11]

It proved organisationally unworkable because in hindsight it is clear that *Beyond the Fragments* meant different things to different groups of feminists and socialists. The book, first published as a pamphlet in 1979, explored how those inspired by the women's movement and other radical socialist movements had organised for change throughout the 1970s. In women's centres, socialist centres, tenants' associations, workers' combine committees and resource centres of all kinds, which were mostly locally based, feminists and socialists had been active outside the institutionalised structures of the left and rejected leninist principles of revolutionary organisation which were concerned above all with questions of leadership; they stressed non-bureaucratic, participatory forms of organisation. *Beyond the Fragments* focused in general on the political implications of socialist feminism, and the assertion of women's interests for the understanding and making of socialism. Looking back, as the strength of localised grassroots struggle was already declining with the election of a far right Thatcher government, the book reflected the fast-fading hopes of the decade which had ended. But, looking forward, it crystallised the confidence some feminists had gained, including its three authors, that we could generalise our politics and didn't need to work only within a separate sphere of women's politics.

So people took up its message in many different ways. The book was criticised by some socialist feminists, for example by Elizabeth Wilson, for failing to stress the *difference* between feminist and socialist goals, and for not addressing the question of how to strengthen the women's movement itself, except 'as part of the woolly mass of libertarians'.[12] But it was also taken up by others, for whom it came to symbolise, against the original aspirations of its authors, the possibility of feminists joining and attempting to influence the totally male-dominated Labour Party. This was a time when the Bennite left was gaining in strength. Tony Benn himself was interviewed in *Spare Rib* and was campaigning to work with groups outside the Labour Party, while many of his better-known supporters then, like Peter Hain, rejected the exclusive emphasis on electoral politics for the need to pursue political activity at all levels. In this context, Jean McCrindle, for example, argued in a *Beyond the Fragments* bulletin in 1982: 'There *is* a structure for women's organisation within the Labour Party that has kept going over the years with pathetically small numbers – and the new influx of younger women partly affected by the women's movement could revive it.'[13] Still others saw *Beyond the Fragments* as justifying their dismissal of class and labour movement politics, though this was completely at odds with the intentions of its authors. We wanted to assert the validity and potential of the experience of the social movements, but alongside the validity and potential of working-class experience and struggle. And some saw *Beyond the Fragments* as confirmation of their own more sectarian libertarianism, in opposition to any and all organisational and political structures.

Debating Feminism Within the Left

Horrified by a second and larger parliamentary victory for Thatcher's government in 1983, even more feminists joined the Labour Party. The problem of there being little autonomous space for feminists to develop and communicate ideas, at least as they related to any political strategy of the women's movement, became even stronger. But I don't think the space for autonomous feminist politics declined *because* women joined the Labour Party, but rather the reverse. Many women, like myself, joined the Labour Party initially because of the absence of any organisational forms of forums for a broader feminist politics outside it. We didn't want to keep our feminism to ourselves. Particularly in local branches of the Labour Party, feminists have argued for a more open, campaigning and educative style of politics.

Despite what we often hear of the strengths of feminist ways of working and organising (frequently from people who have never attempted them), feminists have always had difficulties sustaining such practices except around very immediate and specific goals. At Essex Road Women's Centre in North London, for example, we occasionally joined with other women's groups to hold regional meetings and discuss the work we were doing, but, despite requests that we should keep meeting to share our knowledge and experiences, we were rarely able to follow the meetings up with any consistency or adequate levels of support. And once class and race and other differences between women began to emerge more clearly, feminist ways of organising through an unstructured participatory democracy within small groups became increasingly difficult. Divisive recriminations between women could not be resolved simply by an appeal to sisterhood. Feminism needed other theories which could encompass how sexual oppression exists within and alongside all other relations of oppression and exploitation, but without reducing the latter to a simple offshoot of sexual domination. And we needed other practices, building alliances with groups of women and men, not simply working from our own needs and experiences as women.

Ironically, as I have suggested in earlier chapters, a socialist feminist project which attempts to connect up a feminist analysis and strategy with a more traditional socialist analysis – to investigate how class, and belatedly race, are also *divided* by the hierarchy of gender – has often proved less popular than radical feminism with men on the left and in the Labour Party. This has been as true of those Labour leaders as of marxist theoreticians who, unlike many of their comrades, speak or write of feminism. Ken Livingstone, who has given valuable support to women's struggles in the Labour Party and on local councils, shares many feminists' immediate gut reaction to Andrea Dworkin's analysis of the timeless nature of male power and male violence which she sees portrayed in pornography – an analysis which most socialist feminists reject.[14] Perry Anderson, far more distanced from feminist debate and struggle, argues that the system of sexual domination operates primarily at an individual level, through marriage and the family: 'There is never any overall *centralization* of the structures of women's oppression: and this diffusion of it critically weakens the possibility of unitary insurgence against it.'[15] But from the very beginning socialist feminists argued that male power over women *is* centralised through state policies which make women caring for others in the home financially dependent upon men, as well as its being embedded in other structures of the workplace and the home which cannot be best understood as operating primarily at an individual level. Watching childbirth, pushing prams, putting children to bed, many men now relate sensitively to women and children in ways unthinkable to their fathers – yet the edifice of male power remains.

Women's oppression appears more inevitable and therefore 'natural' if we do see it as operating primarily at an individual level. Anderson's analysis allows socialist men to avoid re-examining their own thought on economic, political and ideological struggle, and to settle for an easier acceptance that men, alas, are tyrannical and obnoxious, that they do abuse women, but then again, socialism is about production; changing the social relations of production is about traditional forms of class struggle, involving the hardest push from the strongest sections of the working class. Men can support women in their struggle against male abuse (or Black people in their struggle against racism) but it is a different struggle.

Significantly, however, in the recent splits which have divided the Labour Party and the Communist Party (CP), feminism has been used by most of the leading protagonists to justify their own perspectives. Angela Weir and Elizabeth Wilson, who are feminists representing a minority split within the CP, have argued that feminism has been used by sections of the left to justify their own moves to the right, and in particular to criticise the trade unions and reject their forms of militancy.[16] From the other side of the CP, Beatrix Campbell has described the split as one between the 'old' and the 'new': traditional labour movement politics versus the politics of those who have rethought their socialism to take into account the analysis and importance of popular social movements – in particular, feminism, the peace and anti-racist movements.[17]

Certainly, some men as well as women both in the CP and sections of the Labour Party have been making increasingly strong criticisms of the traditions of labourism and an economistic class consciousness as inevitably excluding women, Black people and all those with little or no industrial bargaining power. At the same time there has been a return to what can be seen as traditional class politics in recent years, as first Arthur Scargill and the NUM, and then the most economistic and backward-looking Trotskyist group, Militant, in power in Labour-controlled Liverpool Council, became the two most prominent groups to hold out against Thatcher's policies. (They were both defeated.) But there is every reason for feminists to doubt the commitment of many of those who have criticised traditional trade union militancy in the name of feminism and other popular movements, when, like Eric Hobsbawm, for example, they fail to spell out any precise feminist perspectives at all.[18] On the other hand, many men on the left who have been attacked for remaining *within* traditional class politics are explicit in their commitment to feminism. Tony Benn, for example, though now seen as part of the 'old left', is a strong supporter of grassroots activism of all kinds, and has consistently, and in my view very genuinely, emphasised the importance and significance of the women's movement and other popular movements since the late seventies. But preferring an open enemy to opportunistic or mistrusted allies, some feminists have become all the more suspicious of the left and its spokesmen.

The Project of Feminism

Before we can be clear what we are asking men on the left to take on, however, and where they have failed us, we have to be clearer about the project of feminism itself. There are now two increasingly separate projects in contemporary feminism. The first of these, and the one which I have argued throughout this book has come to provide the dominant popular conception of feminism today, is one which stresses basic differences between women and men, and asserts the moral and spiritual superiority of female experience, values, characteristics and culture: women's oppression on this view results from the suppression of this women-centred vision or separate female 'world'. The second project, now less publicly or at least less unambiguously celebrated in the name of 'feminism', is one which stresses the social and economic disadvantages of women and seeks to change and improve women's immediate circumstances, not just in the area of paid work and family life, but by providing funding for women's cultural projects, increasing women's safety in the streets or meeting the special needs of particular groups of women. Many feminists may well support both projects, and certainly a determination to undermine or to shift those notions of 'masculinity' and 'femininity' which were seen as oppressive to or disparaging of women was present from the beginning of the women's liberation movement. But the more recent theorising of women's consciousness or 'subjectivity' – the exploration of ideas of women's separate language, culture and sexuality – have tended to disconnect from, rather than dictate, a concern with many of the immediate political priorities of most women.

What I have tried to establish by analysing the current search for a female biological or psychic experience which is unchanging and universal is that the resulting polarisation between women and men can limit the scope of political struggle and the vision we have of a feminist future. It can mean feminists fail to take in and value our victories or to assess the strength and nature of the forces which determine our defeats. It can also mean we fail to respect the diversity and strengths of women's individual and collective actions for greater autonomy and control over our lives, and fail to reject with conviction actions which oppose such a goal.

In Chapter 1, I examined the popular writing of Mary Daly and Dale Spender, concluding that they offered an exclusively idealist project for feminism. Mary Daly's guidelines for a spiritual voyage into female space express a contempt for the demands of the material world and little interest in women's everyday resistance to oppressive conditions. Dale Spender's documentation of the immediate and 'common' experience of all women explicitly dismisses material change as always in the end serving only to provide new ways for men to exploit women. It is their essentialist insistence upon men's eternal will to domination which creates this shared disinterest in collective political struggle in favour of an alternative emphasis on clearing our heads of 'male ideas' and 'male values' to appreciate the unchanging humanity of women.

A similar type of essentialism appears in the radical/revolutionary feminist analysis of heterosexuality as the single or main cause of women's oppression. Here the penis can serve, and therefore always has served, as a weapon to colonise and subdue women. Its practical implications have been to restrict the focus of feminist activism to an exclusive emphasis on the sexual, and to restrict even the focus on the sexual to the issue of male violence or lesbian separatism. This in turn has placed feminists at odds with each other, reduced the problems of sexist representation to the dangerously ill-defined category of the 'pornographic', and limited the lineaments of male desire to the urge to rape. The promotion of a progressive sexual politics between women and men, let alone the struggle for any more general egalitarian relations between them, enters the dustbin of feminist history, replaced by the cheerless certainty of men's rapacity.

The feminist psychoanalytic exploration of women's consciousness has led, in its Lacanian mould, to a rejection of biological essentialism, only to replace it by a new type of psychic essentialism. Or, in subverting this, post-Lacanian feminists have strengthened biological and idealist accounts of the nature of the 'feminine'. And yet another type of psychic essentialism appears in most of the more recent literature on mothering. It is one which again accepts as unproblematic traditional notions of fundamental sexual polarity. The caring and nurturing nature of women is described as universal because mutual mother-daughter identification is a transhistorical, transcultural effect of the social reality that it is women who mother. But this implies, of course, a universal interpretation of the role of 'mother', and women's successful rather than perhaps ambivalent or conflict-ridden relation to it. Some of the mothering literature does have important political implications for involving men in childcare, but it has also tended to play down the material context which allows successful or unsuccessful, happy or unhappy, parent-child relationships.

Other feminists who have concerned themselves not so much with the project of understanding women's consciousness, but with that of changing women's reality, have pointed out the limitations of the focus on 'female' consciousness. Any feminist perspective which explains women's caring work, for example, in exclusively psychological terms obscures the possibility that there may be no such universal and straightforward nurturing femininity at all; women's mothering capabilities, when present, may be primarily their adjustment to the social and economic arrangements which require them to do the work of caring for others.[19] Such psychological perspectives also tend to obscure not just the possibility but the gloomy probability (once so ardently proclaimed in feminist writings) that women's caring work in our society is often stressful, isolating and undermining of personal confidence. But while this painful reality may be less prominent in feminist writing today, it has ironically become all the more prominent in empirical studies of women's actual experience of mothering.

All the studies which have been undertaken of the effects of isolated mothering confirm that earlier feminist anger. George Brown and Tirril Harris, for example, found that mothers alone with small children were the group most vulnerable to depression; women who have to spend the longest periods of time with young children, alone and without breaks, are likely to be irritable and emotionally unstable.[20] In a recent study of women with pre-school children, Mary Boulton found that although two-thirds of the mothers in her sample found a sense of meaning and purpose in their lives as mothers, half of them nevertheless found childcare a predominantly frustrating and irritating experience. Although this sample of mothers were all living in 'good' social conditions (with husbands, adequate financial support and without the demands of a full-time job) the majority felt overburdened, guilty and anxious.[21] The women who felt 'fulfilled' in their role as mothers (a third of the sample) were balanced by an equal number who felt 'alienated'. And shared parenting, although a superficially appealing solution to the tensions of full-time, isolated mothering, is simply not an economic possibility in most households with children. Nor, Boulton points out, would it necessarily overcome the feelings of isolation, monopolisation and loss of individuality which many of the mothers reported if each parent were still alone in their childrearing. Shared parenting does involve the important ideological work of changing the ideals, attitudes and skills of men, but in the short term the demand for increased provision for childcare, and building up networks of supportive people, would appear more immediate and practical solutions for the problems most women face in mothering.

More frustrating and desperate again are the needs of those many women caring for elderly, disabled or handicapped relatives at home, alone, and mostly financially and practically unassisted by state provision. The one in six women currently caring for the elderly at home, for example, have been found to suffer from both physical and mental stress, while there are also many unnecessary difficulties faced by the elderly who are being cared for.[22] The frustrations of both parties are to a large extent due to the absence of adequate back-up assistance from the state for the needs of either the caregiver or those being cared for in the home, as well as men's failure to share in the work of caring. New social policies and provision, and new rights for carers in the workplace, as well as change in the attitudes of men, are all necessary before we can cease to exploit the work women do caring for others.

From the beginning the women's liberation movement was

concerned with issues of ideology and subjectivity. It is obvious that the construction of sexual difference and of female identity through the sexual and the maternal, and in turn the way our culture conceives of these, are crucial to any understanding of the maintenance of women's social subordination and to many women's internalised self-effacement and submissiveness. I am not suggesting that the project of understanding sexual difference and women's consciousness is the wrong project for feminism, but rather that it can mislead us politically unless we also place it within the historical and political contexts of women's resistance to conditions which confine and exploit us. Any type of essentialist analysis is always likely to divert us from attending to the details of objective conditions, and from the battles of some women to change them.

In earlier days women's liberation insistently emphasised the need to connect theory with practice. The negation, exclusion or stereotyping of women in the scholarly and popular discourses of men, the definition of women in terms of sexuality and motherhood, was something to be constantly confronted and challenged. And in doing so it was easier for some feminists to dismiss the particular pleasures and pains of the female body and its potential to give birth. But in reasserting and celebrating these (as have many feminists who have accepted and appreciated their own femaleness more as they have moved into motherhood) we do not need to return to reductionist accounts of the biological nor to any other type of ahistorical or static psychological essentialism. Some feminists theorising difference, like Chodorow and Irigaray, are at times mindful of these dangers (though other aspects of their work would seem to add to the problem); others like Mary Daly, Dale Spender and Andrea Dworkin disregard the dangers entirely.

The dangers are that focusing on sexual differences as *the* project for feminism denies what was most important about the political project of feminism: all the new issues feminism placed on the *political* agenda. This was not just a question of the dependent, relatively impoverished and sometimes brutalised and sexually abused situation of women compared to men. It raised more general questions: the nature of human 'needs' and how they are met (how we live, relate to and care for each other); the nature of 'work' and how it is recognised and rewarded; the nature of 'politics' and how we organise for change and to what end, the type of society socialists and feminists are trying to create. The activism and aspirations to which such questions gave rise and which feminists in the seventies brought into social movements for change have not disappeared altogether, though the odds against change have lengthened. And they have sometimes reappeared in the struggles of women less directly influenced by feminism.

New Spaces for Feminist Resistance and Reform

In Britain in the eighties the resistance of women has been one recurring source of hope in a very bleak historical period: a period when the Thatcher government has lowered the living standards of the poorest and most vulnerable, destroyed industries and services, undermined trade union militancy and, while dancing attendance on heightened US imperialism, has mobilised every type of racist, nationalistic, individualistic, authoritarian and mean-spirited sentiment throughout Britain. Yet in each and every year of the eighties women have been a significant force of opposition in many of the major struggles. My own dossier of a few of the high points of those years (unfortunately rather London-biased) reveals how women's involvement in political campaigns changes their nature and introduces new issues.

In 1981, when the Law Lords ruled subsidies for public transport illegal, women were at the centre of resistance. For example, socialist feminist Hannah Mitchell initiated what was to become a very popular (though eventually unsuccessful) 'Fares Fair' campaign in London. Public transport users leafletted everybody and used a variety of colourful and creative tactics to oppose higher fares, and attempted – with less response – to win organised trade union support. Women as the main users of public transport met together to discuss how to make public transport safer for women and more accessible for people with babies and prams. A successful spin-off of this campaign was public funding in London for a nightline bus and taxi service for women after dark.[23]

In 1982 vast numbers of people took to the streets in solidarity with the health workers' pay campaign. The resistance to Tory cutbacks in public health care was led by women in public sector unions, who won support both from other trade unions and from the general public. This was also the year in which 300,000 women linked hands to 'embrace' the nine-mile fence surrounding Greenham Common, and express their opposition to Cruise missiles. And in 1983, another 70,000 women went to Greenham with their wire cutters to enable 200 women to invade the base.

The year 1984 is mainly remembered as the year of the miners' strike. Without doubt what was most remarkable about that strike is how different it was from those of the 1970s. What was different, and what drew genuine public support for such a prolonged and bitter struggle – always so likely to end, as it did, in defeat – was women's participation in it, and women's definitions of the issues as they saw them: preserving the life of their communities. It is generally agreed that the strike could not have lasted so long without women's organising and support. Greenham Common supporters, and women's groups everywhere, mobilised to support the strike.

This was also the year when towns and cities throughout Britain and Ireland promoted and publicised an International Feminist Book Fair, and feminists came from around the globe to share their ideas and their writing. Feminist publishing was becoming a cultural success, altering the institution of publishing, if not yet – except for some of the smallest feminist publishers – its economic base.

In 1985, the Ford women sewing machinists, after an 18-year battle, finally won their equal pay claim; a very symbolic victory, for it was a struggle linked to the re-birth of feminism in the late 1960s. And in 1986, with the end of Tory rule finally in sight, attention focused on the Labour Party, and, for some feminists, on its ability to confront the inequalities of sex and race alongside any socialist programme for industrial regeneration and increased public spending. Feminists involved in the pioneering work of the women's committees of local and municipal councils, together with the future Minister of Women's Rights, Jo Richardson, are working hard to ensure that a future Labour government will give real rather than token backing to policies which ensure that employers, educational institutions and local authorities generally are forced to tackle the problems of women's continuing disadvantage.

So although one strand of feminism has retreated to a more subjective politics, many of the practical campaigns and projects of women's liberation in its early days have continued to develop and flourish. At my own local women's centre in the early seventies, health, housing, childcare and employment were the key areas of action and campaigning. In all these areas feminists have entered new forums and remain active, drawing upon those former feminist ideas and ways of organising. Their work in many metropolitan regions was strengthened in the 1980s by the election of left Labour councils, the most dramatic being the election of a Labour GLC in 1981, which sought to work with groups previously excluded 'not only from power but from the left's understanding of and approach to power'.[24] The issues feminists had always raised were the inadequacies of existing services – their undemocratic, authoritarian, disabling, sexist and racist practices. Change as well as expansion (now preservation) were equal priorities for feminists. And in contrast to traditional labour movement campaigns, feminist involvement was always to build up contacts between users and workers in welfare services and to break down the separation between public and private provision in caring relations.

Aspects of such feminist-inspired activism around health care and community provision are exemplified in the current Health Emergency Campaign set up in 1983 with GLC support to co-ordinate the many local campaigns against health cuts in London. This now has branches in all 31 London health districts. It was built from the prior work of socialist feminists like Lucy de Groot in Hackney in London, who have worked to organise joint campaigns between the Borough Council, the Community Health Council and the local trade union council, linking users and workers in the health service to preserve and improve health care provision. Jane Foot and Myra Garrett, two socialist feminists working full time for the campaign, have spoken of the promise and frustrations of their work.[25] Jane Foot describes the tensions of trying to keep a balance between the fast pace of organising needed to defend the continual threat to jobs and services in the NHS and the slower pace of developing alternative policies and approaches to health care. She portrays the desperately overworked, overstretched, harshly disciplined situation of the majority of workers in the health service today (who are mostly women) and yet the amazing work which some trade union activists have put into fighting for their services and linking up with other groups locally, especially women within the National Union of Public Employees (NUPE). At the same time she feels there is now a greater willingness to criticise the welfare state and its provision of services, particularly from the viewpoint of women, of Black and ethnic minorities, and also of pensioners: 'It's the quality and the nature of the relationships within those services that's more an acceptable political issue these days.'

On women's health issues, she describes how the women on the Hackney Community Health Council (CHC) have fought for, and won, a community-based, women-centred, low-technology obstetric service based outside the hospital, one which locates power much more with midwives than with hospital consultants. So a different type of more accessible and more democratic obstetric service is now available for local women in that area. (It involved changes which women like me, who experienced the purgatory of fear, humiliation and isolation in giving birth in the late sixties or early seventies, can only marvel at!) A similar service is being fought for in Tower Hamlets, in a long and bitter struggle, where Wendy Savage, the only female consultant obstetrician at the London Hospital, and one fighting for women's right to choose the obstetric care they want, was suspended on charges of incompetence, charges of which she was completely exonerated in July 1986.

Jane Foot sees the political importance of such health campaigns in their commitment to working with community groups to develop a sense of what the health issues really are, what kinds of service are required and how they should be delivered:

> And it's a very very long process because it's quite unfamiliar territory for a lot of people, and there are few examples to call on. It involves breaching a lot of unbreachable barriers about alternative medicine and the barriers, especially among the left, to criticising the health service and thinking about alternatives.

In her experience the most exciting work has been with pensioners, helping to organise a pensioners' health festival, with massage, meditation, self-defence and self-assertion displays: the whole variety of alternative health work for physical wellbeing. The pensioners (particularly the Pensioners' Press group, which is nearly all women) argued forcefully that they wanted to make a video which would show them not as victims nor simply as people needing services who couldn't look after themselves, but as people whose lives were destroyed only because their resources and potential were completely denied:

> People need to come up with dreams about a health service: how it could meet their needs, would be there when they wanted it, provide the service they wanted, would comfort, would care about them.

In Tower Hamlets Myra Garrett describes a similar 'pull and stress' between defence of the health service and ideas of alternative health care. Once people become involved in health campaigning they begin to question the NHS hierarchy: 'All that lack of democracy and lack of accountability, and no consultation, it all begins to come up as people gain an understanding of how the thing is set up.' Myra Garrett helped to organise a health enquiry into five local estates which revealed the extent to which bad housing, bad water supply and other environmental factors were involved in health. Black women's health groups have worked with the Tower Hamlets health enquiry, where Shamir Dirir, from Somali, has collected evidence on the failure of the health service to meet the specific mental and physical problems of Black women or even to provide women doctors for Muslim women who will not see male doctors. Dirir describes the need for interpreters in the health service and for discussion of the problems of female circumcision.[26]

Besides emphasising women's needs for greater control over fertility, childbirth and healthcare generally, feminist political interventions in the 1980s have borne out most of the earlier feminist analysis of women's position in the family: the strains of isolated mothering, the double workload of employed mothers. Old themes re-emerge with the current research into women's most pressing needs and discontents undertaken in many metropolitan areas throughout Britain in the 1980s. Often funded by the newly established Women's Committees of Labour councils, it aims to highlight women's special burdens and argue for the provision and resources which could begin to alleviate them. The funding for such work, however, has always followed rather than instigated independent activity by groups of feminists outside the structures of the Labour Party. A local survey by Haringey Women's Employment Project (with GLC funding from 1983), for example, discovered that 32 per cent of employed women were the sole earners in their families and 58 per cent of women contributed more than half to the family income.[27] In some areas of the inner London borough up to 60 per cent of women with young children were already working, and three-quarters of those without jobs wanted them if they could find satisfactory childcare. Similar surveys done by the Lewisham Women and Employment Project, set up in 1979 (and funded by the GLC from 1983), established that lack of childcare provision prevented women from pursuing training for jobs, while ensuring that women returning to paid work after caring for children could not find jobs at appropriate levels of ability. For nearly all women, requirements for childcare are inseparable from women's poor employment prospects.

Haringey and Lewisham Women's Employment groups together campaigned for change in employment conditions and childcare provision which would enable both women and men to participate in paid work and caring work in the home. They have both now set up training centres for women in computing, electronic and other technicians' skills which also pay for or provide childcare and pay travel expenses. Other women's training workshops have been established in Sheffield and Leeds during these years.

I suggested in Chapter 2 that much of the local grassroots feminist activism in women's centres, health groups, and around housing and nursery provision had begun to collapse in the late seventies as part of the crisis of radical confidence and increasing fragmentation in more difficult times. But here we see it re-emerging with renewed political confidence and legitimacy in the 1980s, this time, however, through the support of those with authority in existing political structures, through some feminists having formed alliances with, or joined, the political mainstream.

Many feminists have thus come to assert the importance of working within existing political power structures in pursuit of their goals, seeing local government or municipal socialism as an important arena of struggle. In this respect they have departed from much of the revolutionary rhetoric of former times, where working for reforms within existing state structures was more likely to be seen as a betrayal of ideals, perhaps delaying or destroying the revolutionary potential of feminism. Today the majority of politically active socialist feminists talk of struggle in and against the state, participating in and yet attempting to transform its existing sexist, racist and authoritarian social relations and practices. Such feminist involvement has brought the question of social need into economic planning: 'domestic life' and 'the quality of human relationships' are emerging from the silent secrecy of 'the private' to enter the public world of town hall committees and challenge their bureaucratic language.

In its many publications like *Jobs for a Change*, the GLC consistently stressed the contribution of housework and caring to the economic life of society, and argued that men must share the caring. It publicised surveys revealing that in three-quarters of all households men do almost no housework, and in half of them almost no childcare (even when women work full-time).[28] Repeatedly, they posed the question of how men, employers, trade unions and society generally can be made to support a fairer way of caring for children and other dependants, illustrating the policy statement of the GLC that the profit motive and private provision for services 'are inequitable and incapable of providing adequate care for the young and vulnerable'.[29] In its funding of industrial co-ops the GLC policy was to favour, in principle if not always in practice, those attempting to provide workplace creches, like the Asian women's Toys For Lambeth co-op, and other equal opportunities schemes. The Women's Committee for the GLC argued constantly for resources to enable women and men to share jobs and caring more equally, and to reduce the barriers between private caring and public provision. Although it is in its propaganda that it will have made its greatest impact, the Committee did spend most of its budget funding childcare schemes, supporting the National Childcare Campaign and preparing advice booklets for better provision for all women caring for dependants at home. The emphasis of the advice is always on breaking down the isolation of women caring in the home.[30]

In stressing the positive value of public provision for needs, tied in with job creation, the GLC and other metropolitan councils successfully challenged the ideological offensive of the right against state spending, making links between feminism and socialism. The ideas, energy and enthusiasm that this generated are continuing to influence women and men working for change, though some schemes and projects may lose their funding now that the Tory government has dismantled the metropolitan councils which dared to haunt it with the spectre of a socialism that people *wanted*: 'Once you have glimpsed and hoped you remember for the rest of your days, especially if you hold the utopian vision every time you do the washing up,' a GLC document on domestic life and childcare confidently concluded.[31]

It is true, despite such confidence, that many of the more recent engagements of feminists, often sponsored by municipal councils, are beset by the problems of combining feminist ideas of maximum participation, spontaneity and creativity from individual women, with the more tedious and bureaucratic work which funding and supplying a regular service demands. These initiatives, though reaching well beyond the networks of women's centres a decade before, lack the drama and revolutionary fervour of former times. Pragna Patel, Smita Bhide and Rhita Din from the Southall Black Women's Centre, for example, have described how the opening of their centre in 1982, with GLC money, meant a change from 'the high political profile' of the Southall Black Sisters to 'a more muted one'.[32] The lively political debates of the past, often detached from any grassroots work, were now frequently submerged by heavy caseloads and the political compromises demanded by alliances with other groups. Yet overall, they saw the centre as important: 'The main area of our work after funding is going to be organising self-help groups at a grassroots level.'[33] It is the frustrations and problems of day-to-day work with women in their ordinary lives which makes socialist feminist initiatives sometimes seem slow and undramatic, each one inadequate on its own, especially in comparison with the dramatic clash of opposites in radical and cultural feminist rhetoric; yet political change is, in reality, much of the time, a mundane and piecemeal affair.

Each victory for women at a local level, however, has occurred alongside major setbacks more generally. As with its crippling anti-union legislation, the cutbacks of the Thatcher government are often specific attacks on the space available for progressive organisation and resistance. This was most obvious in its petty decision to tax employers' contributions to workplace nurseries, which threatened those few already in existence.

The government's strategy of 'privatisation' of services was one aimed at pushing down the wages and organising strength of the lowest-paid service workers, who are overwhelmingly women, while pushing the burden of caring work back even more on to women in the home. The attempt to abolish wages councils, which set minimum wages in non-unionised low-paid jobs, was also designed to weaken the economic situation of the most vulnerable of workers, most of them women or ethnic minority men and women. (Men make up 91 per cent of skilled manual workers; only 20 per cent of semi-skilled and unskilled jobs are held by white male workers.)[34] Low-paid workers have been progressively worse off since 1980 compared to the better-paid skilled workers. When the government abolished wage protection for cleaners on government contracts in 1984, for instance, wages fell back over 20 per cent – from the pittance of £1.80 an hour to around £1.40.[35] Yet women have continued to resist the worst Dickensian aspects of government policies, with its moves to 'casualise' the labour force and deny workers' rights and trade union protections. Asian women homeworkers in Hillingdon in London, for example, formed a co-operative and started their own training centre to improve their skills and fight for better pay and conditions, some thereby managing to increase their wages from the unbelievable six pence per hour to the more typical low women's wages of £1.50 an hour. And hospital cleaners in Barking in South London stayed out on strike for eighteen months in 1984 and 1985 against a shabby privatisation deal, which, they stressed, undermined not only their pay and conditions but the cleanliness and atmosphere of their hospitals. (They are, as I write, still awaiting the outcome of an industrial tribunal considering their case.)

The Balance of Progress

What can we learn from this extraordinary range of ideas and struggles, with their advances and setbacks, which have engaged women in the eighties? Clearly they have occurred at a time of continuing and often deepening exploitation of large sectors of women in the workforce and the home, both nationally and internationally. Yet this is also a time of continuing and deepening awareness of the special problems that women face.

The principles of women's equality have been raised and supported within most trade unions, political parties (including the Tory Party, whose policies have hit women so hard) and legal institutions. In 1984, for example, Julie Haywood, a cook at Cammell Laird Shipyards in Liverpool, won her industrial tribunal claim for equal pay for work of equal value, comparing her job with that of skilled male colleagues. The 25 per cent increase in pay that this entailed sets a precedent which would affect a huge number of women workers; many unions are now gearing up to fight for it. (But the tribunal did not instruct Haywood's employers to actually pay the increase, which they have so far refused to do, requiring her union to return again to court to win implementation.) Without any doubt, the social discriminations against women are now more visible and the contradictions in their lives are hot issues of debate.

Most Black and immigrant women have remained in the lowest ranks of the low wage hierarchy, where, for example, between 30 and 50 per cent of the worst homeworkers' jobs are done by Asian and Cypriot women.[36] In addition these women have faced heightened racism since the late seventies: increased police raids, police violence, deportations and passport checks attempting to restrict their access to health care, education and other welfare benefits. The long years of institutionalised racism, state violence, physical attacks and social deprivation which sparked off the predominantly Black uprisings in British cities in 1981 produced further anxieties and strains for Black women. One woman from Liverpool described the immediate effects of those days of rebellion:

> Whenever anyone is out now, your family is terrified, thinking you will never get home. It's always been bad here, but we've never known it as bad as this.[37]

If we look at the change in women's economic prospects over the last 15 years we find a strange assortment of statistics. The 1981 census revealed that between 1971 and 1981 jobs for women had increased by 5 per cent while jobs for men fell by 8 per cent; the proportion of women in top managerial and professional jobs had nearly doubled, from 0.6 to 1.1 per cent.[38] In the 1980s almost every new job created in Britain was a part time job for women.[39] Women's overall pay compared to men's has declined since the late seventies.[40] And yet, over the same period, the trade unions have consistently supported maternity rights and abortion rights and in the 1980s have accepted sexual harassment of women as an important issue in the workplace. Ursula Huws concludes her review of the decade 1975-1985 thus:

> Judged by the general level of formal debate and official trade union policies, the recognition of women's special needs in the workplace can be said to have increased steadily throughout the decade.[41]

So, despite improvements in employment opportunities for women, we continue to earn less than men. The recession has increased the relative disadvantage of some women, but particularly poorer working-class and Black women. In other areas women's overall autonomy and control has increased. Women now have greater control over fertility than ever before. (However, we have yet to win the necessary feminist battle to establish women's right to choose to terminate an unwanted pregnancy: only 50 per cent of women now manage to obtain an NHS abortion, and this government has prevented research on a new abortion pill which could be taken in the early weeks of pregnancy.)[42] For most groups in our society, marriage is no longer compulsory to avoid social ostracism and disgrace if a woman chooses to bear a child; illegitimate births increased 100 per cent between 1977 and 1984, almost one birth in six occurring outside marriage. When 59 per cent of those births also register the father's name, we can conclude that more women are choosing to have babies with the help of the father, but outside marriage.[43] The institution of marriage as the literal licence of patriarchy is being eroded.

It is hard to interpret the statistics on violence against women from men: the number of recorded attacks on women has gone up, but almost certainly there has been increased reporting. It does seem likely, however, that there is a real increase in attacks on women, along with the increase in violent crime generally in recent years. At the same time sexual violence against women, incest abuse and sexual harassment have now become accepted political issues, with public funding for counselling of rape and incest survivors in all major cities of Britain. Steps are being taken to make the streets safer for women in many local areas. In response to feminist demands, there is now a new proposal to make rape within marriage a criminal offence from the current Criminal Law Review Committee.[44] Sexual harassment, as I have indicated, has become an issue within trade unions. Yet it remains true that despite legislative and professional interventions against it, and the funding of resources to combat its destructiveness, violence against women is still rampant in our society. And accompanying the greater expression of disgust at male aggression is the continuing cultural celebration of it in the 'Rambo' thuggery which delights the callous wits of callow men. However, Jalna Hanma, a feminist campaigner against men's violence towards women, concludes her review of the decade 1975-1985 with some hope for the future:

> The decade ends with the exposure of a major social problem
> [men's violence against women]. We have the beginning of new
> challenges to a very old system of social relations between men
> and women.[45]

In terms of overall political power there has been little change in the position of women in Britain at the top of any state institutions. The continuing growth of women's political consciousness and activism in local politics and diverse campaigns and movements is not reflected in any parliamentary, legislative, judicial or senior civil service elites, where their representation remains at under 5 per cent.[46] This contrasts with the position in Sweden, Norway, Denmark and Finland, where women's representation in parliament is over 25 per cent.[47]

Such uneven and contradictory advance in the autonomy and wellbeing of women illustrates, for me, the inadequacy of any essentialist definition of the problem. No account of women's situation in terms of any male will to dominate women can explain why women gain greater control over their lives in one sphere only to lose out in another. Men's power over women, traditionally, was exercised most directly in the home, where women's inescapable dependence on men has declined; meanwhile, at least in the long term, men's power in the workforce is undermined by women's role as cheap labour, though in the short term women's lower pay and poorer conditions confirm men's sense of relative power.

Ironically, however, such complexity behind male power, and the absence of any single or simple cause of women's subordination, as well as its highly variable nature both within and between societies, can strengthen rather than undermine essentialist analyses of women's difference from men. Women may succeed in escaping from total dependence on one man into the public sphere of the market economy, only to find their subordination replicated and their home lives all the more demanding. It is hardly surprising, therefore, that the idea of the special nature of woman, which will preclude her easy access into the public sphere, is strengthened in these circumstances. Moreover, it is in the home, as lovers, wives, mothers, daughters and friends caring for those we most cherish, whatever the burdens, inequities and tensions of care, that women are most likely to find at least some sense of meaning in who we are and what we are doing. For it is in relation to the private sphere, of course, that our ideas of femininity are constructed. In our paid work, whatever the sociability, prestige and independence it secures, the meaning and purpose of women's labour is often far less clear.

While the organisation of paid work and work in the home continue to operate in disregard of each other, and while women remain, as for the moment at least we usually wish to remain, pivotal in the latter, we will continue to live out lives which are disjointed and confusing. This disjuncture and confusion can appear to confirm the separate spheres of women and men, the unchanging polarities of sexual difference; thus the pendulum continues to swing between feminist struggles for equality with men and feminist assertions of difference.

Strategies for the Future

Three insights guide my analysis of feminist strategies for the future. The first is the recognition of the personal power and confidence which comes from women's engagement in political struggle, when it is women collectively who direct and control it. The second is the recognition that women's subordination is not a result of a conscious conspiracy by men, or at least not *only* of a conscious conspiracy by men, but is rather embedded in all the social institutions and ideologies of our society. The third is the recognition that the lives of women and men can be as much determined by class, ethnic, regional and national issues as by their sex.

It is not hard to see the importance of collective action in the lives of women. If our memories fail us, the book *Women in Collective Action* (edited by six feminists involved in community work with women) confirms that organising together empowers women.[48] It does so in the context of political struggle where objectives are clear and success seems possible. Women from the South Wales Association of Tenants, who organised to protest against conditions on their council estate from the close of the seventies into the early eighties, speak of how the struggle changed their lives: 'For most of us it meant taking a really close look at ourselves as women, and, whereas before we'd asked what we as women had done for the tenants' struggle, now we asked, "what has the struggle done to us as women"?'[49] Again and again, these Welsh women proclaimed, 'I can't imagine going back to my life before we started this ... I was just a little housewife, but suddenly you find you are a person.'[50]

Black and Asian women who have initiated campaigns against deportations, police violence, discrimination in child benefit provision and racist practices in the education and health service, have also created a strong and militant Black women's consciousness and confidence in recent years. Pratibha Parmar writes:

> Black women together with the rest of the Black community are continuing to fight and struggle against their oppression as Black people living in a racist society. Through their central involvement in this resistance Black women have successfully

demonstrated their strength and militancy and established themselves as a powerful section of the Black community.[51]

The excitement, optimism and sense of power which collective struggle by women generates was also, as I suggested in the last chapter, apparent in all the writings and speeches of the women from Greenham.

But the most recent and extraordinary evidence of the effect of women's collective struggle on women's consciousness and sense of power comes from the women in the pit villages organising together during the miners' strike. These are typical stories:[52]

> I suffer from agoraphobia, and I'd been virtually housebound for 13 years before the strike started. I couldn't even go to the shops on my own ... I've been to psychologists and psychiatrists and even spent money trying to find a cure, but the strike is the only thing that's done it. The only way I can explain it is – it's like being reborn. I know that I've got to keep active after the strike. I've already joined the Labour Party, and we're going to start a women's section.
>
> Pat, Castleford.

> When the strike began I had been on anti-depressants for about twelve years ... Then, suddenly, when we realised that the strike wasn't going to end quickly I found myself getting involved with something outside the home. I had little confidence but quickly I found that I had some skills that were needed. I was in at the deep end and this was the antidote. The support group was the best thing that ever happened to me. Very soon I was helping to organise all sorts of fundraising events and the thanks we got from our community was an enormous boost to my confidence ... people had faith in my ability ... Consequently I broke the depression and all because of a tragic dispute which gave one reason to stand up and fight.
>
> Pat, Sherburn.

> I've had a rough marriage. What I had to put up with! He used to knock hell out of me – he put me in hospital once or twice. I had to wait on him hand and foot ... But since the strike's been on, it's all different. He cleans up now, washes up. I can go out, and when I come in he'll make a cup of tea for me. I couldn't wish for a better husband, and that's God's truth.
>
> Rose, Featherstone.

The women aren't doormats any more.

Kim, Castleford

The women aren't doormats any more, because personality is not a static entity. A subordinate 'femininity' is created and recreated continuously in the taken-for-granted social practices which give men power over women. When women's collective struggles die down – with victory, or more likely in these times, with defeat – the confidence and sense of purpose they generate begins to fade. The challenge women collectively can present to men also recedes with the return of the regular routines that express sexual domination. When Jean McCrindle, for example, recalls the energy and activism of the women against pit closures, which seemed to spread from woman to woman 'like spontaneous bush fire', she also describes the problems of trying to keep the base of the struggle alive today: 'I'm really anxious for it not to become just a memory'.[53] Marina Lewycka, from Yorkshire Women Against Pit Closures, however, points out that a year after the defeat, there is still a committed core of women in every area meeting regularly and at the heart of campaigns against the continuing closure of local collieries, fighting for reinstatement of sacked miners and for better amenities in their communities.[54]

That the collective organisation of women can also begin to shift the thoughts of men, even within the institutions they dominate, was seen in the fact that the NUM were the only large union to support women's demands for an independent political power base within the Labour Party at the Party Conference in 1984 and 1985. (The NUM leadership also strongly, though unsuccessfully, backed the Women Against Pit Closures attempt to gain associate membership of the NUM in July 1985). But all around them their male comrades voted to retain the structures which have kept power in the hands of men. Both the Labour Party and the TUC have passed resolutions committing them to women's equality, and many of the changes which could help achieve it, but neither has yet been able even to change their own internal practices to include more women in positions of power.

Shifting men's power in relation to women is not simply agreeing to a set of principles which promote equality. Pushing on one front will always necessitate a push on another before it can be really effective. Until men more readily agree to sharing the caring and swapping the mopping with women in the home, we will not begin to equalise women's situation in the workforce. Nor will we begin to undermine traditional sexist ideology which sees expressiveness, tenderness, sensitivity and vulnerability as 'feminine'. But women's situation overall will not change until men (and women) see that women's 'part time', underpaid and unprotected position in the workplace, linked with their responsibilities in the home, connects with and sustains other forms of capitalist domination. On an international level, the combination of sexist ideology with the search for ever cheaper forms of labour has enabled the most diabolical abuse of Third World women in the factories, sweatshops and brothels of the Third World.

The unhappy debate, currently being refought with renewed vigour, over whether sex or class provides the most basic axis of oppression under male-dominated capitalism serves merely to mask the interdependence of the one on the other. Women have a particular importance to a capitalist economy as unpaid carers in the home and as a cheap flexible addition to the workforce, where, with less trade union protection, they are easier to hire and fire. But women's central economic role can be masked by ideas about women's separate sphere, which suggest women's apparent unimportance in the economic relations of capitalism. It is women's servicing of men and children in the home which allows their greater exploitation in the workforce, thus maintaining existing capitalist hierarchies of labour. Women's domestic lives are crucial to the maintenance of male dominance. But women's subordinate economic status in the labour market is equally crucial to the maintenance of men's power in the home.

The ubiquity of a gender hierarchy in every social sphere means that most women are likely to feel more comfortable by slotting into rather than challenging their customary subordination to the men of their own social group. The simple numerical absence of women in positions of power and authority over men inevitably boosts the sense of women's difference from men, when gender remains the central defining characteristic of individual identity in our society. Tackling women's routine subordination therefore means finding a way to build a sustained sense of collective power and confidence in women, one which does not evaporate as particular campaigns and struggles decline – as 'normal' life reasserts itself, with its 'normal' separation between waged work and personal life. Drawing upon the recognition of the power which comes from the collective organisation of women and yet seeing the tenacity and interlinked nature of women's institutional subordination, and the different situations of particular groups of women nationally and internationally, takes us back, it seems to me, to the classic arguments of socialist feminism. It takes us back to the need for autonomy *and* alliance, the need to organise ourselves separately as women without cutting ourselves off from other movements of the left.

Most feminists are well aware that women do not overturn existing power structures simply by individually entering the more powerful and privileged terrain of men. Once there, they may merely serve as the exceptions, used to disguise the general exclusion of women. Joining the male elite is anyway demanding, depressing and difficult for many women when it operates through definitions of authority and everyday practices designed to exclude or ignore the situation of most women. Those at the top of any occupational or social institution, for example, are not those who need time off to care for babies or to beautify the home, though they may need it for the Masonic club, the grouse moor or the golf course! Women will change this only by organising together as women and fighting to undermine and remove those definitions and practices which normalise the situation of men with dependent women to service them, whether at home, at work, in the pub or the strip club.

Women-only or women-dominated groups are therefore essential in every social sphere to create and sustain the definitions and practices which express what different groups of women want and need. This is the strength behind training and occupational women's groups like Women in Manual Trades, Women in the Media, women in computer collectives like Microsyster or the women's training centres now established in some of the larger cities in Britain. It is also the reason women in the Labour Party and the Trade Union Congress (TUC) need to continue what can seem a rather tedious campaign for a separate and politically effective power base within those institutions. (Black people have a similar need for Black sections to combat centuries of entrenched racism in the labour movement and the Labour Party.)

Only such organisations of women might be able to create and sustain the confidence and feminist vision necessary to work 'within but against' existing dominant groups – white, male, 'care-free' and technically skilled. But of course women in power in the Labour Party or trade unions could only represent the interests of other women were they also to create open structures of contact with groups on the outside – Black, unemployed, elderly or persecuted sexual minorities. Autonomous organisations of women across and outside different institutional sites are also necessary to tease out the overlapping ideologies and problems of male domination from the ideologies and problems of a capitalist economy. This has become all the more urgent when cultural feminism always tends to collapse capitalist values into 'male' values, and orthodox marxism tends to collapse the problem of male domination into the problem of a capitalist class system.

A Feminist Vision of Socialism

It took the far right in Britain nearly three decades, and the work of dozens of different pressure groups, to overthrow the post-war Keynesian welfare state consensus and assert a new free market philosophy. An anti-sexist socialist alliance today neither should, nor could, return to that old political consensus where skilled, white, heterosexual, able-bodied, men represented the interests of the working class. The left needs a similarly fundamental rethink to come up with its own new vision of socialism. Many socialist feminists have been arguing that the basis for such rethinking needs to begin from the question of how we create a society that can care for all its members while allowing women to live full and creative lives.[55] Some socialist feminists and their supporters have fought for changes which begin to illustrate what such a society might be like. The traditional left has still to produce its new vision. But unless and until the labour movement and the left can take on board a feminist vision which concerns itself with the nature of *all* human relationships, it can never hope to appeal to the majority of people.

'Socialism' in Britain from the late 1920s onwards has been connected with two dominant traditions: the paternalism of the Labour Party and the economism of the labour movement. The former is illustrated, for example, by the post-war nationalisation of sections of British industry, which did improve conditions for its workforce, but left unchanged the former undemocratic, authoritarian structures of management, distant from and unaccountable to its workforce. The same rigidly hierarchical tiers of management were adopted by local government and other institutions of the welfare state, whether in the NHS, the schools or any other state system. In the town halls of local government (until certain recent changes initiated by left Labour councils) different layers of management had little social interaction even with each other or with the elected councillors, and they were altogether out of reach of the public, whose interests they administered. Socialism of this kind acts only on behalf of others, building up a sense of powerlessness in its workforce and the public, alongside indifference if not hostility, rather than support and commitment, for its goals and aspirations.

The labour movement, on the other hand, has rarely fought for control over the nature and goals of industry and services, but rather for some income redistribution between capital and workers, leaving unchallenged all the other social inequalities of disadvantaged groups. Except during certain types of strikes, it has never forged links between the workplace and the world outside. But this bureaucratic and economistic 'socialism' which became dominant after the First World War was once strongly challenged by competing perspectives which are often ignored or dismissed as part of our socialist heritage: syndicalism, working-class feminism and a more utopian and ethical socialism had variously stressed workers' control of production, mutual co-operation and caring and the transformation of all human relationships.[56] Today there are stronger calls from socialist feminists and some male socialists for a renewal of that more democratic and participatory vision of socialism which reaches out to include all social relationships and to give people a sense of greater control over their own lives.

This new vision of socialism which some feminists and other radicals are working for is one which begins from *building the links* between our lives in the workplace and our lives in the home and the community, between control over production and social need. In our society people are systematically deprived of any sense of control over their lives except in the sphere of personal consumption and the home, however restricted these may be by unemployment and low pay. Creativity, meaning and control over our lives reduce to questions of individual taste and parental or familial concerns and obligations. As the miners and women in pit villages were so forcefully reminded in recent years, we are expected to have no control over our working lives or communities. But however much conservative philosophy glorifies private ownership and 'the family' – 'a little bit of heaven on earth' as Margaret Thatcher described home ownership in June 1986, justifying yet another round of public spending cutbacks – human beings do search for a sense of meaning and belonging beyond the personal and the familial. (We see it, ironically, in what is usually only the most regressive and destructive side of nationalism, like the sorry sight of British football fans running riot all over Europe, culminating in murder of Juventus fans in Belgium in 1985.) The manipulation of our desires through media promotion of styles of consumption is so easy and so fiercely defended, just because we now have so little sense of meaning and belonging in any other area of our lives; fashion itself provides forms of communal identity.

The second strand of any new socialist vision is therefore a genuine *participatory* democracy, one in which workers do have a say over the nature and methods of their work, and not only the right (now increasingly being eroded) to struggle over the wages they receive; one in which the public services we all rely upon are not simply bureaucratically controlled from above, but democratised in ways which enable us to experience a measure of control over their organisation and provision. Public resources, whether council estates, hostels, leisure centres, schools or hospitals do not have to be run in ways which deny choice, autonomy and control to those who use them.

Public provision need not provide the stark and brutal contrast with what we assume to be the best (and, given the high levels of domestic violence and misery, conspire to ignore at its worst) in the 'private' provision of care in the home. We belong to more than our 'families' (however sacred they may be to conservative thought), or rather, we should – and our lives would be enriched if we could – feel we belong as well in the public spheres of our streets, neighbourhoods, parks, theatres, cafés, buses and shops, were they planned, resourced and supervised to meet our different needs in consultation with those who use them. Exposing the constraints, monotony, inequalities and frequent abuses inherent in family life, cut off as it is from the life of the community and any concern with the workplace outside the home, feminists have contributed to a new socialist vision of a different type of public provision for need:

> Old people's homes could be a lot more like residential hotels, or else like self-governing communities. A home for the handicapped can be considerably more stimulating for a teenager with Down's syndrome than living alone with her parents. A nursery or children's home can provide positive social experiences of co-operation, companionship and varied activities. It is the overvaluation of family life that devalues these other lives.[57]

I have suggested that some of the popular feminist rhetoric celebrating women's links with 'nature' and nurturing, even calls for men's sharing of household tasks, can undermine other feminist struggles if they occur in isolation from calls for greater public responsibility for caring and for collective resources to replace individual household tasks, offering us more choices in our personal lives. We cannot afford to abandon the feminist critique of 'the family' as the symbol of all that we value and cherish, especially in these times, when it is now all the right has to offer to legitimise its devastation of our public resources and services. As Michèle Barrett and Mary McIntosh have argued, 'Caring, sharing and loving would be more widespread if the family did not claim them for its own'.[58] The feminist exposure of the dishonesty and hypocrisy in family ideology is crucial to any new socialist vision.

These new images of socialism have come, up until very recently and still predominantly, from the left active outside the Labour Party and the labour movement. They represent many of the perspectives and methods of the women's movement, the peace movement, workers' combine committees like those which existed in Ford or Lucas Aerospace, and other alternative technology and alternative media groups. They have all stressed

participatory democracy, and new approaches to the organisation of work and the nature and use of public resources. Mike
Cooley and Hilary Wainwright are two of the better-known
activists who have promoted these ideas for a new type of
socialism stressing popular planning for social need.[59] Hilary
Wainwright has worked with those who produced the *People's
Plan for Docklands*, where, though many of the men have been
defeated in the struggle to keep their jobs, local people, mostly
led by women, are still struggling to control their environment
and build the type of community to which they would want to
belong.[60] Some of the obstacles to the growth of such a
socialism, however, come from the old ideas of socialism within
the Labour Party and the labour movement, and from its
determination to maintain the power and privileges of men.

State provision in all the forms we have known it, most of it
drafted by Labour politicians, has never yet challenged the idea
that it is women, as a sex, who must bear the primary
responsibility of caring for others, a service for which they
receive no guaranteed compensation or support. It has therefore
entrenched rather than undermined male dominance; it has
helped to remove women from any central place of power in
public life and to keep the meeting of human needs cut off from
the organisation of the workplace. And any economic strategy,
however 'socialist' its aims, which, like the capitalist market
itself, fails to analyse and materially value the work done outside
production for profit, cannot create a society which does not
exploit those who give birth and those who are given the job of
caring for others.

Traditional labour movement philosophy has also entrenched
male dominance and other social hierarchies. It is no secret that
its defence of economic differentials and the bargaining power of
'stronger' unions (skilled, white and male) does not necessarily
pull up the wages and conditions of 'weaker' unions; indeed any
such claim is increasingly farcical as the gap between the wages
and conditions of different groups of workers continues to
widen. It is even less of a secret, when women have shouted it
from the rooftops for a decade or more, that the male 'family
wage' has always failed to meet the needs of many women and
their children, though it has always succeeded in denying women
a decent wage of their own.[61] Traditional trade union practices

look increasingly obsolete now that the once-strong manufac-
turing unions, vanquished by technological robots, have seen
their numbers drop and their skills destroyed. Women still have
negligible power within the TUC General Council and it is
estimated that a mere 5 per cent of full time trade union officials
are women.[62] But the determined feminist voice which says the
labour movement will not advance until this changes is
becoming harder to ignore. It is significant, for example, that
women swept the board in the 1986 elections for the executive
of the National Union of Tailors and Garment Workers,
increasing their numbers from three to eleven out of the fourteen
places available. (There has been a similar, though less dramatic
increase in women's executive positions in APEX, ASTMS and
the Inland Revenue Staff Federation.)[63] Angela Coyle recently
summed up the hopes of socialist feminists in the trade union
movement when she wrote:

> Potentially, women could spearhead a new and broader form of
> mass trade unionism ... Women place on the agenda not only
> income distribution, but also questions of working conditions,
> hours of work, consumption and childcare. Paradoxically,
> women's demands now have a wider relevance beyond 'women's
> issues' and could become central to a radical strategy against job
> shortage, poverty and inequality.[64]

Cynthia Cockburn would add to this list that women 'joining
and changing' trade unions, alongside women organising
autonomously to master technology for themselves and
participating in left movements for alternative technologies,
could help to 'domesticate' technology and re-forge the link
between making and 'nurturing'.[65]

Women could spearhead such a movement, in my view, not
because of any eternal qualities of women, but because most
women's problems in the workplace connect directly to their
functions and activities in the home. Women's material interests,
if taken seriously by the trade union movement, are therefore the
most disruptive of traditional labour movement practices which
have maintained rigid divisions between paid work and work in
the home, and preserved existing hierarchies of labour, where
mechanical skills are valued over servicing skills.

I disagree with feminists who, like Beatrix Campbell, have

characterised the labour movement as simply a 'men's movement', at least in the sense that it is a movement which has never acted in the interests of women.[66] Like every other social institution, trade unions have always been dominated by men and are blatantly sexist. They have historically often directly excluded women and failed to support women's struggles; their protection of skilled labour has encouraged practices which discriminate against women and ethnic minorities. Men's behaviour in the workplace, like their behaviour out of it, is often a problem for women, a problem which only a few trade unions, and only after enormous pressure from women, have seriously begun to tackle. There have, however, been struggles where male trade unionists have supported the interests of women workers (from the National Union of Clerks' support for equal pay in the 1890s to support for the health workers' struggle in the 1980s) and where women and men have fought together. Women too, in the past, have supported the now quite anachronistic idea of a male 'family wage'. But with the labour market and employers now turning so firmly towards part-time low-paid female labour to reduce labour costs and to avoid employment protection legislation and other hard-won workers' rights, and with women's share of total employment expected to grow from 45 per cent to 50 per cent by 1990, new labour movement strategies which give power to women are no longer a chivalric option but a forward-looking necessity.[67]

Once we take seriously the feminist question, 'How do we provide for the needs of all, and not at the expense of women?', we set as our goal the wholesale reshaping of society. Feminist writing popping up in local government publications has given us an officially endorsed preview of such a vision, as in sections of the GLC's *London Industrial Strategy*:

> The solution to this quite basic human problem would require absolutely fundamental root and branch changes throughout society, in how work is divided and rewarded, in the hours of paid employment, in how skills are valued and passed on ... In creating new relations of waged work and domestic care the more humanising element of both could be combined and the oppressive aspects of both reduced. Perhaps we might make a future in which the meanings of work, creativity and care are transformed, so work was not onerous toil, creativity not for the favoured few and care the responsibility of a single sex.[68]

It may seem strange to be urging women to participate more actively in trade union politics at a time when union power seems to be in decline and any progress is slow and difficult. But that very decline has led some trade union leaders themselves, like John Edmonds, recently elected general secretary of the boilermakers' union (Britain's second biggest general union), to argue that trade unions must concern themselves with a 'new order of priorities', with the question of 'equal rights' and with 'the needs of workers outside as well as inside the workplace'.[69] The gap between such new trade union rhetoric and changing practices which give women power is still gigantic, but it does create spaces which can be confidently claimed by feminists. Women's struggles in the workplace are not more important than women's strugles against the culture and rituals of male dominance in every area of our lives, but, like the struggles in and around local councils, they provide another way of women moving into the mainstream of political debate and action.

In moving into the mainstream to include the struggle against male domination as part of the struggle for socialism, feminists face the problem of how to keep a balance between the politics of the public sphere (a concern with equality) and the politics of personal life (understanding and valuing the experiences of women). But whereas the problem for women's liberation was once how to assert personal issues as political, the problem has now reversed to one where feminists need to argue that the political does not reduce to the personal. As I have argued, and as the German feminist Barbara Sichtermann has suggested, today 'conflicts of global and apocalyptic proportions are tackled as matters of the heart'.[70] And this is not the analysis women need if we are to win our battles.

Cultural feminists fear that focusing on political action for equality and joining political structures dominated by men inevitably negates or distorts the expression of women's own special experiences and values, perhaps even making women more aggressive and competitive, more like men. (However, we know from our own women's conferences that women can be just as aggressive and competitive as men, once they begin to feel more powerful.) But working in political structures dominated by men does not, and should not, if it is to be successful, preclude women from organising autonomously. The success of any feminist struggle begins to change women's relations with men, both in and outside political forums, shifting the conditions which enable men to dominate women – whether in the workplace, in the home, or in society generally. A feminist politics which can reach out to all women, as distinct from the privileged few, must concern itself with material inequalities – with questions of income, resources and the control of resources. This means struggles in and around the state and work around trade unions, however wearing and slow these may be. Such struggles are of equal importance to sexual politics and ideology if only because they are inevitably linked: economically independent women find it easier to make choices, to leave brutal men, assert a lesbian lifestyle if they want to, and decide if, when and how they wish to mother.

When by far the greatest difference between women and men is the social inequality of women, to suggest that avoiding public forums is necessary to preserve women's difference from men is to suggest preserving virtues and values which require exclusion and subordination in order to flourish – hardly something to celebrate. New cracks keep appearing in the interlinking structures of men's power and privileges in relation to women. It is in deepening these cracks that feminists can work to strengthen the power of women to participate in creating the type of future we want for ourselves and others.

Strategically, this means feminists fighting for minimum wages, shorter 'working' hours, leave for caretakers and an independent income for those caring for dependents in the home. It means policies for the recruitment, promotion and training of women, particularly for jobs which have excluded women. It means shifting state funding for industry, and state intervention in industry, to create jobs geared to social needs, and the re-evaluation of existing notions of 'work' and 'skill' which value and reward what are currently men's activities over those of women.

Concretely, it means women gaining real power in the women's sections of the Labour Party and the TUC, but, as centrally, creating and supporting policies which open up these institutions to the ideas and activities of radical groupings of women (and men) on the outside. It is from such activities, as we saw in health, transport, women against pit closures or women fighting institutionalised racism, that most of the creative rethinking about socialism, or any other progressive vision, has come. We need feminist ideas to travel all the way up and all the way down our present hierarchies of power.

Ideologically, this means challenging all our assumptions of masculinity and femininity which express notions of dominance and submission, with the heterosexual male as the central, self-asserting, authoritative representative of 'humanity'. And this takes us back to sex, and to violence, and to the politics of the personal: to the reshaping of desires where women's bodies are no longer defined through reproduction and reduced to passive sexual commodities for men, and where men's bodies are no longer defined through the phallus, and used as the symbol of a masculinity which is coercive and oppressive to women. Women and men might then begin to enjoy once again those childhood pleasures as both object and subject of desire, might escape from their restricting and compulsive sexual obsessions into more mutual sexual encounters.

It is true that the current leadership of the Labour Party and the trade unions show little commitment towards making any of these changes. And yet, the only leaders they have with any imagination, and any following at all, like Ken Livingstone, are quite certain of the need for them:

> I have always thought that the Labour Party's almost exclusive concentration on the employed male white working class was a weakness. My own view is that you can't transform society on that basis. You need a coalition which includes skilled and unskilled workers, the unemployed, women and Black people, as well as the sexually oppressed minorities ... This means that *we* have to change. I'm opposed to cynical attempts to co-opt the women's movement just because we can get votes out of it. The Labour Party must listen to what the women are saying and then change itself.[71]

Livingstone's politics and the aspirations of so many who worked with the GLC are not properly on the socialist agenda. But the only hope for socialism is to put them there.

However, feminists too need to accept that part of their struggle must involve an alliance with men to transform the social inequalities, and the dangerous and destructive tech-nologies, of existing capitalist economies. Political engagement 'with' and 'against' men, whether in the Labour Party, the trade unions, the autonomous Black, anti-nuclear, ecological, anti-racist or other progressive social movements and groupings of the left, is the umbrella strategy feminists need to pursue. There is, after all, nothing so unusual in one's closest allies in one area being one's most immediate, and therefore most irritating, opponents in another.

The real problem with the popular 'new feminism' which sees women as essentially virtuous and men as essentially vicious is that it serves the forces of reaction as surely as it serves the forces of progress. Margaret Thatcher calls upon women's special qualities to suggest her own greater integrity, sincerity and depth of feeling.[72] Over the three years I have been writing this book some of the fiercest clashes between radical and socialist feminists have died down, a change also reported by other European feminists.[73] In these pages I have tried to bring these and other clashes between feminists to life, not to rekindle the confrontation but to face rather than to deny our disagreements, and in facing them to see which of the many different varieties of feminism we do share and can support. The issues which have preoccupied feminists in recent years, sexuality, motherhood and nationalistic aggression, can be transformed by a progressive movement of women, but only through an analysis which brings them into the wider political arena of an anti-capitalist, internationalist movement which supports those fighting imperialist domination in the Third World. It is an analysis which would highlight rather than ignore the conflicts and contradictions women face, and have always faced, in their lives as women. Femininity has always been at least partially at odds with itself, heterogeneous, contradictory and changing, its expression varying along with class, race, age, sexual orientation and individual biography. So too has masculinity. There is no unifying female experience which could in itself change or save the world: women's patriotism, as well as men's, could once again be mobilised to help destroy it.

The future is not female. But feminism, a feminism seeking to transform socialism and end men's power over women, has a crucial role to play in its construction.

Endnotes

Introduction

1. Hannah Kantor et al, *Sweeping Statements*, London, The Women's Press, 1984.
2. Cynthia Cockburn, *Machinery of Dominance: Women, Men and Technical Know-How*, London, Pluto Press, 1985.

1. Compensations of the Powerless

1. Virginia Woolf, 'Men and Women' in (ed.) M. Barrett, *Women and Writing*, p. 65, London, The Women's Press, 1979.
2. Deborah Cameron, *Feminism and Linguistic Theory*, pp. 142-3, London, Macmillan, 1985.
3. Quoted in Sally Alexander and Sue O'Sullivan, 'Sisterhood Under Stress', *Red Rag*, 8, 1975, p. 19.
4. See, for example, Organisation for Economic Co-operation and Development, *Women and Employment: Policies for Equal Opportunities*, Paris, 1980.
5. Rebecca West, 'The Sin of Self-Sacrifice' in (ed.) J. Marcus, *The Young Rebecca*, p. 235, London, Virago, 1982.
6. Robin Morgan, 'Feminism is the Key to our Survival and Transformation' in *The Anatomy of Freedom*, p. 283, Oxford, Martin Robertson, 1982. Ronald Reagan, 'Why if it wasn't for feminism, we men would still be walking around in skin suits carrying clubs'. Quoted in S. Brownmiller, *Femininity*. p. 208, New York, Linden Press/Simon & Schuster, 1984.
7. Roger Scruton, 'The Case Against Feminism', *The Observer*, London, 22 May 1983.
8. Mary Wollstonecraft, *A Vindication of the Rights of Woman* (1792), London, Penguin, 1978.
9. Susan Griffin, *The Roaring Inside Her*, p. 175, London, The Women's Press, 1984.
10. Kingsley Amis in (ed.) J. Green, *A Dictionary of Contemporary Quotations*, p. 54, London, Pan Books, 1982.
11. Juliet Mitchell, *Woman's Estate*, p. 162, Harmondsworth, Penguin, 1971.
12. Susan Griffin, in (eds) L. Caldecott and S. Leland, *Reclaim the Earth*, p. 1, London, The Women's Press, 1983.
13. Marilyn Strathern, 'No Nature, No Culture: the Hagen Case' in (eds) C. MacCormack and M. Strathern, *Nature, Culture and Gender*, p. 177, Cambridge, Cambridge University Press, 1980.
14. Raymond Williams, *Keywords*, p. 186, London, Fontana, 1976.
15. Raymond Williams, *Problems in Materialism and Culture*, p. 76, London, Verso, 1980.

16. Adrienne Rich, *Of Woman Born*, p. 39, London, Virago, 1977. Susan Griffin, *Woman and Nature*, p. 217, London, The Women's Press, 1984.

17. Ann Oakley, *Taking it Like a Woman*, p. 72, London, Jonathan Cape, 1984.

18. Adrienne Rich, op. cit., p. 39.

19. Jo Spence, 'What Do People Do All Day?', *Screen Education*, 29 (1978/79).

20. Susie Orbach, *Fat is a Feminist Issue*, London, Hamlyn, 1981.

21. ibid., p. 84.

22. Dale Spender, 'No Matter What' in (ed.) J. Holland, *Feminist Action*, p. 14, London, Battle Axe Books, 1984.

23. Robin Morgan, *Going Too Far*, p. 93, New York, Random House, 1978.

24. Judith Arcana, *Every Mother's Son*, p. 17, London, The Women's Press, 1983.

25. Elizabeth Wilson, 'Interview with Andrea Dworkin', *Feminist Review*, 11, 1982, p. 24.

26. Adrienne Rich, 'Afterword', in (ed.) L. Lederer, *Take Back the Night*, p. 313, New York, William Morrow & Co, 1980.

27. Michelene Wandor, *The Body Politic: Women's Liberation in Britain 1969-1972*, London, Stage One, 1972.

28. Sheila Rowbotham, *Woman's Consciousness, Man's World*, p. xiv. Harmondsworth, Penguin, 1973.

29. Valerie Charlton, 'The Patter of Tiny Contradictions', *Red Rag*, 5, 1973, p. 5.

30. Sheila Rowbotham, op. cit., p. 38.

31. Juliet Mitchell, *Woman's Estate*, op. cit., pp. 56-7.

32. See Nell Dunn, *Living Like I Do*, London, Futura, 1977; Ray Gordon, 'Diary of a House Husband', *Achilles Heel* 2, 1979; Lynne Segal et al, 'Living Your Politics: A Discussion of Collective Living Ten Years On', *Revolutionary Socialism* 4, 1979.

33. Andrea Dworkin, 'Taking Action' in *Take Back the Night*, op. cit., p. 288.

34. Angela Hamblin, 'What Can One Do with a Son?' in *On the Problem of Men*, p. 241, London, The Women's Press.

35. Mary Daly, *Pure Lust*, p. 379, London, The Women's Press, 1984.

36. Mary Daly, *Gyn/Ecology*, p. 394, London, The Women's Press, 1979.

37. See Meaghan Morris, 'A-Mazing Grace: Notes on Mary Daly's Poetics', *Intervention* 16 (Australia), 1982.

38. Mary Daly, *Gyn/Ecology*, op. cit., p. 22.

39. ibid., p. 339.

40. Mary Daly, *Pure Lust*, op. cit., p. 4.

41. ibid., p. 4.

42. ibid., p. 363.

43. ibid., p. 378.

44. ibid.

45. Meaghan Morris, op. cit., p. 72.

46. Mary Daly, *Pure Lust*, op. cit., p. 366.

47. Mary Daly, *Gyn/Ecology*, op. cit., p. 59.

48. ibid., p. 8.

49. ibid., p. 334.

50. Mary Daly, *Pure Lust*, op. cit., p. 384.

51. ibid., p. 385.

52. ibid., p. 110.

53. ibid., p. 385.

54. Audre Lorde, 'An Open Letter to Mary Daly' in (ed.) C. Moraga, *This Bridge Called My Back*, p. 97, Massachusetts, Persephone Press, 1981.
55. ibid.
56. Dale Spender, *For the Record*, op. cit., p. 205.
57. Statement made by Mary Daly in discussion after her speech in Sydney, 24 August 1981.
58. Meaghan Morris, op. cit.
59. See Deborah Cameron, *Feminism and Linguistic Theory*, p. 143, London, Macmillan, 1985.
60. Susan Griffin, *The Roaring Inside Her*, op. cit., introduction.
61. Dale Spender, *Women of Ideas (and What Men Have Done To Them)*, p. 8, London, Routledge & Kegan Paul, 1982.
62. Dale Spender, *For the Record*, op. cit., p. 16.
63. ibid., p. 192.
64. Dale Spender, in (ed.) R. Rowland, *Women Who Do and Women Who Don't – Join the Women's Movement*, p. 209, London, Routledge & Kegan Paul 1984.
65. Dale Spender, *Women of Ideas*, op. cit., p. 737.
66. ibid.
67. Dale Spender, *For the Record*, op. cit., p. 3.
68. Dale Spender, *Time and Tide Wait for No Man*, London, The Women's Press, p. 2, 1984.
69. Dale Spender, *Women of Ideas*, op. cit., p. 30.
70. Jill Julius Matthews, *Good and Mad Women*, p. 5, Hemel Hempstead, Allen & Unwin, 1984.
71. Dale Spender, in *Feminist Action*, op. cit., p 19.
72. Cicely Hamilton, *Marriage as a Trade* (1909), London, The Women's Press, 1981.
73. See Anne Phillips, *Divided Loyalties: Dilemmas of Sex and Class*, London, Virago (forthcoming).
74. Dale Spender, in *Feminist Action*, op. cit., p. 12.
75. See the Islander columns in the *New Statesman* during 1985.
76. Dale Spender, *Man Made Language*, 1980, London, Routledge & Kegan Paul.
77. Maria Black and Rosalind Coward, 'Linguistic, Social and Sexual Relations', *Screen Education* 39, 1981.
78. Deborah Cameron, op. cit.
79. ibid., pp. 99-100.
80. Dale Spender, *For the Record*, op. cit., p. 110.
81. ibid., p. 177.
82. ibid., p. 109.
83. ibid., p. 5.
84. Carol Smart, *The Ties That Bind*, p. 157, London, Routledge & Kegan Paul, 1984.
85. Liz Stanley and Sue Wise, *Breaking Out: Feminist Consciousness and Feminist Research*, p. 174, London, Routledge & Kegan Paul, 1983.
86. Dale Spender, *For the Record*, op. cit., p. 29.
87. ibid., pp. 172-3.
88. ibid., p. 51.
89. Sheila Rowbotham, quoted in Spender, ibid., p. 165.
90. ibid., p. 180.

91. ibid.
92. ibid., p. 205.
93. Genevieve Lloyd, *The Man of Reason*, p. 104, London, Methuen, 1984.
94. Dale Spender, in *Women Who Do and Women Who Don't*, op. cit., p. 210.
95. Michelene Wandor, 'The Impact of Feminism on the Theatre', *Feminist Review* 18, 1984, p. 91.
96. Dale Spender in *Feminist Action*, op. cit., p. 6.
97. Dale Spender, *For the Record*, op. cit., p. 114.
98. Elizabeth Fox-Genovese, 'Placing Women in History', *New Left Review*, 133, May-June 1982, p. 29.
99. Hilary, 'Have You Been Raped Then?' *Sweeping Statements*, p. 9, London, The Women's Press, 1984.
100. Jayne Egerton, 'The Goal of a Feminist Politics ... The Destruction of Male Supremacy or the Pursuit of Pleasure?' *Sweeping Statements*, op. cit., p. 199.
101. ibid.

2. Not Advancing but Retreating

1. Michèle Barrett, 'Rethinking Women's Oppression: A Reply to Brenner and Ramos', *New Left Review*, 146, 1984, p. 128.
2. Sue O'Sullivan, 'Passionate Beginnings: Ideological Politics 1969-72', *Feminist Review* 11, 1982, p. 70.
3. Shaila, with support from Third World/Black Feminist Group and the Black Lesbian Group, 'Angry Opinion' in *Sweeping Statements*, p. 87, London, The Women's Press, 1984.
4. Herbert Marcuse, 'On the Need for an Open Marxist Mind', *The Listener*, 9 February 1978, p. 171.
5. André Gorz, *Farewell to the Working Class*, pp. 85-6, London, Pluto Press, 1982.
6. Robin Morgan, *The Anatomy of Freedom*, p. 285, Oxford, Martin Robertson, 1982.
7. ibid.
8. Ken Livingstone, 'Fifth Column', *New Socialist* 19, September 1984.
9. Angela Coyle, *Redundant Women*, London, The Women's Press, 1984. Sue Sharpe, *Double Identity*, Harmondsworth, Penguin, 1984.
10. Brian Jackson, *Fatherhood*, p. 128, London, George Allen & Unwin, 1983.
11. Marge Proops, *The Guardian*, 10 September 1984.
12. ibid.
13. Ruth Milkman, 'Women's Work and Economic Crisis', *Review of Radical Political Economics*, vol. 8 no. 1, 1976.
14. Veronica Beechey, 'The Shape of the Workforce to Come', *Marxism Today*, August 1985.
15. See Anne Phillips, *Divided Loyalties: Dilemmas of Sex and Class*, London, Virago (forthcoming).
16. Barbara Ehrenreich, *The Hearts of Men*, London, Pluto Press, 1983.
17. Ellen Willis, 'Radical Feminism or Feminist Radicalism', in (eds) S. Sayres et al, *The 60s Without Apology*, p. 93, Minneapolis, University of Minneapolis Press/Social Text, 1984.
18. Angela Weir and Elizabeth Wilson, 'The British Women's Movement',

New Left Review 148, December 1984.

19. Lee Comer, *Wedlocked Women*, pp. 274-5, Leeds, Feminist Books, 1974.

20. Private communication from Marsha Rowe.

21. Editorial, *Red Rag*, 4, 1973, pp. 1-2.

22. Maria Dalla Costa and Selma James, *The Power of Women and the Subversion of the Community*, Bristol, Falling Wall Press, 1972.

23. Diana Adlam et al, 'Socialist Feminism 1979: an Assessment', *Scarlet Woman*, July 1979, p. 14.

24. See Barbara Ehrenreich, op. cit.

25. Editorial, *Red Rag* 5, (1973), p. 2.

26. Veronica Beechey, 'On Patriarchy', *Feminist Review* 3, 1979. Sheila Rowbotham, 'The Trouble with "Patriarchy" ', *New Statesman*, 28 December 1979.

27. Editorial, *Scarlet Woman*, July 1979, p. 34.

28. Conference Paper 3, *Women and Socialism* (collected papers of conference), 1974, p. iii, unpublished.

29. Ann Fiander et al, 'Forward to the Building a Mass Women's Liberation Movement', paper at the Mile End Socialist Feminist Conference, 1974, unpublished.

30. Editorial, *Scarlet Woman*, July 1975, p. 5.

31. Barbara Ehrenreich, 'Life Without Father', *Socialist Review*, vol. 14, no. 1, January-February 1984, p. 49.

32. See chapter 4.

33. Editorial Statement, *m/f* 1, 1978, p. 5.

34. 'Proposed Guidelines for Sunday Workshop Discussion' for Socialist Feminist Conference 1979, *Scarlet Woman*, July 1979.

35. Sally Alexander et al, 'Points for Discussion at Socialist Feminist Conference 1979', *Scarlet Woman*, July 1979, p. 18.

36. ibid., p. 19.

37. Diana Adlam et al, op. cit., pp. 15-16.

38. Conference planning paper for Socialist Feminist Conference 1980 (unpublished).

39. Barbara Norden, 'Socialist Feminists', *Spare Rib* 140, September 1984, p. 29.

40. See Lynne Segal, 'A Local Experience', in S. Rowbotham et al, *Beyond the Fragments*, London, Merlin. 1980.

41. See Sheila Rowbotham et al, *Beyond the Fragments*, op. cit.

42. Ann Karpf, 'Do the Glossies Gloss over Feminism?', *New Statesman*, 6 November 1985, p. 19.

43. Personal communications from women active in GLC funded women's centres in boroughs in South London and North London.

44. Pratibha Parmar, in 'Can Black and White Women Work Together?' *Spare Rib* 168, July 1986, p. 20.

45. bell hooks, *Feminist Theory from Margin to Center*, Boston, South End Press, 1985.

46. See, for example, bell hooks, ibid., p. 4.

47. Maxime, '1984: Black Women So Far …' *Spare Rib* 138, January 1984, p. 3.

48. Valerie Amos and Pratibha Parmar, 'Challenging Imperial Feminism', *Feminist Review* 17, 1984, p. 3.

49. ibid., p. 4.

50. Parita Trivedi, 'To Deny Our Fullness: Asian Women in the Making of History', *Feminist Review*, ibid., p. 17.
51. Michèle Barrett and Mary McIntosh, 'Ethnocentrism and Socialist Feminist Theory', *Feminist Review* 20, 1985, p. 25.
52. *Working for Children in Wandsworth*, GLC Popular Planning Unit, Conference Report, 1985.
53. See 'Can Black and White Women Work Together?' op. cit., p. 20.
54. Floya Anthias and Nira Yuval-Davis, 'Contextualising Feminism – Gender, Ethnic and Class Divisions', *Feminist Review* 15, 1983.
55. Black Women's Group (Brixton), *Women's Struggle*, p. 1, London, Rising Free Bookshop, undated.
56. Gloria I. Joseph, 'Black Mothers and Daughters' in (eds) G.I. Joseph and J. Lewis, *Common Differences: Conflicts in Black and White Feminist Perspectives*, p. 80, New York, Doubleday, 1981.
57. Adrienne Rich, 'Compulsory Heterosexuality and Lesbian Existence', *Signs: Journal of Women in Culture and Society* vol. 5, no. 4, 1980, p. 643.
58. Jill Johnstone, *Lesbian Nation: The Feminist Solution*, New York, Simon & Shuster, 1973.
59. Sally Alexander and Sue O'Sullivan, 'Sisterhood Under Stress', *Red Rag* 8, 1975, p. 19.
60. Cynthia Cockburn, *Brothers: Male Dominance and Technological Change*, London, Pluto Press, 1983.
61. Ruth Cavendish, *Women on the Line*, London, Routledge & Kegan Paul, 1982.
62. Karen Durbin, 'A Weight Off my Head', in (ed.) M. Rowe, *Spare Rib Reader*, p. 27, Harmondsworth, Penguin, 1982.
63. Gayle Rubin, 'Thinking Sex: Notes for a Radical Theory of the Politics of Sexuality' in (ed.) C. Vance, *Pleasure and Danger*, p. 267, London, Routledge & Kegan Paul, 1984.

3. *Beauty and the Beast I*

1. Lal Coveney et al, *The Sexuality Papers*, p. 9, London, Hutchinson, 1984.
2. R.W. Connell, 'Theorising Gender', *Sociology* vol. 19 no. 2, (1985), p. 265.
3. Cora Kaplan, 'Wild Nights' in *Formations of Pleasure*, p. 34, London, Routledge & Kegan Paul, 1983.
4. Catherine MacKinnon, 'Feminism, Marxism, Method, and the State', *Signs* vol. 7 no. 3, Spring 1982, p. 516.
5. Havelock Ellis, quoted in Jeffrey Weeks, *Sexuality and its Discontents*, p. 62, London, Routledge & Kegan Paul, 1985.
6. Michel Foucault, *The History of Sexuality, Volume 1, An Introduction*, London, Allen Lane, 1979.
7. Judith Williamson, 'Packaging the Punch', *Women's Review* 1, 1985, p. 4.
8. Lesbians Against Pornography, 'A Blow Job for Men is a Con Job for Women', *City Limits*, March 16-22 (1984), p. 7.
9. Adrienne Rich, 'Compulsory Heterosexuality and Lesbian Existence' in *Signs*, vol. 5, no. 4, 1980, p. 191.
10. Martha Vicinus, *Independent Women*, p. 291, London, Virago, 1985.

11. Catherine Hall, *Adultery*, programme for Channel 4 TV, 29 November 1985.
12. Beatrix Campbell, 'Feminist Sexual Politics', *Feminist Review 5*, 1980.
13. Lynne Segal, ' "Smash the Family"? Recalling the Sixties' in (ed.) L. Segal, *What is to be Done about the Family?*, Harmondsworth, Penguin, 1983.
14. Beatrix Campbell, 1980, op. cit.
15. Germaine Greer, *The Female Eunuch*, London, MacGibbon & Kee, 1970.
16. Ellen Willis, *Beginning to See the Light*, p. 12, Boston, South End Press, 1981.
17. Deirdre English, 'Talking Sex – Communications on Sexuality and Feminism', *Socialist Review 58*, July-August 1981, p. 45.
18. Tape of programme of Australian Broadcasting Commission 1982 (personal possession).
19. Mary Ingham, *Now We are Thirty*, p. 177, London, Methuen, 1981.
20. Every feminist I have consulted has wholeheartedly endorsed this observation.
21. Sheila Rowbotham, 'The Role of Women in the Revolution defined by some Socialist Men' (1968), in (ed.) L. Mohin, *One Foot on the Mountain*, p. 210, London, Onlywomen Press, 1979.
22. Anne Koedt, 'The Myth of the Vaginal Orgasm', in (ed.) L. Tanner, *Voices from Women's Liberation*, p. 159, New York, Mentor, 1970.
23. Pat Whiting, 'Female Sexuality: Its Political Implications', in (ed.) M. Wandor, *The Body Politic*, p. 189, London, Stage One, 1972.
24. Angela Hamblin, 'The Suppressed Power of Female Sexuality', *Shrew: Women's Liberation Workshop Paper*, vol. 4, no. 6, December 1972, p. 10.
25. Beatrix Campbell, 'Sexuality and Submission', in S. Allen et al, *Conditions of Illusion*, p. 108, Leeds, Feminist Books, 1974.
26. Rosalind Delmar, 'What is Feminism?' in *The Body Politic*, op. cit., p. 118.
27. Monica Sjoo, 'A Woman's Right over Her Body' in *The Body Politic*, ibid., p. 181.
28. Shulamith Firestone, *The Dialectics of Sex*, p. 138, London, Paladin, 1971.
29. Kate Millett, *Sexual Politics*, London, Abacus/Sphere, 1972.
30. Cora Kaplan, 'Radical Feminism and Literature: Rethinking Millett's Sexual Politics', *Red Letters 9*, 1979.
31. Roger Scruton, *The Observer*, 22 May 1983.
32. Enoch Powell, *The Guardian*, 12 August 1985.
33. Germaine Greer, *The Female Eunuch*, op. cit., p. 316.
34. ibid., p. 316.
35. ibid., p. 260.
36. ibid., p. 317.
37. Anthony Storr, *Human Aggression*, p. 177, Harmondsworth, Penguin, 1970.
38. Angela Weir, 'Battered Women: some Perspectives and Problems' in (ed.) M. Mayo, *Women in the Community*, London, Routledge & Kegan Paul, 1977.
39. Anna Coote and Tess Gill, *The Rape Controversy*, p. 3, London, National Council for Civil Liberties Pamphlet, 1975.
40. *No Turning Back*, London, The Women's Press, 1981.
41. Sue Cartledge and Joanna Ryan, *Sex and Love*, London, The Women's Press, 1983.
42. Anna Coote and Beatrix Campbell, *Sweet Freedom*, p. 222, London, Pan Books, 1982.

43. Jeffrey Weeks, *Sexuality and its Discontents*, op. cit.
44. William Masters and Virginia Johnson, *Human Sexual Response*, Boston, Little, Brown & Co., 1966; William Masters and Virginia Johnson, *Human Sexual Inadequacy*, Boston, Little, Brown & Co., 1977.
45. Shere Hite, *The Hite Report*, p. 229, New York, Dell, 1976.
46. ibid., p. 270.
47. Betty Dodson, *Liberating Masturbation*, distributed by Betty Dodson, New York, 1972; Lonnie Barbach, *For Yourself: The Fulfilment of Female Sexuality*, New York, Signet, 1975; Barbara Seaman, *Free and Female*, Greenwich, Conn., Fawcett Publications, 1972.
48. See Lynne Segal, 'Sensual Uncertainty, or Why the Clitoris is Not Enough', in *Sex and Love*, op. cit.
49. Verena Stefan, *Shedding*, p. 20, London, The Women's Press, 1979.
50. Shere Hite, op. cit., p. 386.
51. Eleanor Stephens, 'The Moon Within Your Reach', *Spare Rib*, 42, December 1975, p. 15.
52. Personal communication from Marsha Rowe (editor of *Spare Rib* anthology).
53. Robin Morgan, *Monster*, p. 84, London, private edition, 1973.
54. Sheila Shulman, 'Pome to Jackie', in (ed.) L. Mohin, *One Foot on the Mountain*, p. 214, London, Onlywomen Press, 1979.
55. Anja Meulenbelt, *For Ourselves*, London, The Women's Press, 1981.
56. ibid., p. 8.
57. ibid., p. 95.
58. ibid., p. 134.
59. See *Sex and Love*, op. cit., for examples of the difficulties of both lesbian and heterosexual relationships.
60. Editorial Collective, *Scarlet Woman* 13, May 1981, p. 29.
61. Adrienne Rich, 'Compulsory Heterosexuality', op. cit.
62. See Wendy Clark, 'The Dyke, the Feminist and the Devil', *Feminist Review* 11, 1982.
63. Susan Griffin, 'Rape: the All-American Crime', *Ramparts*, September, 1971.
64. Leeds Revolutionary Feminist Group, 'Political Lesbianism: the Case against Heterosexuality', in *Love Your Enemy*, p. 5, London, Onlywomen Press, 1981.
65. ibid., p. 8.
66. ibid., p. 67.
67. Lal Coveney et al, *The Sexuality Papers*, op. cit., p. 49, London, Hutchinson, 1985.
68. See Lesley Rimmer, *Families in Focus*, p. 31, London, Study Commission on the Family, 1981.
69. Leeds Revolutionary Feminist Group, op. cit., p. 7.
70. Nancy Friday, *Men in Love: Men's Sexual Fantasies*, London: Arrow Books, 1980; Shere Hite, *The Hite Report on Male Sexuality*, London, MacDonald, 1981.
71. Justine Jones, 'Why I Liked Screwing or Is Heterosexual Enjoyment Based on Sexual Violence?', in (eds) D. Rhodes and S. McNeill, *Women Against Violence Against Women*, p. 57, London, Onlywomen Press, 1985.
72. ibid.
73. ibid.
74. Lal Coveney et al, op. cit., p. 14.

75. See Susan Ardill and Sue O'Sullivan, 'Upsetting an Applecart: Difference, Desire and Lesbian Sadomasochism', *Feminist Review* 23, 1986.
76. Angela Davis, *Women, Race and Class*, p. 173, New York, Random House, 1981.
77. Andrea Dworkin, *Pornography*, op. cit.
78. Peggy Reeves Sanday, 'The Sociological Context of Rape: a Cross-Cultural Study', *Journal of Social Issues*, vol. 37, no. 4, 1980.
79. Steve Lukes, *Power: A Radical View*, London, Macmillan, 1974.
80. Delia Dumaresq, 'Rape – Sexuality in the Law', *m/f* 5, 6, 1981.
81. bell hooks, op. cit., p. 75.
82. Andrea Dworkin, *Pornography*, op. cit., p. 123.
83. ibid., p. 15.
84. ibid.
85. Mary Louise Ho, 'Patriarchal Ideology and Agony Columns' in (eds) S. Webb and C. Pearson, *Looking Back: Some Papers from the British Sociological Association 'Gender and Society' Conference*, Department of Sociology, Manchester 1984.
86. ibid.
87. Andy Moye, 'Pornography', in *The Sexuality of Men*, 1985, p. 62, London, Pluto Press.
88. ibid.
89. Elizabeth Wilson, *What is to be Done about Violence against Women?*, p. 166, Harmondsworth, Penguin, 1983.
90. Lal Coveney et al, op. cit., p. 13.
91. Rosalind Coward, 'Sexual Violence and Sexuality', *Feminist Review* 11, 1982.
92. D.L. Mosher, 'Psychological Reactions to Pornographic Films', in *Technical Reports of the Commission on Obscenity and Pornography*, vol. 8, Washington D.C., U.S. Government, 1970.
93. E. Donnerstein and G. Barrett, 'The Effects of Erotic Stimuli and Male Aggression towards Females', *Journal of Personality and Social Psychology*, 1978.
94. E. Donnerstein, 'Aggression, Erotica and Violence against Women', *Journal of Personality and Social Psychology*, 1980.
95. N.M. Malamuth, 'A Longitudinal Content Analysis of Sexual Violence in the Bestselling Erotic Magazines', *Journal of Sex Research*, 1980.
96. *Committee on Obscenity and Film Censorship*, November, p. 78, London, HMSO, 1979.
97. Quoted in Joan Smith, 'Mrs Whitehouse's Private Member', *New Statesman*, 13 December 1985, p. 10.
98. ibid.
99. Liz Kelly, 'Feminist vs Feminist', *Trouble and Strife*, Winter 1985.
100. Tony Eardley, 'Pin-ups Come Down on Building Site', *Achilles Heel* 4, 1980.
101. Rosalind Coward, op. cit. p. 19.
102. See Ellen Seiter, 'Feminism and Ideology: the *Terms* of Women's Stereotypes', *Feminist Review* 22, 1986.
103. See Sue Cartledge and Joanna Ryan, *Sex and Love: New Thoughts on Old Contradictions*, London, The Women's Press, 1983; Ann Snitow et al (eds), *Desire*, London, Virago, 1984; Carol S. Vance (ed.), *Pleasure and Danger*, London, Routledge & Kegan Paul, 1984; Rosalind Coward, *Female Desire: Women's Sexuality Today*, London, Paladin, 1984.
104. Barbara Ehrenreich, in *In These Times* vol. 7, no. 40. 1983.

105. Jeffrey Weeks, op. cit.
106. Liz Heron, 'The Other Face of Feminism', *New Statesman*, 1 April 1983.

4. *Beauty and the Beast II*

1. Hester Eisenstein, Introduction to (eds) H. Eisenstein and A. Jardine, *The Future of Difference* p. xviii, Boston, G.K. Hall & Co., 1980.
2. bell hooks, op. cit. p. 135.
3. Hazel and Alice, 'Custom-Made Woman Blues' (Rounder Records 0027).
4. Naomi Weisstein, 'Psychology Constructs the Female, or the Fantasy Life of the Male Psychologist', in (ed.) M. Garskof, *Roles Women Play*, p. 71, Belmont, California, Brooks/Cole, 1971.
5. Martina Horner, 'Femininity and Successful Achievement', in Garskof, op. cit., p. 107.
6. Judith Bardwick and Elizabeth Douvan, 'Ambivalenc: the Socialization of Women', in (eds) V. Gornick and B. Moran, *Women in Sexist Society*, New York, Signal, 1971.
7. Phyllis Chesler, 'Women in the Psychotherapeutic Relationship', in Gornick and Moran, op. cit., p. 383.
8. Eleanor Maccoby, *The Development of Sex Differences*, Stanford, Stanford University Press, 1966.
9. Ann Oakley, *Sex, Gender and Society*, p. 158, London, Temple Smith, 1972.
10. ibid., p. 170.
11. ibid., p. 204.
12. Northern Women's Group Education Study Group, 'Sex Role Learning: A Study of Infant Readers', in M. Wandor, *The Body Politic*, op. cit., p. 149.
13. See Oakley, op. cit., p. 207.
14. R.W. Connell, *Which Way is Up?*, Chapter 10, London, Allen & Unwin, 1983.
15. Juliet Mitchell, *Women and Psychoanalysis*, Harmondsworth, Penguin, 1974.
16. Jacqueline Rose, 'Femininity and its Discontents', *Feminist Review* 14, p. 9, 1983.
17. Sigmund Freud, 'Female Sexuality', (first published 1931) in Penguin *Freud* 7, p. 17, Harmondsworth, Penguin, 1973.
18. Sigmund Freud, 'Some Psychical Consequences of the Anatomical Distinction between the Sexes', in Penguin *Freud* no. 7, p. 340, Harmondsworth, Penguin, 1973.
19. See Juliet Mitchell, Introduction to (eds) J. Mitchell and J. Rose, *Feminine Sexuality*, p. 16, London, Macmillan, 1982.
20. Dalston Women's Study Group, 'Was the Patriarchy Conference "Patriarchal"?' in *Papers on Patriarchy*, p. 76, Brighton, Women's Publishing Collective, 1976.
21. The papers were by Rosalind Coward et al, 'Psychoanalysis and Patriarchal Structures'; and Cora Kaplan, 'Language and Gender', both in *Papers on Patriarchy*, op. cit.
22. Juliet Mitchell, 1974, op. cit., pp. 377-81; Rosalind Coward et al., op. cit., p. 16.
23. Elizabeth Wilson, 'Psychoanalysis: Psychic Law and Order', *Feminist Review* 8, 1981, p. 76.
24. Jacqueline Rose, op. cit., p. 19.

25. ibid., p. 9.
26. Elizabeth Cowie, 'Fantasia', *m/f* 9, 1984.
27. Susan Griffin, *Pornography and Silence*, London, The Women's Press, 1981.
28. Tania Modleski, *Loving with a Vengeance*, p. 45, London, Methuen, 1984.
29. ibid., p. 47.
30. Rosalind Coward, *Female Desire*, pp. 187-97, London, Paladin, 1984.
31. Quoted in Tania Modleski, op. cit., p. 38.
32. See Elaine Marks and Isabelle Courtivron, *New French Feminists*, Brighton, Harvester, 1981; and Ann Rosalind Jones, 'Writing the Body: Towards an Understanding of L'Ecriture Féminine' in (ed.) E. Showalter, *The New Feminist Criticism*, London, Virago, 1986.
33. Luce Irigaray, *The Sex Which Is Not One*, p. 28, New York, Cornell University, 1985.
34. ibid., p. 28.
35. See Elizabeth Cowie et al, 'Representation vs Communication' in (ed.) Feminist Anthology Collective, *No Turning Back*, London, The Women's Press, 1981; Gayle Greene and Coppélia Kahn (eds), *Making A Difference*, London, Methuen, 1985.
36. Cora Kaplan, 'Pandora's Box: Subjectivity and Sexuality in Socialist Feminist Criticism', in Greene and Kahn, op. cit., p. 152.
37. See Toril Moi, *Sexual/Textual Politics: Feminist Literary Theory*, London, Methuen, 1985.
38. Ann Rosalind Jones, 'Julia Kristeva on Femininity: The Limits of a Semiotic Politics', *Feminist Review* 18, 1984.
39. See Julia Kristeva, *About Chinese Women*, London, Marion Boyars, 1977.
40. See Nancy Chodorow, *The Reproduction of Mothering*, p. 48, London, University of California Press, 1978.
41. Dorothy Dinnerstein, *The Mermaid and the Minotaur*, New York, Harper & Row, 1976; Adrienne Rich, *Of Woman Born*, op. cit.
42. Lee Comer, op. cit.
43. Brent Against Corrie Pamphlet Group, *Mixed Feelings*, January 1980.
44. Quoted in Caroline Osborne, 'Review of Post-Partum Document', *Feminist Review* 18, 1985, p. 137.
45. Nancy Chodorow, op. cit., p. 110.
46. ibid., p. 181.
47. ibid., p. 291.
48. Nancy Chodorow, 'On The Reproduction of Mothering: A Methodological Debate', *Signs*, vol. 6, no. 3, 1981, p. 501.
49. See Sally Berry et al, 'Letter from the Women's Therapy Centre Study Group', *m/f* 3, 1979, p. 111.
50. Luise Eichenbaum and Susie Orbach, *Outside In, Inside Out*, p. 43, Harmondsworth, Penguin, 1982.
51. Luise Eichenbaum and Susie Orbach, *What Do Women Want?*, p. 75, Glasgow, Fontana, 1984.
52. *Outside In, Inside Out*, op. cit., p. 59.
53. Liz Heron (ed.), *Truth, Dare or Promise*, p. 1, London, Virago, 1985.
54. Carolyn Steedman, *Landscape for a Good Woman: A Story of Two Lives*, London, Virago, 1986.
55. bell hooks, op. cit., p. 140.
56. Jean Bethke Elshtain, 'Symmetry and Soporifics: A Critique of Feminist Accounts of Gender Development', in (ed.) B. Richards, *Capitalism and Infancy*,

p. 74, London, Free Association Books, 1984.
57. Sigmund Freud, 'Two Case Histories', 1909, Standard Edition, vol. x, pp. 259-60.
58. Nancy Chodorow, 'Gender, Relation, and Difference in Psychoanalytic Perspective', in Eisenstein and Jardine, op. cit., p. 16.
59. ibid., p. 14.
60. Nancy Chodorow, *Signs*, op. cit., p. 503.
61. See Iris Young, 'Socialist Feminism and the Limits of Dual Systems Theory', *Socialist Review 50/51*, 1980; Roger Gottlieb, 'An Exchange: Mothering and the Reproduction of Power', *Socialist Review*, 78, 1984.
62. Cynthia Cockburn, 'The Material of Male Power', *Feminist Review* 9, 1981.
63. Nancy Chodorow, *Signs*, op. cit., p. 502.
64. Adrienne Rich, 'Sibling Mysteries', in *The Dream of A Common Language*, p. 52, London, Norton & Co., 1978.
65. Rose Lamb Coser in *Signs*, Spring 1981, op. cit., p. 488.
66. Carol Gilligan, *In a Different Voice*, London, Harvard University Press, 1982.
67. ibid., p. 172.
68. Jane Flax, 'Theorizing Motherhood', *Women's Review of Books*, vol. 1, no. 9, 1984, p. 13.
69. See Marx and Engels, *The German Ideology Part 1: Feuerbach*, p. 47, London, Lawrence & Wishart, 1982.
70. Ethel Spector Person, 'Sexuality as the Mainstay of Identity: Psychoanalytic Perspectives', *Signs*, vol. 5, no. 4, Summer 1980, p. 26.
71. R. Emerson Dobash and Russell Dobash, *Violence Against Wives*, London, Open Books, 1980.
72. Andy Metcalf and Martin Humphries, *The Sexuality of Men*, p. 7, London, Pluto Press, 1985.
73. R.W. Connell, *The Social Basis of Sexual Politics*, Sydney, George Allen & Unwin, forthcoming.
74. R.W. Connell, 'Men's Bodies' in *Which Way is Up*, op. cit.
75. R.W. Connell, ibid.; Andrew Tolson, *The Limits of Masculinity*, London, Tavistock, 1977.
76. Ann Snitow, 'Mass Market Romance: Pornography for Women is Different', *Radical History* 20, 1979, p. 145.
77. Janice Winship, ' "A Girl needs to get Street-wise": Magazines for the 1980s', *Feminist Review*, 21, 1985, p. 21.
78. ibid., p. 42.
79. Martin Durham, 'Common Grounds', letter to *New Socialist*, 33, 1985, p. 47.
80. Ann Oakley, *Subject Women*, pp. 250, 251, Oxford, Martin Robertson, 1981.
81. Madeleine Simms and Christopher Smith, 'Young Fathers: Attitudes to Marriage and Family Life', in (eds) L. McKee and M. O'Brien, *The Father Figure*, London, Tavistock, 1982.
82. Eichenbaum and Orbach, 1984, op. cit., p. 178.
83. Denise Riley, 'The Serious Burdens of Love? Some Questions on Childcare, Feminism and Socialism', in (ed.) L. Segal, *What is to be done about the Family?*, p. 153, Harmondsworth, Penguin, 1983.
84. Diane Ehrensaft, 'When Women and Men Mother', *Politics and Power* 3, London, Routledge & Kegan Paul, 1981.
85. Ruth Wallsgrove, 'Thicker than Water: Mothering and Childcare', *Trouble and Strife*, 7, 1985, p. 21.
86. ibid.

87. See Colin Brown, *Black and White in Britain: the Third PSI Survey*, London, Heinemann, 1984.

88. Denise Riley, op. cit., p. 155.

89. Adrienne Rich, *Of Woman Born*, op. cit., p. 14.

90. Eichenbaum and Orbach, 1984, op. cit., p. 193.

91. ibid., p. 194.

92. Interview with Susie Orbach, *The Guardian*, Women's Page, 2 April 1985.

5. *Beauty and the Beast III*

1. Ann Snitow, 'Holding the Line at Greenham', *Mother Jones*, February/March 1985, p. 47.

2. Jean Bethke Elshtain, 'On Beautiful Souls, Just Warriors and Feminist Consciousness', in (ed.) J. Steinhem, *Women and Men's Wars*, p. 342, Oxford, Pergamon Press, 1983.

3. Ross Poole, 'Structures of Identity: Gender and Nationalism', in *War/Masculinity*, p. 78, Sydney, Intervention Publications, 1985.

4. Women Oppose the Nuclear Threat (WONT), 'Something in Common', in (ed.) Cambridge Women's Peace Collective, *My Country is the Whole World*, London, Pandora, 1984.

5. In *The Greenham Factor*, pamphlet, London, Greenham Print Prop (undated).

6. Petra Kelly, 'Women and the Future', in *My Country is the Whole World*, op. cit.

7. For example, Leonie Caldecott and Stephanie Leland (eds), *Reclaim the Earth*, London, The Women's Press, 1983.

8. Lilian Mohin, in *Breaching the Peace*, p. 25, London, Onlywomen Press, 1983.

9. Ruth Wallsgrove, 'Greenham Common Women's Peace Camp – So Why Do We Still Feel Ambivalent?', *Trouble and Strife* 1, 1983, p. 4.

10. Ann Snitow, op. cit., p. 33, 1985.

11. Alice Cook and Gwynne Kirk, *Greenham Women Everywhere*, p. 5, London, Pluto Press, 1983.

12. Cook and Kirk, op. cit.; Barbara Harford and Sarah Hopkins (eds), *Greenham Common: Women at the Wire*, London, The Women's Press, 1984.

13. Harford and Hopkins, op. cit., p. 3.

14. ibid., p. 22.

15. Brenda Whisker, in *Breaching the Peace*, op. cit.

16. See Cynthia Enloe, *Does Khaki Become You?*, p. 87, London, Pluto Press, 1983.

17. Crystal Eastman, in Cambridge Women's Peace Collective, op. cit., p. 106.

18. Olive Schreiner, in *Cambridge Women's Peace Collective* ibid., p. 81.

19. Quoted in Jill Liddington, 'The Women's Peace Crusade', in (ed.) D. Thompson, *Over Our Dead Bodies*, p. 187, London, Virago, 1983.

20. Quoted in Liddington, ibid., p. 192.

21. See Sheila Rowbotham, *Friends of Alice Wheeldon*, London, Pluto Press, 1986.

22. Sandra Gilbert, 'Soldier's Heart: Literary Men, Literary Women, and the Great War', *Signs*, vol. 8, no. 3, Spring 1983.

23. ibid., p. 429.

24. ibid., p. 439.
25. ibid.
26. Angus Calder, *The People's War*, p. 310, London, Granada, 1982.
27. Vera Brittain, *Testament of youth*, p. 290, London, Virago, 1978.
28. ibid., pp. 291-2.
29. Wilfred Owen, in Introduction to (ed.) E. Blunden, *The Poems of Wilfred Owen*, p. 41, London, Chatto & Windus, 1955.
30. Vera Brittain, op. cit., p. 138.
31. W.B. Yeats, 'An Irish Airman Foresees his Death', in (ed.) A.N. Jeffares, *W.B. Yeats Selected Poetry*, p. 69, London, Macmillan, 1962.
32. See Anne Wiltsher, *Most Dangerous Women*, p. 210, London, Pandora, 1985.
33. Virginia Woolf, *Three Guineas*, p. 83, Harmondsworth, Penguin, 1982.
34. ibid., p. 125.
35. Emmeline Pethick-Lawrence, in Cambridge Women's Peace Collective, op. cit., p. 113.
36. Di Parkin, 'Women Warriors in the Second World War', in R. Samuel, *Patriotism and the Making of British National Identities*, London, Routledge (forthcoming).
37. ibid.; Cynthia Enloe, op. cit.
38. Di Parkin, op. cit.
39. ibid.
40. Angus Calder, op. cit., p. 310.
41. Andrea Dworkin, *Pornography*, op. cit., p. 51.
42. ibid., p. 68.
43. Dworkin, for example, dedicates *Pornography* 'For John Stoltenberg'.
44. Jill Johnstone, *Lesbian Nation: The Feminist Solution*, New York, Simon & Schuster, 1973.
45. Shulamith Firestone, *The Dialectic of Sex: The Case for Feminist Revolution*, New York, William Morrow, 1970.
46. Brian Easlea, *Fathering the Unthinkable: Masculinity, Science and the Nuclear Arms Race*, London, Pluto Press, 1983.
47. Andrea Dworkin, *Pornography*, op. cit.; Mary Daly, op. cit., p. 366.
48. Harford and Hopkins, op. cit., p. 119.
49. ibid., p. 119.
50. ibid., p. 166.
51. Cook and Kirk, op. cit., p. 42a.
52. Harford and Hopkins, op. cit., p. 109.
53. Martha Gellhorn, *The Face of War*, p. xv, London, Virago, 1986.
54. Robert Ardrey, *The Hunting Hypothesis*, p. 15, London, Fontana, 1977.
55. See Paul Hirst and Penny Woolley, *Social Relations and Human Attributes*, p. 69, London, Tavistock, 1982.
56. Richard Leakey and Roger Lewin, *People of the Lake*, p. 120, New York, Avon, 1979.
57. John Keegan, *The Face of Battle*, pp. 314-15, New York, Vintage Books, 1977.
58. ibid., p. 317.
59. Lynda Birke and Jonathan Silvertown, *More Than the Parts: Biology and Politics*, p. 2, London, Pluto Press, 1984.
60. For example, Charlotte Perkins Gilman, *Herland*, London, The Women's Press, 1979.

61. Sir Julian Huxley, Introduction to Konrad Lorenz, *On Aggression*, p. ix, Methuen, 1967.
62. Lorenz, op. cit., pp. 207-8.
63. ibid., p.209.
64. ibid., pp. 109-10.
65. ibid., p. 239.
66. Birke and Silvertown, op. cit., p. 136.
67. ibid., p. 138.
68. Steven Rose, 'Biological Reductionism: Its Roots and Social Functions', in Birke and Silvertown, op. cit., p. 29.
69. S.C. Washburn, 'Human and Animal Behaviour', in (ed.) A. Montagu, *Sociobiology Examined*, p. 274, London, Oxford University Press, 1980.
70. See Hirst and Woolley, op. cit., pp. 62-6.
71. Rosalind Coward, 'The Sex Life of Stick Insects', in *Female Desire*, op. cit.
72. E.O. Wilson, *On Human Nature*, p. 19, Cambridge, Mass., Harvard University Press, 1978.
73. M. Sahlins, *The Use and Abuse of Biology*, London, Tavistock Press, 1977; A. Montagu (ed.), op. cit.
74. Gayle Rubin, 'The Traffic in Women: Notes on the "Political Economy" of Sex', in (ed.) R. Reiter *Towards an Anthropology of Women*, p. 169, New York, Monthly Review Press, 1975.
75. E.O. Wilson, op. cit., p. 99.
76. ibid., p. 111.
77. ibid., p. 105.
78. Steven Rose, op. cit., p. 30.
79. ibid., p. 32.
80. Cynthia Enloe, op. cit.; Chapkis, W. (ed.), *Loaded Questions: Women in the Military*, Amsterdam, Transnational Institute, 1981.
81. Douglas Bothing, *In the Ruins of the Reich*, London, Allen & Unwin, 1985.
82. Quoted in Angus Calder, review of Roger Holmes, *Firing Line*, in *London Review of Books*, 20 June 1985.
83. Cynthia Enloe, op. cit., p. 150.
84. ibid., p. 154.
85. ibid., p. 155.
86. Mary Kaldor, 'The Armament Process', in (eds) D. MacKenzie and J. Wajcman, *The Social Shaping of Technology*, p. 267, Milton Keynes, Open University Press, 1985.
87. John Palmer, 'Military R&D Is Shoving Civil Research to One Side', *The Guardian*, 8 July 1986, p. 25.
88. Donald MacKenzie, 'Militarism and Socialist Theory', *Capital & Class*, 19, 1983, p. 43.
89. Mary Kaldor, *The Baroque Arsenal*, p. 42, London, Deutsch, 1982.
90. Hilary Wainwright, 'The Women Who Wire Up the Weapons', in *Over Our Dead Bodies*, op. cit., p. 140.
91. Michael Kidron, *Western Capitalism since the War*, Harmondsworth, Penguin, 1970; Paul A. Baran and Paul M. Sweezy, *Monopoly Capital*, Harmondsworth, Penguin, 1966.
92. Ron Smith, 'Aspects of Militarism', *Capital & Class*, 19, 1983.
93. ibid.
94. ibid.
95. Nottingham WONT, 'Working as a Group: Nottingham Women Oppose

the Nuclear Threat', in (ed.) L. Jones, *Keeping the Peace*, p. 28, London, The Women's Press, 1983.

96. See, for example, Stuart Hall, 'The Whites of their Eyes: Racist Ideologies and the Media', in (eds) G. Bridges and R. Brunt, *Silver Linings*, London, Lawrence & Wishart, 1981.

97. Ross Poole, op. cit., p. 79.

98. See William Broyles Jun., 'Why Men Love War', *Esquire* Magazine, November 1984.

99. Ross Poole, op. cit., p. 78.

100. Docklands Development Forum, *The People's Plan for the Docks*, Newham Docklands Forum, 1983.

101. Jean Bethke Elshtain, op. cit., p. 341.

102. Sara Ruddick, 'Pacifying the Forces: Drafting Women in the Interests of Peace', *Signs*, vol. 8, no. 3, 1983, p. 479.

103. ibid., p. 479.

104. ibid., p. 481.

105. Ian McEwan, *Or Shall We Die? An Oratorio*, London, Cape, 1983.

106. Petra Kelly, *Fighting for Hope*, p. 104, London, Chatto & Windus, 1984.

107. Hilary Wainwright, *Over Our Dead Bodies* op. cit., p. 144.

108. Virginia Sapiro, *The Political Integration of Women*, pp. 161-2, London, University of Illinois Press, 1985.

109. Sheila Rowbotham, 'What Do Women Want? Women-Centred Values and the World As It Is', *Feminist Review*, 20, 1985.

110. Virginia Woolf, *Three Guineas*, op. cit., p. 121.

111. Virginia Woolf, *The Voyage Out*, p. 212, Harmondsworth, Penguin, 1970.

112. Michèle Mattelart, *Women, Media and Crisis: Femininity and Disorder*, London, Comedia Publishing Group, 1986.

113. Kristina Luker, *Abortion and the Politics of Motherhood*, Berkeley, University of California Press, 1984.

114. Quoted in Mary Daly, *Pure Lust*, op. cit., p. 212.

115. Lynne Spender, in Robyn Rowland, op. cit., p. 128.

116. Barbara Norden, 'Many Visions – Many Hands', *Spare Rib*, 158, September 1985, p. 8.

117. See Ann Snitow, op. cit.

118. Tony Parker, *Soldier, Soldier*, London, Heinemann, 1985.

6. *Neither Foes nor Loving Friends*

1. Melissa Benn, 'Ten Years On', *Women's Review of Books* 2, December 1985, p. 5.

2. Charlotte Bunch, quoted in Kumari Jayawardena, *Feminism and Nationalism in the Third World*, p. iv, Institute of Social Studies, The Hague, Netherlands, 1982.

3. Marilyn French, *Beyond Power*, London, Cape, 1986.

4. ibid., p. 17.

5. ibid., p. 488.

6. ibid., p. 489.

7. ibid., p. 19.

8. Hester Eisenstein, *Contemporary Feminist Thought*, pp. 125-35, London, Unwin Paperbacks, 1984.
9. Beatrix Campbell et al, 'Feminism and Class Politics', in *Feminist Review 23*, 1986, p. 16.
10. Melissa Benn, op. cit., p. 5.
11. Sheila Rowbotham, Lynne Segal and Hilary Wainwright, *Beyond the Fragments: Feminism and the Making of Socialism*, London, Merlin, 1980.
12. Elizabeth Wilson, 'Beyond the Ghetto: Thoughts on "Beyond the Fragments – Feminism and the Making of Socialism" ', *Feminist Review*, 4, 1980, p. 38.
13. Jean McCrindle, 'Women and the Labour Party', *Beyond the Fragments Bulletin* 3, p. 17.
14. Ken Livingstone, 'Fifth Column', *New Socialist* 19, p. 6. 1984.
15. Perry Anderson, *In the Tracks of Historical Materialism*, p. 92, London, Verso, 1983.
16. Angela Weir and Elizabeth Wilson, 'The British Women's Movement', *New Left Review* 148, 1984.
17. Beatrix Campbell, 'Politics Old and New', *New Statesman*, 8 March 1985.
18. Eric Hobsbawm, 'Labour's Lost Millions', *Marxism Today*, October 1983; 'Labour Rump or Rebirth', *Marxism Today*, March 1984.
19. Janet Finch and Dulcie Groves, *A Labour of Love: Women, Work and Caring*, p. 20, London, Routledge & Kegan Paul, 1983.
20. George Brown and Tirril Harris, *Social Origins of Depression*, London, Tavistock, 1978.
21. Mary Boulton, *On Being a Mother*, London, Tavistock, 1983.
22. Alan Walker, 'Care for Elderly People: a Conflict between Women and the State', in Finch and Groves, op. cit.
23. The GLC-funded Safe Women's Transport and the Stockwell Lift Service, two local transport services run by women for women. See Valerie Wise, 'Goodbye to All This?' *Women's Review* 3, January 1986, p. 5.
24. Quoted in Sheila Rowbotham, 'Sharing and Caring', *New Statesman*, 15 January 1984.
25. The following quotes from Jane Foot and Myra Garrett are from interviews conducted by Sheila Rowbotham (available in History Workshop Archives, London).
26. Shamir Dirir was also interviewed by Sheila Rowbotham.
27. *Women's Employment in Haringey: A Programme for Action*, discussion paper prepared by Haringey Women's Employment Project, 1983.
28. *Jobs For a Change*, March 1985.
29. Quoted in Sheila Rowbotham, 1984, op. cit., p. 11.
30. Valerie Wise, in *Women's Review* op. cit., p. 4.
31. 'Domestic Work and Childcare', in *The London Industrial Strategy*, GLC, p. 214, 1985.
32. Rahila, 'Southall Black Sisters', *Outwrite* 47, May 1986, p. 8.
33. ibid.
34. See *Jobs For a Change* no. 15, p. 3.
35. ibid.
36. ibid.
37. Black woman living in Liverpool 8, in (ed.) A. Curno et al, *Women in Collective Action*, p. 97, London, Association of Community Workers in the UK, 1982.

38. Heather Joshi, 'Unfair Shares', *The Guardian*, 8 May 1984.
39. Philip Stephens, 'Slipping Backwards to a Low Wage Service Economy', *Financial Times*, 7 July 1984.
40. Joshi, op. cit.
41. Ursula Huws, 'Women and Employment' in (eds) G. Ashworth and L. Bonnerjea, *The Invisible Decade*, p. 60, Aldershot, Gower, 1985.
42. Alison Frater, 'A Woman's Place is in the Hospital', *New Statesman*, June 1986, p. 8.
43. See *The Economist*, 16 June 1984, p. 22.
44. Jalna Hanmer, 'Violence to Women: From Private Sorrow to Public Issue', in Ashworth and Bonnerjea, op. cit., 1985.
45. ibid., p. 51.
46. Joni Lovendreski, *Women in European Politics: Contemporary Feminism and Public Policy*, Brighton, Harvester, 1985.
47. ibid.
48. A. Curno et al, op. cit.
49. South Wales Tenants' Association, 'Coming Alive Hurts', in A. Curno et al, op. cit., p. 27.
50. ibid., p. 28.
51. Pratibha Parmar, 'A Revolutionary Anger', ibid., p. 93.
52. North Yorkshire Women Against Pit Closures, *Strike 84-85*, Leeds, North Yorkshire Women Against Pit Closures, 1985.
53. Jean McCrindle and Sheila Rowbotham, 'More than Just a Memory', *Feminist Review* 23, p. 121.
54. Marina Lewycka, 'The Way We Were', *New Socialist*, 36, March 1986.
55. For example, Anna Coote, 'A New Starting Point', in *The Future of the Left*, Cambridge, Polity Press, 1984; Anne Phillips, *Hidden Hands*, London, Pluto Press, 1983.
56. See E.P. Thompson, 'Postscript 1976' in *William Morris, Romantic to Revolutionary*, London, Merlin, 1977; Stuart Hall, 'The State: Socialism's Old Caretaker', *Marxism Today* 11, November 1984; Sheila Rowbotham, *Friends of Alice Wheeldon*, op. cit.
57. Michèle Barrett and Mary McIntosh, 'The Family Wage: Some Problems for Socialists and Feminists', *Capital & Class*, 11, 1980.
58. ibid., p. 80.
59. Mike Cooley, *Architect or Bee?* Langley Technical Services, 1980; Hilary Wainwright and Dave Elliott, *The Lucas Plan: A New Trade Unionism in the Making?* London, Allison & Busby, 1982.
60. *The People's Plan for the Royal Docks*, London, Newham Docklands Forum and GLC Popular Planning Unit, 1983.
61. Michèle Barrett and Mary McIntosh, 1980, op. cit.
62. Helen Hague, 'Women and Unions', *Marxism Today*, June 1986, p. 5.
63. ibid.
64. Angela Coyle, *Redundant Women*, p. 147, London, The Women's Press, 1984.
65. Cynthia Cockburn, *Machinery of Dominance: Women, Men and Technical Know-How*, p. 257, London, Pluto Press, 1986.
66. Beatrix Campbell, article in *The Guardian*, 9 August 1982.
67. John Lloyd, 'Radical Changes in Work Forecast', *Financial Times*, 13 June 1986.
68. *The London Industrial Strategy*, op. cit., p. 138.

69. John Edmonds, 'Uniting the Fragments', *New Socialist*, June 1986, p. 19.

70. Barbara Sichtermann, *Femininity: the Politics of the Personal*, p. 1, Cambridge, Polity Press, 1986.

71. Ken Livingstone/Tariq Ali, *Who's Afraid of Margaret Thatcher? Ken Livingstone in Conversation with Tariq Ali*, p. 66, London, Verso, 1984.

72. 'Woman to Woman', Margaret Thatcher interviewed by Miriam Stoppard on London television (ITV), 19 November 1984.

73. See Sue Lees and Mary McIntosh, 'European Forum of Socialist Feminists', *Feminist Review*, 23, p. 140, 1986.

Index

abortion, 41, 50, 52, 75, 81-2, 136, 147, 228
academic feminism, 52-3, 115, 131-2
Addams, Jane, 169
aggression, 181-2, 185, 186
AIDS, 74
Allende, Salvador, 200
Althusser, 52
Amis, Kingsley, 5
Amos, Valerie, 62
Anderson, Perry, 211
anti-imperialism, 54-5, 62, 191
anti-sexist men, 150-2, 155
Arcana, Judith, 3-4, 12
Ardrey, Robert, 179, 180
arms production, 189-93
Asian women, 62, 64, 224, 226, 227, 231
Astell, Mary, 24-5
Australian Broadcasting Commission, 77

Balint, Michael, 134-5
Bandaranaike, Mrs, 176
Barbach, Lonnie, 92
Bardwick, Judith, 118-19
Barking, 226
Barrett, G., 110
Barrett, Michèle, 38, 63-4, 239
Barrow, General, 189
battered women, 12, 85-6, 168
BBC, 112, 199
Becker, Howard, 31
Benn, Melissa, 204, 208
Benn, Tony, 39, 209, 212-13
Beyond the Fragments, 208-10
Bhide, Smita, 225
biological reductionism, 179-87
Birke, Lynda, 180
Birmingham conference (1973), 46
Birmingham conference (1978), 56, 66, 96
Black, Maria, 27-8
Black Dwarf, 78-9
Black feminism, 21, 54, 61-5, 102, 159, 225, 231-2
Black Lesbian Group, 38
Blake, William, 27

bodily states, 8-11
The Body Politic, 13
Bonney, Rosanne, 77
Boulton, Mary, 216
Boycott, Rosie, 45
Breaching the Peace, 164, 167
British Aerospace, 191, 198
Brittain, Vera, 171, 172-3
Brixton Black Women's Group, 64
Brown, George, 215-16
Brownmiller, Susan, 103, 130
Bunch, Charlotte, 204

Calder, Angus, 175
Camden Council Women's Unit, 64
Cameron, Deborah, 1, 28-9
Cammell Laird Shipyards, 227
Campbell, Beatrix, 55, 76, 80-1, 88, 208, 212, 241-2
Capara, Fritzof, 39
capitalism, 44-5, 47-9, 76, 83, 191, 234
Cartledge, Sue, 87-8
Catholic church, 18, 22
Cavendish, Ruth, 67
censorship, 104, 112-13
Charlton, Valerie, 14
Chesler, Phyllis, 118-19
Chicago, Judy, 68
Chicago Women's Liberation Union, 51
childbirth, 41, 82
childcare, 16, 64, 83, 136, 156-61, 215-16, 223, 224-5; *see also* mothering
Chiswick Women's Centre, 85
Chodorow, Nancy, 135, 136-7, 139, 141-4, 146, 147, 151, 156-7, 160, 217
Christie, Julie, 14
Churchill, Winston, 104, 112
CND, 191, 199, 201
Cockburn, Cynthia, 67, 144, 241
Cockran, Mrs, 11
Coleman, Gwen, 170
Comer, Lee, 45, 135
Committee on Obscenity and Film Censorship, 111

266